Maths is essential

'To be successful in business today, leaders must focus on the fundamentals. That means being skilled at mathematics beyond the basics. Leaders need more than financial acumen to read a balance sheet. They need sharp, analytic math skills that help them interpret numbers, identify trends, and shape strategy.'

Anne Mulcahy, *Xerox Chairman and CEO*

'Numeracy and mathematical skill are absolutely essential for a successful business career. In more than 35 years of working life in the City of London, I have seen over and over again the importance of a solid grounding in mathematical techniques. Today, this is truer than ever with computers offering sophisticated analytical tools that can only be harnessed properly by understanding the underlying mathematical concepts. In that spirit, this book should offer its readers an extra advantage in today's competitive business world.'

Marcus Agius, *Chairman, Barclays*

'An understanding of mathematics is now regarded as essential for working in the modern world of business. Clare Morris should be commended for her excellent text on *Essential Maths*. The book is extremely well written. The style is very user friendly. The text should be regarded as essential reading for any business student who has a weakness in handling numbers.'

Alan Mabbett, *University of Central England Business School, UK*

'A comprehensive guide for those who tuned out to maths at school.'

Dr Christine Blight, *Coleg Menai, UK*

'Clare Morris has produced a text that will prove to be popular with students, because of its clear approach. This is an excellent text that will prove to be an invaluable resource. Many of our business degree students have developed an aversion to maths during their secondary education. Teaching them the necessary business maths skills can be an arduous task. That task will be made easier by Clare Morris's book. She combines a common sense approach with good and relevant examples. I can see it being a boon to my teaching on a range of business courses.'

Geoff Jones, *Hugh Baird College, UK*

'Written in a friendly and approachable style, *Essential Maths* can really help students to learn – especially those who hate maths, or think they do.'

Andrew Goudie, *Salford Business School, University of Salford, UK*

ESSENTIAL MATHS
for Business and
Management

Clare Morris

with Emmanuel Thanassoulis

First published 2007 by PALGRAVE MACMILLAN
Houndmills, Basingstoke, Hampshire RG21 6XS and
175 Fifth Avenue, New York, N.Y. 10010
Companies and representatives throughout the world

PALGRAVE MACMILLAN is the global academic imprint of the Palgrave Macmillan division of St. Martin's Press, LLC and of Palgrave Macmillan Ltd. Macmillan® is a registered trademark in the United States, United Kingdom and other countries. Palgrave is a registered trademark in the European Union and other countries.

ISBN-13: 978-1-4039-1610-5
ISBN-10: 1-4039-1610-1

This book is printed on paper suitable for recycling and made from fully managed and sustained forest sources. Logging, pulping and manufacturing processes are expected to conform to the environmental regulations of the country of origin.

A catalogue record for this book is available from the British Library.

A catalog record for this book is available from the Library of Congress.

10 9 8 7 6 5 4 3 2 1
16 15 14 13 12 11 10 09 08 07

Printed and bound in China

Contents

Contents

Figures and Tables

Figures

Tables

Preface

In the 13 years which have elapsed since the publication of the original volume of this book, there have been many changes in the world of business education. The original volume was intended to act as a self-study refresher course which students could follow in order to revise the necessary mathematics prior to entering a BA Business Studies or an MBA programme. It is now more common for mathematics of this kind to be incorporated into an assessed course within programmes of this kind. This new version of the book is thus conceived primarily as a text for such courses, though it should still serve also as a self-study tool for those who wish to revise their mathematics independently.

The book has therefore been completely rewritten, to give a much greater focus on business applications. Some of the less widely useful topics covered in the first edition, such as integration, have been omitted in order to allow for a more thorough and in-depth treatment of other areas. More exercises and case studies have been incorporated (and further resources of this kind can be found on the companion website).

The book now includes elements, such as the specification of prerequisite knowledge and learning outcomes, which have become the norm within higher education programmes. Also included are 'Pause for reflection' sections intended to encourage, not only effective learning, but reflection on the learning process. In this way it is hoped that the book will instil good habits in the study of mathematics which will persist should readers proceed to more advanced work in the subject.

Two things, however, have not changed. First, anything with 'mathematics' or 'quantitative' in the title still causes concern to many students embarking on business courses. The book is aimed at building confidence, particularly in those readers who may hitherto have classed themselves as 'not much good with maths', as well as helping them to develop their skills.

Second, the book acknowledges that, while many of the topics covered might be found in a school-level mathematics course, they need to be covered in a quite different manner for an audience of adults whose primary interest is in business and management. A less formal, more 'conversational' style has therefore been adopted, which it is hoped will render the ideas more readily accessible.

My thanks go to my editor, Martin Drewe, for his patience and support throughout the preparation of this new edition, and to Sonia Taylor for her careful checking of the examples and solutions. I am indebted to numerous colleagues with whom I have had constructive discussions about teaching quantitative methods at this level, and to the many students who have helped me to refine my ideas on the subject, particularly those taking the University of Gloucestershire's module 'Confidence Counts' who were kind enough to complete questionnaires concerning their experience of the course. I am also aware of the contribution of Emmanuel Thanassoulis to the original version of the book. However, since I have carried out all the revisions, any errors which have crept in are also entirely my responsibility.

Clare Morris
February 2007

Microsoft product screen shot(s) reprinted with permission from Microsoft Corporation.

CHAPTER 1

Business and maths – what's the link?

Intended learning outcomes

By the end of your work on this chapter you should:

- understand why anyone aiming at a business career needs to be reasonably proficient in certain areas of mathematics
- have had a chance to reflect on your previous experiences of studying mathematics, and on the strengths and weaknesses of your personal learning style
- have begun to develop your skills at reading about and writing mathematics
- be aware of the use and limitations of spreadsheets and calculators when carrying out mathematical processes.

1.1 Why do I need this book? Business without maths

When you learned that maths – possibly disguised as something like 'Quantitative Methods' – would form part of your business or management course, I wonder if like many students you found yourself thinking, 'Why on earth do I have to do that?' Let's see if I can convince you that successful business people really do need to be comfortable with maths.

Just try to imagine for a moment what it would be like to set out to run a business without using any mathematics – in other words, any numerical information. For a start, you would not be able to run your business legally, since all registered companies (in the UK at least) have to file accounts once a year with Companies House. You would not be able to measure how well the business was doing, except in a vague, impressionistic sort of way. You would probably not even be able to get the business started, because financial support for new businesses from lenders depends on business plans – and business plans contain forecasts, budgets, estimated dates when the company will break even, all of which need to be expressed in mathematical terms.

Now you may be thinking that you don't have any ambitions to start your own business, or to be a chief executive. You're more interested in working in a particular business function. It's easy to see why maths is important for someone intending to work in a technical area – accounting, say, or engineering – but perhaps your aim is to go into a career in hotel or leisure management, food retailing or human resource management. Surely you can avoid working with numbers in those areas? And anyway, aren't there specialists who can deal with any numerical work which does arise?

The quotes below, taken from the website http://www.mathsatwork.com/real.html, show how people working in those areas find that in fact they do need to use maths, and particularly arithmetic, in their everyday work.

From Debbie Adams, Senior Restaurant General Manager, Pizza Hut (UK) Ltd:

> It is important to understand where our sales have come from each day and what they mean.
>
> I need to understand average spend per customer or table, net and gross values of items, VAT calculations, and percentages (e.g. If we forecast sales of £1,000 and they actually total £1,277, the percentage increase). I also need to pay members of staff, calculating the numbers of hours worked, how much they get paid per hour, employees' national insurance contributions, holiday pay, and any other benefits or deductions.
>
> Analysing the business on a daily and weekly basis is key. For example, if we tell the company we think we are going to make £X and we come in under that, they aren't going to be too happy.
>
> I use simple maths, adding, subtracting, averages, ratios and percentages, but it is the understanding of maths that is a prerequisite of the job.

From Joe Dybell, Supply Chain Controller, Tesco:

> I am the controller of the Tesco supply chain, therefore the role uses maths to calculate and forecast the company sales figures. This is then related to how we set up the

systems, by calculating how much stock to order and send, and informing the 24 distribution centres how much work they have to do on a daily basis.

As the answer is never right or wrong, I use maths to demonstrate improvements in sales, customer service level and wastage by week or by year.

My job is ideal for someone who enjoys numbers and playing with numbers. They need to be able to identify trends in complex information and then test theory to see if they hold true.

And from Tess Toole, working in human resources for the Royal Liver Insurance Company:

My job is to pay the 500 or so people that work at Royal Liver Building for Royal Liver Assurance. I basically gather together all payments and all deductions and input them into the computer system. The computer calculates the net pay for each person. This is gross pay less income tax, national insurance and pension contributions, if applicable. The money due to each person is automatically sent into their bank accounts and payslips are produced which I send out.

Maths is obviously a very large part of my job. I use it to calculate small sums to find out how much overtime a person is due and to calculate how much pension contributions a person would pay. I use it in the large and complicated calculations involved in manually calculating the whole of the employees' wages.

I won't pretend that I'm a maths genius and that I do all these sums in my head – of course I don't. For the amount of calculation that I do a calculator is a must. Knowing how to subtract, divide, get percentages and averages is essential regardless of whether or not a calculator is used. You have to know what buttons to press to get the answer you want!

As these quotes make clear – and as most people working in business would testify – there is hardly any area of business where mathematics can be totally avoided.

But don't worry: as these quotes also make clear, we are not talking about rocket science here. None of the people quoted would claim to be expert mathematicians. They are simply intelligent people who have put their mind to acquiring skills which are an enormous asset to them in their everyday work. There is no reason why you too should not acquire those skills; the aim of this book is to help you to do so. The rest of this chapter is intended to provide a foundation for your learning, by offering some ideas about effective ways to learn maths.

1.2 How to learn mathematics

Insight from the experts

There are some telling phrases in each of the quotes above, which can start us thinking about good and less good ways to learn about mathematics.

Debbie says, 'it is the understanding of maths that is a prerequisite of the job'. In other words, not just mechanically carrying out procedures, but understanding what you are doing and why you are doing it. More about this a bit later in the section.

Joe says, 'the answer is never right or wrong'. This is something which perhaps distinguishes maths used in a business context from the kind of 'maths for its own sake' you may have studied before, and which many students can find unsettling at first. Because we are dealing with practical problems, the calculated answer may not tell the whole story, or there may be a range of possible 'right answers' from which we must choose on business, rather than mathematical, grounds. Very often later in this book you will find that exercises don't end with a numerical answer, under which you can draw a neat line and wait for someone to tick it as correct; instead, you will be asked 'What does this mean in practical terms?' So you need to get used to linking the maths with other aspects of the problem, and using your knowledge of other business areas – and your ordinary common sense – alongside the mathematical techniques you've learned.

Finally, Tess says, 'I won't pretend that I'm a maths genius and that I do all these sums in my head ... You have to know what buttons to press to get the answer you want!' The advent of calculators and spreadsheet packages has taken a lot of the drudgery out of mathematics, but it certainly hasn't removed the need to understand what's going on. In fact, it is even more important now to have a 'feel' for the kind of answer you expect to get, so that you are not totally at the mercy of the machine. For this reason, you'll find sections called 'For Excel users' at the end of most of the chapters in the book, showing how the material of the chapter links to various Excel functions.

Pause for reflection

Decide whether you agree or disagree with the following statements (be honest!):

- My main objective in studying this course is to pass the assessment.
- I don't like just accepting what my lecturer tells me.
- I like to work things out for myself.
- Maths is all about knowing the right methods.

What kind of learner are you?

If you agreed more strongly with the second and third statements above than with the other two, then your approach to learning will stand you in good stead in your study of this course. Just listening to someone telling you things about mathematics (or for that matter, reading about them in a book) will never give you a really secure understanding of the subject. To achieve that you must try the ideas out for yourself with pen and paper, and think about what you are doing while you are doing it.

If you agreed more strongly with the first and last statements – well, there is nothing wrong in wanting to pass the assessment – you'd be silly if you did *not* want to pass! But if you let 'being able to do the questions' rather than 'understanding what's going on' drive the way you try to learn maths, you will never achieve a feeling of real confidence in your ability; and if you learn 'methods' in a mechanical way, you will be flummoxed by the first example you come across that isn't exactly like one you've done before.

Most of you will probably feel that you don't fall neatly into one or the other category. You'll find some topics interesting, and want to get a deeper insight into the underlying ideas; other parts of the subject will stimulate you less, and you may feel that you just have to get on and plough through examples in the hope that 'the penny will drop' while you're doing this, as it often does.

Nevertheless, throughout this book I will be seeking to reinforce the kind of learning that involves understanding, and to discourage the kind that reduces maths to formulae and recipe-like 'methods'. You may find this irritating at times, but I promise it will pay off in the end.

Lose the label!

There is one other aspect of your study of maths which needs to be considered: your previous experiences of the subject, at school and maybe at college, in a professional training course or at work. Many people, by the time they start a higher education course, have already labelled themselves 'bad at maths', perhaps because they've been told this by a teacher, or because they have done badly in an exam. This happens with many subjects, of course – from the age of about seven I have carried an invisible label 'bad at sports' around my neck! – but it's particularly prevalent with maths. It's not unknown for public figures such as MPs to admit cheerfully that they 'never could do sums'.

However, you need to throw away this label before we go any further. One of the main objectives of this book is to give you not just mathematical skills, but confidence in using those skills, and you will never gain that confidence while you retain the idea that you are 'bad at maths' in the same unchangeable way that you have blue or brown eyes, or are tall or short. In any case, the kind of maths we will be studying in this course is probably quite different from that which you have met before, in that it is 'maths for a purpose' and not just 'maths for its own sake'. Many students find that concepts that made little sense when encountered in the abstract are perfectly easy to understand when they have a practical context.

So lose the label. If you had the ability (as you obviously did) to get on to your higher education course, then you have the ability to learn and understand this kind of mathematics.

Pause for reflection

Think about your earlier experiences of studying mathematics. Write down three things you enjoyed or were good at, and three that you did not enjoy or found difficult. Can you see anything that links the topics in the two groups? (For example, if you enjoyed work with graphs, geometry, and statistical diagrams such as pie charts, this might indicate that you are someone who relates well to pictorial or visual ideas.)

Compare your lists with those of one or two other people in your learning group. How similar are they? If this suggests that there are common areas which everyone is anxious about, explore why this might be.

A short list of tips for studying maths

- Always have a pencil and paper to hand when you're reading a maths book or your notes, so that you can try out calculations, fill in gaps in mathematical arguments, and scribble down summaries of what you are reading in your own words. This is the only way you will get, to use a fashionable word, 'ownership' of the ideas you're reading about.

- Never let anything go past which you don't understand, in the hope that it will make sense later. Maths is a cumulative subject, in which one topic builds on another, so if you don't understand something today, that may well prevent you from understanding something more important tomorrow.

- Don't be afraid to ask about things you don't understand. Your lecturer will be pleased that you are making the effort, not annoyed because you didn't understand first time.

- Everyone – and I mean everyone – makes mistakes with maths – not major conceptual errors, but little slips in arithmetic. Don't lose faith in your lecturer when he/she does so! And if you find something in a textbook – including this one! – that you can't follow, don't immediately assume it's your fault, just possibly an error could have crept in. Textbook authors and lecturers are no more infallible than the rest of humanity.

- Most learning follows a spiral process, so don't feel that once you have learned something you should never need to revisit it. Often when you return to a topic you will find that your understanding is deeper, due perhaps to something else you have learned subsequently.

1.3 The language of mathematics

Many people feel that the fact that maths is generally written in a special language forms an obstacle to their enjoyment of the subject. This language tends to involve numerous symbols, rather than the English sentences that we are used to with other subjects.

It's certainly true that the language of maths, just like French or Russian, takes a bit of getting used to. But I'm sure that no one will have any difficulty in reading the statement $3 + 2 = 5$ as 'three plus two equals five'. The symbols $+$ and $=$ are familiar because you have known how to interpret them for a long time, and you understand that they are simply symbolic ways of writing 'plus' and 'is equal to'. In the same way, the other symbols that we will encounter are shorthand notations for other mathematical operations, and in time you will become as adept at interpreting them as you are today with $+$ and $=$.

I will try to make a point, every time we encounter a new piece of notation, of explaining how it should be read. This isn't just being pedantic; it is very hard to feel you really understand a concept when you don't even have a proper way of putting it into words. You'll also find a glossary at the end of the book – that's a list of all the terms and symbols used in the text, with an explanation of their meaning.

You can make your mathematical work a great deal easier to follow – both for anyone else who needs to look at it, and for yourself when you come to look back at it later – by making sure that you put in plenty of explanation of what is going on. You should be able to read well-written mathematics as you would ordinary English. So, for example, suppose that you want to write down the calculation of your wages when you have worked 35 hours at £8.80 per hour plus 5 hours overtime at £13.20 per hour. You could just write

$$35 \times 8.80 + 5 \times 13.20 = 374$$

(or indeed input the whole calculation straight into a calculator) and there would be nothing wrong with this, but to make it clearer what is going on, it would be better to write:

35 hours at £8.80 per hour = £308
5 hours at £13.20 per hour = £66
So total pay = £308 + £66 = £374.

It's true that in this simple case, you might not need so much detail, but the point I am making is that it never does any harm to put in more rather than less explanation.

Whatever you do, don't string together lines of mathematics with = signs between things which aren't equal – a common failing which can lead to a lot of confusion. For example, with the above calculation you might be tempted to write

$$35 \times 8.8 = 308 + 5 \times 13.2 = 66 + 308 = \ldots$$

If you unpick this, it includes the statement '$35 \times 8.8 = 308 + 13.2$', which is manifestly not true. Of course, it's not difficult to unravel what is meant, but nevertheless writing down untrue statements is not good practice, and in more complex situations can send you off in totally the wrong direction.

Get into the habit, then, of trying to read your maths aloud – if you can't do this, or if you have to resort to 'little three up in the air' or 'strange squiggly symbol' – you need to have another look at the way it's written.

One final point: like any other subject, maths has its own particular terminology, sometimes using words that will be new to you, sometimes using ordinary English words but in a special sense. Students sometimes get irritated by this. I have heard a student rep ask in a course committee why lecturers had to use so many long words, and why they couldn't use ordinary English. The answer, I'm afraid, is that while it's often possible to give a reasonable explanation of an idea in 'ordinary English', there are some concepts that simply have to be given a new name. And at the time when many of these concepts were being invented, everyone who had been through higher education learned Latin and Greek, so the names tend to be derived from those languages, which is perhaps why they sound strange to us today.

For instance, the top of a fraction is known in mathematics as the *numerator* (we'll come across this term again in Chapter 2). OK, you could refer to 'the number on the top of the fraction' – but it might be a whole algebraic expression rather than just one number. So it is much more efficient to refer to the numerator – and once you know what it means, the term is no stranger than, say, 'television' – another word derived from Latin and Greek.

Pause for reflection

Write down as many symbols and technical terms as you can remember from your previous study of maths. Then try to define in words what each of them means.

Compare your list with those of other people in your learning group. Are there things on your list that aren't on theirs, or vice versa? If so, explain to each other what the unfamiliar ones mean. If you are doubtful about any of them, check your understanding with your tutor.

You should now be aware that you already have quite a wide 'mathematical vocabulary', which will give you a good start for your further study.

1.4 Spreadsheets and calculators

We heard, in the quote from insurance company employee Tess Toole at the start of this chapter, that 'for the amount of calculation that I do a calculator is a must'. Calculators, and spreadsheets such as Excel, are an essential tool for carrying out arithmetical work, particularly where large volumes of information are involved.

However, like any other tool such as an electric drill, calculators and spreadsheets need to be used in an informed way if they are not to cause potential damage. There are two aspects to this:

(a) You need to know how to get the tool to do what you want it to do. With a calculator, this involves reading and working through the instruction book which comes with the machine – and which many users promptly lose or throw away. It is not possible in this book to give detailed instructions on how to carry out particular calculations, since different calculators vary in the details of their operation. However, you will find links to some useful sites on the companion website. With a spreadsheet, finding out how it works probably involves doing an introductory course. This may be provided within your overall programme, but if not you can find some very helpful free online courses on the Microsoft Office online training website at http://office.microsoft.com/en-us/training/default.aspx. The audio course 'Get to know Excel: create your first workbook' is a good place to begin. You will find a link to this site on the companion website associated with this book.

(b) You need to know exactly what the tool is doing as a consequence of the buttons you press or the instructions you give. So, for example, if you put the calculation $3 \times 6 + 4$ into a cell in an Excel spreadsheet, you need to be aware that the multiplication will be carried out before the addition, so that the answer will be 22 and not 30. We'll be coming back to this point in the next chapter.

The sections called 'For Excel users' at the end of most chapters of this book will assume that you already have the skills outlined under (a) above. In other words, they assume you understand the basics of how to use a spreadsheet: to enter data, move things around the sheet, copy and paste cells, and so on. We shall then focus on the further skills you need to get Excel to help with the concepts covered in the chapter.

So if you're hoping to use Excel to help you with your course – or if this is a compulsory element of the course – then it might be a good idea, before going any further, to check that you are comfortable with the basic skills.

1.5 | ... and a word about the Web

The Internet is a wonderful resource, and you will find many references to specific websites throughout this book.

However, if you have become reliant on searching the Web, copying and pasting information (with due acknowledgement, of course) as part of your assessed work in other subjects, then a word of warning is perhaps needed. If you simply search on a word such as 'quotient' (don't worry if you don't know what that means, as it will be covered in the next chapter), you will find literally millions of hits, some of which are relevant to the simple mathematical use of the term, and others not. Even where a web page does give a simple definition (for example, a Wikipedia page), it may move on quickly to more advanced uses of the term. So you could frighten yourself quite unnecessarily by trying to use a site where the level of discussion is too advanced.

It is also as well to remember that nothing on the Web is guaranteed to be correct. Although your searches may come up with handouts and course materials from many universities across the globe, these may contain errors (in my experience, sometimes serious ones). Even where the material is sound, different uses of notation and terminology can lead to confusion and misunderstanding.

So it is as well not to rely too heavily on seeking out web-based information to support your study of maths. Better to stick to books and other resources recommended in your course reading list, or by your course tutor.

For further exercises and multiple choice revision questions visit the companion website: www.palgrave.com/business/morris

CHAPTER 2

Arithmetic – working with numbers

Intended learning outcomes

By the end of your work on this chapter you should:

- be able confidently to carry out arithmetic operations involving positive and negative numbers, fractions, decimals and percentages
- have developed your ability to estimate roughly what the result of a calculation should be
- know how to round numbers to a given number of decimal places or significant figures, and be able to make a sensible decision as to how many figures to quote in a practical context
- be aware of a range of symbols for mathematical operations and understand their meanings
- be comfortable in reading and writing arithmetical expressions, and understand the technical terminology which is used in this context.

Prerequisites

There are no prerequisites for this chapter. Much of the work covered here should be in the nature of revision of things you already know.

2.1 Why do we need arithmetic?

> ### Before you start
>
> Write a list of all the arithmetical operations you already know how to carry out – addition, subtraction, working with fractions, and so on. Make sure you include those which you need to carry out on a calculator, like taking the square root, if you've come across that. You may be surprised at the length of the list! What this means is that a good deal of the material in this chapter may be more a matter of revision than of learning new concepts.

Whether we are aware of it or not, arithmetic pervades both business and everyday life. Just think how many colloquial expressions make reference to arithmetical ideas: 'It doesn't add up'; 'It's just a matter of putting two and two together', and so on.

Businesses rely on the use of arithmetical operations: the four basic functions (addition, subtraction, multiplication and division), together with percentages, fractions and decimals. In functional areas from accounting to personnel, and in sectors from manufacturing to hospitality, people are routinely carrying out calculations as part of their everyday work. Of course, as we saw in the quote from Tess at the beginning of Chapter 1, not all these calculations are carried out by hand. They may be done using a calculator, or using a spreadsheet, or hidden away in the depths of a computer program which carries out a complex function such as a payroll calculation.

But even the most complex computations are made up of a relatively small range of arithmetical operations. In this chapter, you will have the opportunity to remind yourself how these operations work, perhaps learn about some which are new to you, and practise your skills so that you gain confidence in working with numbers.

Because many of the ideas covered in this chapter are basic, underpinning most applications of mathematics in business, you won't find as many explicitly business-related examples as in later chapters. This may make the work seem a bit 'dry', but I'm afraid that's unavoidable – it's a bit like having to understand the *Highway Code* before you can safely go out and start doing the exciting things like actually driving a car!

2.2 The spectrum of numbers

Numbers in business problems often arise as a result of either counting or measuring things. When we count, we do so in whole numbers – 0, 1, 2, 3 and so on – for which the technical term is *integers*. We can think of these as strung out along a line, as shown in Figure 2.1 – conventionally we show increasing values moving to the right.

The numbers used for counting are all positive – we could write +1, +2, +3 and so on, but we don't usually bother – but we can also think of negative numbers (–1, –2, –3 and so on) extending to the left of zero. Because these numbers are not used for counting –

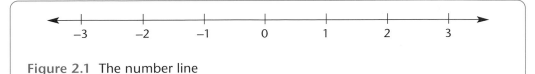

Figure 2.1 The number line

you would not say 'There are minus three sheep in that field' – it's not quite so easy to get a 'feel' for what they mean. But they can be very important, and have a very real practical meaning in business situations. For example, if a company is in debt to its bank to the tune of £10,000, then its bank balance could be represented as –£10,000. Accountants sometimes, rather confusingly, show this as (10,000), but this notation is not used in mathematics.

It's not only in a financial context that negative numbers have a practical meaning. Another example is provided by the large-scale construction going on at the time of writing in connection with the London Olympics in 2012. Since the project must be completed by that time, you sometimes see references to 2006 being 'year minus 6', meaning that it is six years before the target date.

Test your understanding

Think of a couple more practical applications for the idea of a negative number.

One obvious question is 'What happens in the gaps between the whole numbers?' The answer, of course, is those gaps are filled with numbers which are not integers – such as 3½, 4.637, or 0.00001. However, a discussion of those numbers will have to wait until later in this chapter.

Research has shown that people think about numbers in many different ways. Some actually 'see' them, though they often find it hard to explain just what it is that they see. People with what is called 'synaesthesia' may even associate different colours with different numbers, and there are others who have the ability to remember very long lists of numbers quite easily, or to carry out extraordinarily complex calculations very fast in their heads.

You might like to reflect on how you think about numbers. More prosaically, it is important that you start to think about roughly what you expect the results of a calculation to be, so that if you happen to press the wrong button on your calculator, you will spot the mistake and be able to correct it. At the simplest level, this means realising that if you multiply two 'big numbers' together, you will get an 'even bigger number' – for example, $623 \times 486 = 302,778$. If you carry out this calculation on a calculator but, as I did just now, don't press the last 6 quite hard enough, so that you're actually multiplying 623×48, you should realise that the answer 29,904 isn't as big as it should be. I shall be encouraging you to develop this skill throughout the book.

2.3 Arithmetic with whole numbers

Positive whole-number arithmetic

Addition and *multiplication* of positive whole numbers should not cause you any problems, even if you have to resort to a calculator where large numbers are involved. Thus 28 + 46 = 74, 12 × 15 = 180, and so on. (I don't propose to go here into the processes of 'long multiplication' and other hand-calculation methods, since I assume that you'll actually be using a calculator to carry out most of your arithmetic.)

Subtraction is easy when we subtract a smaller number from a larger one, as in 17 – 8 = 9. However, subtracting a larger number from a smaller one will give a negative answer: 7 – 11 = –4. You can see how this works using the number line in Figure 1.1; addition is represented by a move to the right, subtraction by a move to the left. So we start at +7, seven steps to the right of zero; then to subtract 11, we move 11 steps to the left, ending up at –4. Another way to think of this is that the difference between 11 and 7 is 4, but because we are taking the bigger number from the smaller one, the answer is negative. It's equivalent to a situation where you have £7 in your pocket, but you owe someone £11, so you are actually in debt by £4.

Division is no problem with positive numbers when the number being divided is an integer multiple of the number we're dividing by: 44 divided by 11 is 4, because 11 × 4 = 44. However, if that isn't the case – for instance, with 44 divided by 12 – the answer will be a fraction, and we'll therefore defer discussion of that idea until we get to Section 2.5.

Arithmetic with negative whole numbers

We've really already covered addition and subtraction involving negative numbers in the previous section, since this can be dealt with by using the number line as described there. Thus if we have –16 + 20, then we are starting 16 steps to the left on the line, and then moving 20 steps to the right for the '+20', ending up at +4.

An alternative way to think of this is to realise that the order in which we write sequences of additions and subtractions doesn't matter, so that –16 + 20 is completely equivalent to +20 – 16 which comes to +4 as before. (Remember that we don't generally write the + in front of a number like +4; if there's no sign, the number is assumed to be positive.)

It's when we get to multiplication and division involving negative numbers that many people start to feel somewhat nervous, perhaps because they remember from their earlier study of mathematics that this is where things start to become less obvious. In fact, there are two perfectly simple rules in this case:

- **Multiplying or dividing two numbers with the same signs (that is, two pluses or two minuses) gives a positive answer.**
- **Multiplying or dividing two numbers with different signs (that is, one plus and one minus) gives a negative answer.**

Let's look at some examples first, and then think about why the rules might work in this way.

> –2 × 8: here there are different signs (because the 8 is really +8), so the answer will be –16.
>
> 12 divided by –6: again two different signs, so the result is –2.
>
> (–7) × (–9): the two signs are the same, so the result is +63 or just 63. We put the brackets in here because we don't generally write two signs next to each other: –7 × –9 looks odd to a mathematician. The brackets are there to keep the signs apart, and to show that the minus sign belongs with the number – we're multiplying 'minus seven' by 'minus nine'.

Now, why does this make sense? At first sight, it might appear to be a pretty mysterious rule, just cooked up by mathematicians to make students' lives difficult! However, if we go back to the idea of a negative quantity as a loss or a debt, then it makes perfect sense. If a construction company is losing £120,000 a week on a big development project which has overrun – and such figures are by no means uncommon – then over a four-week period it will lose £480,000. Writing the weekly loss as –120,000, we can calculate the loss over the four-week period as –120,000 × 4, which must be equal to –480,000. So to make sense in practical terms the multiplication of the negative number by the positive one must give a negative answer.

Test your understanding

Work out the following to make sure that you can handle whole-number arithmetic:

1. 11 + 18   2. 13 − 4   3. 23 − 27   4. −7 + 4   5. 12 − 9 + 3
6. 3 × 12   7. 27/3   8. −4 × 7   9. (−4) × (−7)   10. 50/(−10)

Combinations of arithmetic operations

So far we have considered the individual arithmetic operations one by one, but of course they often need to be combined.

Consider, for example, a company which is putting together engineering components to sell on to car manufacturers. Each component consists of three washers costing 2p each, two plates costing 15p each, and a bolt costing 40p. What will be the total cost of the component?

Clearly we need to add together 3 × 2p, 2 × 15p and 40p – the combined cost of the three washers, two plates and a bolt. That comes to 6p plus 30p plus 40p, or 76p in total. We could write the whole calculation as 3 × 2 + 2 × 15 + 40, where in order to get the correct answer we must carry out the multiplications before the additions. This gives us an important rule: multiplication takes place before addition. More generally, in fact we can say that:

- multiplication and division take place before addition and subtraction, and
- multiplication and division have equal priority, as do addition and subtraction.

This is an important rule to remember, as it's the one that is built in to the operations of spreadsheets such as Excel. If you were to put the expression above, $3 \times 2 + 2 \times 15 + 40$, into one cell of a spreadsheet, the resulting figure would be 76, in line with this rule.

If you want to remind yourself of the order in which the operations take place, you can write $(3 \times 2) + (2 \times 15) + 40$, to emphasise that the multiplications in the brackets have to be done first. This isn't essential, but you might find it helpful. Later on, as we encounter other kinds of arithmetic operations, we shall see how they slot into this ordering of priorities.

Test your understanding

Work out the results of the following calculations:

1. $2 + 12/4$ 2. $6 \times 5 - 11$ 3. $5 \times 6/15$ 4. $(10 + 6)/4$ 5. $8 \times (7 + 2)$

Zero – a special number

The number zero is not quite like other numbers. In relation to the operations we've considered thus far, it has the following special properties:

- Adding zero to a number, or taking it away from a number, leaves the number unchanged: so $4 + 0 = 4$, and $7 - 0 = 7$.
- Multiplying any number by zero gives an answer of zero – for example, $0 \times 16 = 0$, and $0 \times 250{,}436 = 0$. This makes sense because, to put it colloquially, 'any amount of nothing is still nothing'.
- Division by zero is not possible within the ordinary number system. If you have a calculator you can confirm this by trying to carry out a calculation such as 20 divided by 0. The calculator should display an error message. The same will happen if you put this calculation into a cell of a spreadsheet. So if you find yourself trying to divide something by zero in the middle of a complex calculation, something must have gone wrong!

Notation and terminology

The familiar signs + and – for addition and subtraction are used universally. The multiplication sign is generally written as '×' in print and on calculators, but most computing languages, and spreadsheets such as Excel, use the asterisk symbol '*' to avoid possible confusion with the letter 'x'. Thus $2 * 3 = 6$.

There is more diversity in how division is indicated. You are probably most familiar with the sign '÷', which is used in school-level texts and on some calculators. However, the oblique line or 'slash', with symbol '/', is preferred in many computing languages. And as we will see in the next section, the notation ½, which is usually interpreted as showing a fraction, can also be viewed as a division.

Thus $12 \div 6 = 12/6 = \dfrac{12}{6} = 2$.

You also need to be familiar with the technical terms used for various elements of a calculation. This may seem to be a nuisance, but there's nothing unusual in a subject having its own special terminology. You'll come across the same thing in accounting, economics and many other subjects which are studied as part of business and management. Learning to use the terminology of mathematics is as important a part of your study of the subject as learning to carry out calculations correctly.

So:

- We refer to the result of adding a set of numbers as their *sum*: 12 is the sum of 3, 4 and 5.
- The result of a subtraction is a *difference*: 2 is the difference between 12 and 10.
- The result of a multiplication is a *product*: 10 is the product of 2 and 5.
- In a division, the number being divided is the *dividend*, the number we are dividing by is the *divisor*, and the result of the division is the *quotient*. In the calculation 12/6 = 2, 12 is the dividend, 6 the divisor, and 2 the quotient.

You may have noticed that a multiplication can 'undo' the effect of a division: 30/6 = 5, and 5 × 6 = 30. So multiplying by 6 reverses the effect of dividing by 6. In the same way, addition reverses the effect of subtraction: 16 – 9 = 7, and 7 + 9 = 16, so adding 9 gets us back to where we started. We say that the operations addition and subtraction, and of multiplication and division, are *inverses* of each other. We'll be coming back to this idea later on when we look at solving equations.

One final point about addition and subtraction: we actually use the + and – signs for two rather different purposes. In the case of an expression such as 11 + 2, the plus sign represents an operation, or an instruction to do something with the two numbers – in this case, add them together. But in the number +6, the plus is simply an indication of the positive sign of the number. The same is true with the minus sign: in 17 – 3, it's an operation, but in the number –8, it's an indication that this is a negative number. Of course, the two things are very closely related, but it's as well to remember that there is a difference. For that reason, I would not recommend you to read the minus as 'take away': 17 take away 3 is all very well, but calling –8 'take away 8' doesn't make sense.

Test your understanding

Find

1. The sum of 10, 7 and 4.

2. The sum of 10, 7 and —4.
3. The product of 18 and 3.
4. The product of —2 and 11.
5. The divisor in the calculation 28/4.
6. The quotient in the calculation 16/(—4).

2.4 Fractions and their arithmetic

As mentioned above, the positive integers are used when counting things. The number of students on a course, the number of outlets of a retail chain, or the number of product lines carried by a supermarket would all be positive integers.

However, when we *measure* something rather than counting, we don't necessarily get a whole-number answer. For example, a construction company working out the amount of concrete it needs for a building project may well end up with an amount which is not a whole number of tonnes. Suppose that three and a half tonnes are needed. This can be expressed as 3½, or as 3.5 (don't worry if you are rusty on decimals, as we'll be coming back to this later), so the point representing the amount would lie between 3 and 4 on our number line. In fact, the spaces between the integers are entirely filled with such numbers. Some can be written in an exact form, like 3½, or 2.86. Some appear as *recurring* decimals – you may recall that if you try to write 1/3 as a decimal, it comes out as 3.333... and the string of 3s goes on forever. There are even some numbers where the decimal representation continues indefinitely, never repeating itself – if you've studied geometry you will have encountered π, the ratio of the circumference of a circle to its diameter, which is a number of this kind.

We will concentrate in this section on fractions, but before we do so, you may be wondering why we need to bother with fractions, since most of our calculations will be done using a calculator, and most calculators work with decimals. There are several answers to that point: one is that fractions are often easier for people to interpret. So saying 'about a quarter of our customers take more than three months to settle their accounts' will be more meaningful to most people than saying 'the proportion of customers who take more than three months to settle their accounts is 0.255'. Another, more theoretical reason is that many numbers that cannot be expressed precisely as decimals – like 1/7, which your calculator will tell you is 0.142857142857... – have very simple fractional representations.

Fractions are particularly useful when we want to talk about chances or probabilities: a common way to express such ideas is to say things like 'I reckon there's about a 1 in 5 chance that this project will overrun.' You may well find yourself studying the concepts of probability later on in your course.

Writing and talking about fractions

The fact that we generally write a fraction in the form ½ or 11/23 makes it clear that fractions are really nothing more than divisions: ½ is 'one divided by two' and so on. We'll be returning to this point when we discuss decimals later in the chapter.

We call the 'number on the top' of a fraction the *numerator*, and the one 'on the bottom' the *denominator*. As with the technical terms we've already encountered, the main reason for using these names is that 'numerator' is a good deal more concise than 'number on the top'.

Fractions are not restricted to numbers less than 1; 17/4 is a perfectly respectable fraction. In fact any fraction where the numerator is bigger than the denominator represents a number bigger than 1. It would be possible to write 17/4 in the form 4¼, though we don't usually use this form in mathematics.

Many different combinations of numerator and denominator can be used to represent the same number: 6/12, 18/36 and 4/8 are all equivalent ways of writing ½. In each case, the fraction represents the same proportion of the whole – whether we have six twelfths, four eighths or whatever, what we really have is a half.

The equivalence of all these representations of ½ can also be demonstrated by the process known as *cancelling* or *cancellation*, which means dividing the top and bottom of the fraction by the same number. For instance, we can divide the top and bottom of 18/36 by 3, which gets us to 6/12, and if we divide the top and bottom of 6/12 by 6, we reach ½. This process does not alter the value of the fraction. When it's not possible to carry out any further cancellation, as is the case with ½, we say that the fraction is *in its lowest terms*.

Adding and subtracting fractions

The one phrase that most people can recall from their study of fractions at school is *common denominator*. Fractions that have a common denominator – that is, the same number on the bottom – can be added directly: thus 2/5 + 4/5 = 6/5, 1/8 + 3/8 = 4/8 = ½, and so on. Notice that the denominator stays the same. Saying 'two fifths plus four fifths equals six fifths' is rather like saying 'two dollars plus four dollars equals six dollars' – the 'currency' in one case is dollars, and in the other, its fifths.

Now, just as it's not possible to add amounts of money expressed in different currencies, so fractions with different denominators can't be added directly. If you want to find the total cost of an Anglo-Swiss project, where the British part of the project is costed in pounds sterling and the Swiss part in Swiss francs, you need to convert both to a common currency – euros, perhaps – before adding them together. In the same way, fractions need to be converted to a common 'currency' by ensuring that they have the same denominator – which is where the phrase 'common denominator' comes in. The same will be true if we want to subtract rather than add the fractions.

So if we want to add 2/7 and 3/4, one possibility is to make 28 the denominator of both fractions. We can do this by multiplying the top and bottom of 2/7 by 4, to get 8/28, and multiplying the top and bottom of 3/4 by 7, to get 21/28. Then 8/28 + 21/28 = 29/28. (Just as with cancelling, multiplying top and bottom of a fraction by the same number doesn't change the value of the fraction.)

Pause for reflection

Why do you think we opted for 28 as the common denominator here?

You probably spotted that 28 is the product of 7 and 4, which are the denominators of the two fractions. This approach always works, though it doesn't always give the simplest result. For example, consider 5/6 – 3/4. We could use the 'rule' we've just established, and write this as 20/24 – 18/24 = 2/24, which cancels to 1/12. But we could also write 5/6 as 10/12, and 3/4 as 9/12, so that 10/12 – 9/12 = 1/12 as before. We call 12 the *lowest common denominator* of the two fractions, because 12 is the smallest number into which both 6 and 4 will divide.

If you find it tricky to spot the lowest common denominator in a particular case, use the 'multiply the two denominators' rule – you can always cancel at the end of the calculation.

Test your understanding

Work out the following, cancelling the answers to their lowest terms where possible:

1. 2/3 + 2/5   2. 4/9 – 1/6   3. 1/10 + 3/10   4. 1/12 – 1/3   5. 1 1/3 + 2 1/4
6. Find the sum of 8/9 and 2/3.
7. Market research indicates that two-thirds of a department store's customers prefer to pay by credit card; one-eighth use a debit card, and the remainder pay cash. What fraction pay cash? If the store deals with 18,000 transactions per week, how many debit card payments will there be?
8. An experienced project manager for a construction company is asked to assess the likelihood that a new building will be completed on time (where 'on time' means within a specified three-month period). He estimates that the chance of the project being completed early is one in four, while the chance that it will be late is one in ten. What is the chance that the building will be completed on time?

Multiplying fractions

This is the easiest of all operations with fractions – we just multiply the tops and the bottoms of the fractions separately, and then cancel if possible:

3/5 × 8/9 = 24/45 = 8/15 (cancelling by 3)
11/4 × 7/8 = 77/32, and so on.

It's worth mentioning what happens when we multiply a fraction by a whole number, as in 8 × 7/12. There is sometimes a temptation to multiply both the top and the bottom of the fraction by the 8 – but of course, this will leave the fraction unchanged. All becomes clear if we note that any whole number like 8 can be written as 8/1, and so the multiplication is really 8/1 × 7/12 = 56/12 = 14/3, cancelling by 3.

Dividing fractions

It's probably easiest here to give you the rule first and then demonstrate how it works. To divide, say, 4/5 by 3/10, we turn the divisor – the 3/10 in this case – upside down and then multiply: 4/5 ÷ 3/10 = 4/5 × 10/3 = 40/15 = 8/3 (what did we do in that last step?). You can check that this is indeed the correct result by multiplying the 8/3 by 3/10: 8/3 × 3/10 = 24/30 = 4/5, which is correct.

The rule is often abbreviated to 'invert and multiply'. One particularly useful consequence is that 12 ÷ 3 = 12 ÷ 3/1 = 12 × 1/3, so that dividing by 3 and multiplying by 1/3 are equivalent. The same thing would apply for a division by any whole number.

We can now summarise the processes for working with fractions:

- To add or subtract fractions, use a common denominator.
- To multiply fractions, multiply the numerators and denominators separately.
- To divide fractions, invert the divisor and multiply.

Test your understanding

Evaluate the following:

1. 11/12 × 3/7   2. 1/15 ÷ 5/6   3. 2 × 3/8   4. 16 ÷ 1/4
5. Divide 6 by 3/4   6. What is the product of 3/4 and 8/9?
7. 3 1/4 × 4 1/2   8. 4/5 ÷ 2
9. A small independent bakery makes, among other things, wholemeal loaves. Each batch of these loaves takes three-quarters of an hour to cook. If 22½ hours of oven time per week is available for making these loaves, how many batches can be cooked?
10. The infant mortality rate (IMR) is an important indicator of the standard of living in a country. In 1953 in the UK, 28 out of every 1000 live babies born died within their first year of life. What is this rate as a fraction in its lowest terms? In 1993 the corresponding rate, to the nearest whole number, was 8. Express this rate as a fraction with the same denominator as your figure for 1953. By what factor did the rate reduce over the 40-year period?

2.5 | Using decimals

What are they and why do we need them?

From time to time, stories surface in the media about plucky greengrocers who are refusing to 'bow to Brussels' by weighing their apples in kilograms, and insist on using pounds and ounces. Most of the world, however, now uses the decimal system of weights, measures and money, which is one reason why anyone involved in business needs to have a good understanding of decimals.

Pause for reflection

1. Write down as many examples as you can of measurements that use decimal units – for example, weights are usually given using grams and kilograms, where a kilogram contains 1000 grams. Compare your list with that of other members of your group.
2. Think about what you already know about decimals, not only from possible previous study of the subject, but also from your everyday use of money and measurement systems.

But what *are* decimals? The old-fashioned usage 'decimal fractions' gives us a clue – they are really just a special kind of fraction. The 'decimal' part is derived from the Latin word 'decem' meaning ten, so what we have is a particular kind of fraction based on tens. To see why these particular fractions have been given a special status, we need to look a little more closely at the way we write our numbers.

The number system commonly in use today is in fact based on what are called powers of ten – 10, 100, 1000, and so on (we'll be looking more closely at the idea of a power in Chapter 3). When we write a number such as 243, what this really means is (working from the right) $3 \times 1 + 4 \times 10 + 2 \times 100$ – the digits of the number tell us how many units, tens, hundreds and so on are involved. The further to the left we go, the higher the power of ten – thus 4923 = three units plus two 10s plus nine 100s plus four 1000s.

This is by no means the only possible system. If you are studying computing you may have come across binary (based on 2) or hexadecimal (based on 16) systems, and in the course of history different civilisations have chosen to write their numbers in many different ways. However, for most practical purposes the ten-based decimal system is pretty well universal.

But what happens if we want to use the decimal system to represent a fraction – a number smaller than 1? Just as we can add digits to the left-hand end of a number to represent higher powers of 10, so we can add them to the right to represent fractions based on 10 – tenths, hundredths and so on. However, we need a way of marking whereabouts in the number we change from powers of 10 to fractions – and that's the function of the decimal point. So when we write 243.96, the 2, 4 and 3 are interpreted as already explained, the decimal point marks the transition to the fractional part of the number, and then we have 9 tenths plus 6 hundredths. Altogether the number is $2 \times 100 + 4 \times 10 + 3 \times 1 + 9 \times 1/10 + 6 \times 1/100$.

If we have a number which is less than 1, such as 6/10, it's clear that there will be no figures before the decimal point, so the number will just be .6 when written. However, because it's rather easy to overlook the decimal point when we write the number in this way, the convention is to put a zero in front of it, giving 0.6. In a similar way, a fraction such as 4/1000 will become 0.004 – no tenths, no hundredths, and four thousandths.

An alternative notation

You may come across an alternative way of writing large and small numbers, based on the decimal number system we've just been discussing. This is so-called 'scientific notation', and you'll find it used on calculators to show numbers which are too large or too small to fit within the usual 8-character display window; it's also available within Excel.

The notation is best illustrated by some examples. Consider the number 22,400,000, which could be written as $2.24 \times 10,000,000$. A calculator using scientific notation would display this as 2.24E07, indicating that the 2.24 is to be multiplied by a 1 followed by 7 noughts. Similarly 186,400,000 can be shown as 1.864E+08, and so on.

The convention is that the decimal place in a number written in scientific notation is always placed after one digit. If the number has too many non-zero digits to be fully displayed, then most calculators will round it off, so that 186,545, 000 would become 1.87E+08 in an 8-digit display (see Section 2.6 for more about rounding).

When it comes to small rather than large numbers, the method is similar: 0.000463 can be written as 4.63/10,000, which in scientific notation becomes 4.63E–04. The 'E–04' indicates that the 4.63 is to be divided by a 1 followed by 4 noughts – it's the minus sign which indicates that a division rather than a multiplication is required. In the same way, 0.0000525 would appear as 5.25E–05.

The E here stands for 'exponent', a term which we will discuss more fully in Chapter 4. Also in that chapter it will become clear why the minus sign is used to indicate a division.

Test your understanding

1. Express the following numbers as a sum of powers of ten, as we did with the numbers 243.96 and 4923 above:

   462, 5003, 11.4, 7.12, 53,289.

2. Write the following fractions as decimals:

   17/100, 141/1000, 140/1000, 3/100, 114/100.

3. Write the following numbers in scientific notation for a calculator with an 8-digit display:

   53,700,000   442,226,000   0.000775.

Adding and subtracting decimals

As long as you remember to keep the decimal points lined up, so that all the tenths, hundredths and so are also lined up vertically, this should not cause any problems, For example:

$$
\begin{array}{r}
1.3 \\
2.97 \\
0.04 \\
\underline{10.5} \\
14.81
\end{array}
$$

This of course is exactly what we do when adding amounts of money – you could interpret this addition as £1.30 plus £2.97 plus 4 pence plus £10.50. (Notice that we can add a zero to the right-hand end of the number without making any difference – but see Section 2.6 on 'Accuracy and rounding' below for more about this.)

Multiplying decimals

Most of the time you will probably be using a calculator or spreadsheet to carry out anything other than the simplest decimal multiplication. However, if you find yourself having to multiply decimals by hand, then the easiest way is as follows: begin by ignoring the decimal points, and just multiplying the numbers in the ordinary way. So to multiply 0.03 by 0.008, start by saying $3 \times 8 = 24$ or 24.0. Then, to decide where to put the decimal point in the answer, move the decimal point to the left by a number of places equal to the total of the numbers of figures after the point in the separate numbers being multiplied. Here there are two decimal places in 0.03, and three in 0.008, so we need five in the answer – thus we move the point in 24.0 five places to the left, to get a final result of 0.00024.

This may seem a bit mysterious, but it's actually just a consequence of the way the fractional equivalents of the decimals work. If we wrote 0.03 as 3/100 and 0.008 as 8/1000, and then multiplied the two fractions, we would have $3/100 \times 8/1000 = 24/100,000 = 0.00024$, just as we obtained above.

The process works in the same way even if we are multiplying numbers greater than 1. So to multiply 3.2 by 25, begin by multiplying 32 by 25, giving 800 or 800.0. Then count the decimal places involved: 3.2 has one figure after the point, 25 has none, so the total is one. We thus need to move the point one place to the left in the answer, giving 80.00 or simply 80. You can check with your calculator that this is correct.

Dividing decimals

First let's consider the division of a decimal by a whole number – for example, 0.12/3. If we write this in fractional terms, it becomes (12/100)/3, which the rules for division of fractions tell us is equal to $(12/100) \times (1/3) = 4/100 = 0.04$ (cancelling by 3). But this is exactly the answer which we would get from dividing the 0.12 by 3 in the normal way, simply inserting the decimal point at the appropriate place in the calculation.

To see how more generally we can divide one decimal by another, consider 4.148/0.04. We can multiply both top and bottom of this fraction by 100, to get 414.8/4, without altering the value of the fraction; we chose 100 here because this has the effect of making the denominator into a whole number. Now we can proceed as described in the last paragraph, to get 103.7 as the answer.

Multiplication and division by powers of 10

Because decimals are based on powers of 10, multiplications and divisions by 10, 100, 1000, and so on follow a particularly simple pattern. Take 5.8×10: if we use the rule for multiplication of decimals, we get 58 (check that you can see how this works). So multiplication by 10 has just moved the decimal point one place to the right. In the same way, multiplication by 100 moves it 2 places to the right, and so on.

The reverse is true when we divide by a power of 10: $0.5/10 = (5/10)/10 = (5/10) \times (1/10) = 5/100 = 0.05$, so we have moved the point one place to the left. Similarly division by 100 moves the point two places to the left, and so on.

Moving between fractions and decimals

Fractions and decimals are interchangeable since, as we now know, a decimal is just a special kind of fraction. We've already seen how to write a decimal as a fraction with a power of 10 in the denominator. To go the other way – for instance, to write a fraction such as 3/8 as a decimal – just carry out a decimal division in the normal way: $3/8 = 3.0/8 = 0.375$.

Sometimes, when we carry out this process, we find that the division never actually comes to an end, no matter how long we carry on, so that we are left with what's called a *recurring* decimal. One simple example of this is the decimal representation of 1/3, which is 0.33333... – however many times we divide by 3, there is always a remainder of 1. We say that the 3 *recurs* here. With other fractions, it may be a whole group of figures which recurs rather than a single digit – try to convert 1/11 into a decimal to see how this arises.

Is all this really necessary?

As mentioned above, you will probably reach for your calculator as soon as calculations with decimals are required, so is there really any point in getting to grips with all this hand-calculation theory? The answer is that, while you may not need to develop skills in carrying out complex decimal arithmetic manually, it is helpful to be familiar with ideas such as how the number of decimal places in a product is determined. This will enable you to answer the question 'Is this as reasonable answer?' when looking at the results which emerge from your calculator, and could save you from the consequences of a slip of the finger on the keys.

Test your understanding

1. $0.24 + 3.791$ 2. $4.6 - 8.92$ 3. $11 + 0.04 + 1.3$ 4. $16.09 - 12.36$
5. $2/0.1$ 6. 10.4×20 7. 16.71×0.05 8. $173.42/0.12$
9. What is 8/9 as a decimal?
10. How many Norwegian kroner will I receive in exchange for a sum of £102.19, on a day when the rate of exchange is 12.14 kroner to the pound?

11. What is 0.325 as a fraction in its lowest terms?
12. If the dollars to sterling exchange rate is 1.90 dollars to the pound, and a company wishes to buy a machine costing $13,492, what will be the equivalent price in £?

2.6 Accuracy and rounding

Pause for reflection

If you were asked 'How much money have you got in the bank?' how accurate an answer do you think you would give? Would it be correct to the nearest £10, £1, penny ...?

If the chair of the Board of Marks & Spencer were asked for the value of the company's assets, what sort of accuracy do you think he or she would quote in the answer?

Would the same degree of accuracy be required in the two situations above, and if not, why not?

How accurate do numbers need to be?

The activity above should have brought home to you the fact that different levels of accuracy in quoting figures are required for different purposes. Although calculators and spreadsheets will display the results of calculations to a high degree of accuracy, it is very often not appropriate to quote the figures in such detail. There is no simple answer to the question 'How accurate should my answer be?' – it is a matter of judgement. However, there are two general points to be borne in mind.

(a) How are you going to be using the figures? If you just want to convey an idea of the general size of something, it can be quite distracting to quote very detailed figures. For example, if you are describing the floor area of an office that you are hoping to rent out to clients, it is pointless to say that it is 1246.97 square metres – a statement such as 'about 1250 square metres' would be much more sensible.

If, on the other hand, you are quoting the interest rate which will be paid on an investment, then the third or fourth decimal place might be crucial. The difference between annual rates of 12.5% and 12.53% may look trivial, but when the sum invested is, say, £100,000, the extra 0.03% results in an additional £30 earned over a year – quite a substantial amount.

(b) How accurate were the figures which went into the calculation? Roughly speaking, a calculation is only as accurate as its least accurate component. And there are some figures that almost by definition can't be known with complete accuracy – the population of a large city might be a case in point. Babies are being born around the clock, and at the same time people are dying, so that any figure is only 'correct' for a tiny period of time. In such a situation, to quote a figure which *appears* extremely precise would be an example of what is sometimes called 'spurious accuracy'.

How can we specify the accuracy we require?

The accuracy to which a number is being quoted can be described in three ways.

(a) We can indicate how many decimal places are to be quoted. For example, we might ask for the answer to a calculation 'correct to two decimal places'. Thus, if the accurate answer works out to 4.983, then correct to two decimal places we would give 4.98. This is because 4.983 is closer to 4.980 than to 4.990. On the other hand, if the answer were 4.987, then we would quote 4.99 correct to two decimal places, because 4.987 is closer to 4.990 than 4.980. The usual rule is that figures ending in 1, 2, 3, 4 are rounded downwards, while those ending in 5, 6, 7, 8, 9 are rounded upwards. This does create a slight bias, in that, if we are rounding off a large number of figures, rather more of them will be rounded up than down, but generally that's not a serious concern.

There is one slightly technical point to note here. You might think that adding zeroes to the end of a decimal number doesn't make any difference to its value – so 44.9000 should mean the same as 44.90 or 44.9. However, conventionally, if you write 44.9000 it will be assumed by anyone looking at the figure that this is correct to four decimal places; 44.90 will be taken as correct to two decimal places, and so on. So adding extra zeroes to the end of numbers is not a good idea unless you really want them to be interpreted in this way.

(b) Method (a) of course is only useful if we are dealing with decimal numbers. Another, more general method is to round off 'to the nearest 10' (or 1000, or whatever). This is particularly useful when dealing with large numbers. So we would say that £4576 to the nearest £10 is £4580, while £82,240 to the nearest £100 is £82,200. The rules for rounding in this way are very similar to those in (a) above: 5, 6, 7, 8, 9 get rounded up, while 1, 2, 3, 4 get rounded down. Thus £845 to the nearest £10 will be £850, not £840.

(c) The third method involves the concept of *significant figures*. This is perhaps best illustrated by an example: in the number 604,400, the first four digits – 6, 0, 4, 4 – are significant in the sense that they convey information about the value of the number; the zeroes on the end are not significant, since they are simply there to indicate the size of the number. So if we are asked to quote 604,400 to three significant figures, the answer will be 604,000. In the same way, 0.00406 to two significant figures becomes 0.0041 – the zeroes at the front are not significant. Generally speaking a zero is only significant if it is 'sandwiched' between two non-zero digits.

Rounding with calculators and spreadsheets

Many calculators will let you set the number of decimal places to be given in answers, and within Excel and other spreadsheets you can format the contents of a cell to show a preset number of decimal places. However, you need to take care. While Excel, and some calculators, will round off to the required number of decimal places properly in accordance with the rules we've given above, others simply truncate the figure – that is, chop off the unwanted figures without any proper rounding (thus, for example, turning 9.77 into 9.7 rather than 9.8 when one decimal place is required). So be sure that you know which way your chosen tool is operating.

Test your understanding

1. Find 8.9266, 24.36879, 0.004572, −32.66, to three decimal places.
2. What are 10,170, 0.03064, 2.6666, −17.94, to three significant figures?
3. Weekly takings of three branches of a retail store are quoted as £24,279 (correct to the nearest pound), £18,730 (to the nearest ten pounds) and £19,350 (to the nearest £50). If you wanted to add the three figures together, how accurate would the answer be?

2.7 Making sense of percentages

Pause for reflection

More use is probably made of percentages in the media, in business and in everyday life than of any other aspect of arithmetic. Compile a list of the places where you've seen percentages cited recently – for example, in advertising for credit cards ('0% for six months'), in newspaper stories about the economy ('Inflation tops 2% for second consecutive month') and so on.

Unfortunately it is also very easy to misuse percentages. Think again about the applications in the list you've compiled, and ask yourself whether any of them are inappropriate.

What are percentages?

Just as decimals are fractions based on powers of ten, so percentages are fractions whose denominator is always 100. So when we write 32%, what we mean is 32/100 – the % sign is what remains of the /100 scribbled very quickly!

Percentages have become very widely used because it is much easier to work with fractions with a nice standard denominator like 100 than with awkward numbers like 19 and 27, particularly when we are interested in making comparisons. To most of us, a statement like 'Last year we offered jobs to 47 out of 93 applicants; this year the figure is 38 out of 80' doesn't convey very much. You might spot that the proportion of applicants offered jobs has fallen a little, since 47 is just over half of 93, while 38 is less than half of

80, but it's difficult to go much further than this because the numbers involved are not 'nice', and the total numbers of applicants in the two years are different.

However, if we are told that the proportion of applicants being offered jobs last year was 51%, whereas this year it's 48%, we get a much better idea of the change. This is simply because we are now comparing figures on a common basis – 51 out of every 100 compared with 48 out of 100 – and moreover a basis which, being a nice round number, is easier to visualise. This is why the use of percentages is so widespread.

Calculating percentages

We use the idea of a percentage in two quite different contexts.

Finding one quantity as a percentage of another

For instance, in the example above, we want to convert 38 appointments out of 80 applicants to a percentage, so we are asking 'What is 38 as a percentage of 80?' This is equivalent to converting the fraction 38/80 to 'something'/100. If we write x to stand for the 'something', then we have $38/80 = x/100$. This is a very simple equation, and although we shall not be covering solution of equations formally until Chapter 5, you can probably see that here $x = 38/80 \times 100 = 47.5$. So 38 is 47.5% of 80, and we can say last year, 47.5% of applicants got jobs.

The process we have gone through here can be generalised to give a formula for calculating any number as a percentage of another:

To express a as a percentage of b, calculate a/b × 100.

Thus 6 as a percentage of 24 is $(6/24) \times 100 = 25\%$, 9 as a percentage of 27 is $(9/27) \times 100 = 33\%$ (to the nearest whole percentage) and so on.

To find a given percentage of a quantity

The reverse of the calculation in the previous section occurs when we want to find a certain percentage of a number. For example, the VAT rate in the UK at the moment is 17.5%, and so to find the VAT to be added to a bill of £60, we need to find 17.5% of £60. Since 17.5% is the same thing as 17.5/100, we need to calculate $17.5/100 \times 60 = £10.50$. The general version of this is:

To find a% of b, calculate (a/100) × b

So if you are getting 3.4% per annum interest on a savings account, and you have £2000 in the account at the start of the year, by the end you will have $(3.4/100) \times 2000 = £68$ interest to be added to the account.

What you can and can't do with percentages

Whenever you hear someone mentioning a percentage, you should ask 'percentage of what?' Sometimes the answer will be clear from the context. If the menu in a restaurant says '15% service charge will be added' it's pretty clear that it means '15% of the total bill'. However, if there's any doubt, then the base for the percentage calculation needs to be made clear – for example 'house prices are now 8% higher on average than they were this time last year' or 'only 4% of our total number of customers complained about poor service last month'.

A consequence of this is that you can't carry out arithmetic with percentages in the same way as you would with other kinds of number. If 30% of a company's female workforce, and 10% of males, work part-time, that doesn't mean that the total percentage for the company is 40%. To get the correct answer, you would need to know how many males and females are employed in total. If there are 200 females and 100 males, then there will be 60 female part-timers and 10 males, so the total number of part-timers is 70 out of a total workforce of 300, which (check this!) comes to about 23%.

A common, but mistaken, belief about percentages is that 'you can't have a percentage bigger than 100'. Of course, this is clearly false; since, as we now know, a percentage is simply a fraction with 100 as the denominator, a percentage greater than 100 just represents an amount bigger than 1. So, if a company had 60 customers in its first year of operation, and 150 in its second year, then it's perfectly correct to say that there has been a 150% increase in the numbers of customers – the numerical increase is 90, and 90 as a percentage of $60 = (90/60) \times 100 = 150\%$.

One common application of percentages is the addition or subtraction of a fixed percentage from a number. For example, suppose that a restaurant has a policy of adding a 60% mark-up to the price of a bottle of wine, and that the proprietor wishes to calculate how much she should be charging for a bottle that cost her £6.50. The long-winded way of doing this is to say that 60% of $£6.50 = 6.50 \times 60/100 = £3.90$, and then add this to the original price of £6.50 to get a total of £10.40. However, it's much more efficient to note that adding 60% to the original price is equivalent to taking 160% of that price – the original 100% plus the extra 60% – and so to find 160% of $£6.50 = 6.50 \times 160/100 = 10.4$ or £10.40, as before. Similarly, if a store wants to reduce the price of a washing machine costing £440 by 25% in a sale, then the sale price will be 100% – 25% or 75% of the original, and so sale price = $£440 \times 75/100 = £330$.

The reverse of this calculation, however, is a bit more tricky. Suppose you are told that the sale price is £330, and that this represents a reduction of 25% on the original price. There is a temptation to say that the original price must therefore have been £330 plus 25% of £330, which comes to £412.50 – but this is clearly not correct, since we know the answer should be £440. Can you see where things have gone wrong?

The answer, of course, lies in that question 'percentage of what?' which we should ask when looking at the 25%. The answer is that the reduction is not 25% of the sale price – it's 25% of the original price. So £330 must be 75% of the original, and if you remember that 75% is three-quarters it's easy to see that one-quarter of the original price must therefore be £110, giving an original price of £440. (There is a more formal way to work this out, but as it would involve the solution of a small equation, which won't be covered until Chapter 5, we won't pursue it here.)

Percentages with your calculator

Some calculators have a % key, which can save you the trouble of entering the ×100 and /100 in the two types of percentage calculation. Different models of calculator have % keys which operate in slightly different ways, so you need to read the instruction booklet for your particular model to find out exactly how to use this function – or try experimenting using the calculation of 3 as a percentage of 24 (which should be 12.5%) and 8% of 250 (which should give an answer of 20).

Interchanging decimals, fractions and percentages

As we've seen, both decimals and percentages are just different ways of writing fractions. It can be helpful to remember the decimal and percentage equivalents of certain common fractions, so here is a list:

Fraction	Decimal	Percentage
1/2	0.5	50%
1/3	0.3333...	33.3% to one decimal place
1/4	0.25	25%
3/4	0.75	75%
1/5	0.2	20%

Try adding a few more rows to the table using other simple fractions, to make sure you understand the conversion process.

Test your understanding

1. Find the following: 12% of 75, 20% of 120, 7.5% of 80, 140% of 16, 80% of 8.
2. What are 3 as a percentage of 8; 16 as a percentage of 40; 90 as a percentage of 50; 1 as a percentage of 5; 12 as a percentage of 32?
3. What will a price of £2.50 become if a 16% mark-up is added?
4. A construction company bills a customer for £22,450. However, a penalty clause in the contract makes the company liable to a reduction of 12% for late completion. How much will it actually receive?
5. The price of a camera including VAT of 17.5% is £90. What was the price before VAT was added?
6. A firm has 237 male and 161 female employees. What percentage of its workforce is male?
7. Last year 346 customers of a small building society defaulted on their mortgage payments; this year the figure was 279. By what percentage has the number of defaulters decreased? Do you think this is a useful measure? If not, suggest a measure which would be more useful, and indicate what additional information, if any, you would need in order to calculate it.
8. If there is a steady 3% per annum growth in the population of a country, by what

> percentage will its population increase over a ten-year period? (You may find it simplest to investigate the effect of this rate of growth on a hypothetical population of, say, 10,000 people.)
> 9. What are the following as decimals: 42%, 3%, 5/8, 6/5, 110%?
> 10. Express the following as percentages: 0.225, 0.04, 2.4, 3/4, 13/20.

2.8 | Some new arithmetic operations

The basic operations of arithmetic – addition, subtraction, multiplication and division – together with the use of the = sign to represent equality, are so familiar that most of us probably don't even recall when we first learned their meaning.

Later on in this book, we shall encounter new types of arithmetical operation, represented by new and unfamiliar symbols. For example, I shall introduce a symbol to mean 'add up this whole series of numbers'. This can be rather disconcerting at first, but if you feel anxious at the prospect, remind yourself that all such symbols are simply shorthand for things that can be expressed in English. Thus = can be read as 'is equal to'. This should help to demystify the symbols used in mathematical expressions.

2.9 | Putting it all together

At the time I'm writing this, the Derbyshire Building Society, with which I have an account, is advertising its First Online Savings Account. Information from the Society's website tells me that the account offers a gross (that is, before deduction of tax) interest rate of 4.75%, and that interest is paid annually on 28 February.

Suppose that Sally Jones, a sole trader running a marketing consultancy, decides that she will put £100 per year into this account, for a period of three years, with a view to saving for a replacement for her present laptop computer. She will make her first payment on 1 March 2007. How much will she have in her account on 28 February 2010?

We shall have to assume – though this isn't part of the information given by the building society – that the interest rate is guaranteed to stay at 4.75% for the three-year period. Then we can carry out the calculation year by year as follows:

On 1 March 2007, Sally has £1000 in her account.
On 28 February 2008, 4.75% of this amount is added as interest. We know that 4.75% of $1000 = 1000 \times 4.75/100 = 47.5$, so the total in the account at that point is £1047.50.
On 1 March 2008, Sally deposits a further £1000, so she now has £2047.50 in her account.
On 28 February 2009, interest amounting to 4.75% of £2047.50 is added – that's $2047.50 \times 4.75/100 = £97.26$, giving a total in the account of £2047.50 + £97.26 = £2144.76.
Another £1000 is added on 1 March 2009, giving £3144.76 in the account.

Finally, on 28 February 2010, interest amounting to 4.75% of £3144.76 is added – that's 3144.76 × 4.75/100 = £149.38. So the account now contains £3294.14.

Sally now discovers that the top-of-the-range laptop she wants to buy costs £3500. By what proportion do her savings fall short of the total price?

The shortfall is £3500 – £3294.14 = £205.86. As a proportion of the price of £3500, this is 205.85/3500 = 0.059 or about 5.9%.

We've used various arithmetic operations in these calculations, including the appropriate rounding of the figures bearing in mind that they represent amounts of money. The step-by-step process which we've used isn't in fact the most efficient way of doing the calculation – we could make use of a formula that tells us how the interest accumulates – but to do that we would need algebra, which is the topic of the next chapter.

2.10 For Excel users

Arithmetic within Excel follows exactly the same rules as the hand calculations we have discussed in this chapter. In particular, the conventions about multiplication and division taking precedence over addition and subtraction, and about the use of brackets, apply.

What have I learned?

Look back at the list of 'Intended learning outcomes' at the start of this chapter. How do you feel that the understanding which you have developed matches up against that list? Are there any arithmetical processes about which you used to feel confused, but which you now understand? And are there any about which you still don't feel very confident? Share you views on this with other students on your course, and with your tutor. You may be worrying about things that aren't going to be very important in your particular course, or perhaps your understanding is better than you think it is.

Exercises

Evaluate the following:

1. 6 × 1/12 – 3/4   2. 47.2 × 0.3   3. 0.06/0.03   4. 16% of 800
5. 24 – 4 × 3   6. 27 as a percentage of 60   7. 7/8 of 72
8. Add 15.5% to 43.2, giving your answer correct to one decimal place.
9. Find the product of 12 and 9.
10. Find the quotient of 36 and 4.

Case Study: N-Press Printing

You are working on a placement with N-Press Printing, a small printing company which produces advertising posters, handbills and flyers. You have been asked to examine the growth of the company over the past few years, and to compare its performance with that of its major competitor, PrinTidy.

You have been given the following information by N-Press's management.

Year	2004	2005	2006
Turnover of N-Press(£)	213,000	220,000	227,000
Turnover of PrinTidy (£)	231,000	234,000	237,000

(a) To what level of accuracy does it appear these figures have been rounded?
(b) By approximately what percentage per year does N-Press's turnover appear to be growing?
(c) How would you characterise the growth of PrinTidy?
(d) If N-Press carries on growing at the same rate, roughly when will its turnover break the £250,000 per year barrier?
(e) If both companies continue to expand at the same rate, roughly when will N-Press overtake PrinTidy? How confident would you feel about this prediction?
(f) What kind of use could N-Press's management make of the results of your work?

For further exercises and multiple choice revision questions visit the companion website: www.palgrave.com/business/morris

CHAPTER 3

Introducing algebra

Intended learning outcomes

By the end of your work on this chapter you should:

- be able to explain why algebra can be a useful tool in a business context
- be confident in manipulating algebraic expressions involving powers, roots, brackets and arithmetical operations
- be able to express simple practical problems in algebraic terms
- be familiar with the terminology used to interpret algebraic expressions.

Prerequisites

Before starting work on this chapter you need to feel confident about:

- the basic operations of arithmetic covered in Chapter 2
- the rules for priority of arithmetic operations introduced in Section 2.3.

3.1 Why do we need algebra?

Before you start

Think for a moment about the ideas which the word 'algebra' conjures up in your mind. Then write down a couple of sentences which capture these ideas. (Keep these somewhere safe – you'll need to revisit them at the end of the chapter.)

What kind of ideas did you come up with? Maybe you felt like Jane, who said 'Algebra always seemed like something mysterious – these minus signs kept appearing, and I didn't know why.' Or perhaps Asha's comments ring a bell with you: 'When we learned a new method, I could do the exercises just after the lesson, but then I just forgot it all.'

Both of these students are expressing common, and perfectly reasonable, worries about algebra. Whereas arithmetic – as discussed in Chapter 1 – deals with numbers which are concrete and meaningful, algebra seems to operate in a mysterious realm of letters which can mean anything we want them to, and which are combined according to strange laws known only to mathematicians.

Of course, this isn't really the case at all, as I hope I shall convince you in this chapter. The key really lies in how you approach your study of algebra. If you try to learn 'methods' parrot-fashion, without thinking about *why* they work, you are giving yourself a very difficult task – a bit like trying to learn a poem in a language you don't speak.

Arithmetic, as discussed in Chapter 2, is all we need if we are always going to be operating with numbers. Here are some examples where this might be the case:

- An accountant preparing the profit and loss statement of a company for the financial year – the values of sales, interest charges, depreciation and so on are all known quantities for a given year, and so all the accountant needs to do is to perform the right arithmetical operations on these quantities to arrive at the profit or loss figure for the year.
- A sales department preparing an invoice for a customer. Once the amounts of various items ordered by the customer are known, together with their prices, plus any discounts, delivery charges, and so on, the calculation of the total amount owed is a matter of arithmetic.

In other cases, however, we do not know the actual values of the quantities we're dealing with. Sometimes the quantity could take a whole range of possible values and we want to find which is the best one to choose (as in trying to determine the most profitable quantity of an item to manufacture); in other cases we won't find out the value until some later date (like, say, the value of a share this time next year).

In such a situation, using letters to represent the (unknown) numbers in our problem has two big advantages:

1. It enables us to examine the problem in more detail without having to know what the numbers involved are.
2. It can give us results which are completely general so that they are true for any values of the quantities involved.

For instance, suppose you have 250 shares in a company, and you want to say something about the total amount you would receive if you sold them at this time next year. Of course you don't know what the selling price of each share will be at that time, but if you use the letter P to represent the price in £ on the day you sell the shares, then you can say:

Total (in £) received for 250 shares = $250 \times P$

This simply expresses the fact that to find the total you receive, you multiply the number of shares you've got by their selling price on the day – but it's a great deal shorter and simpler!

Two things to notice here which we'll return to later:

1. We've been very careful about specifying the *units* – £ in this case – in which the unknown price is measured.
2. We've used a letter which means something – P for price – rather than the *x*s and *y*s you may have been used to from school algebra. This is generally a good idea – it helps you to remember what the letters stand for.

Test your understanding

1. Use the expression above for the total received to find out how much you'll get if the price per share is (a) £2 (b) £2.50 (c) 50p.
2. Can you modify the expression for the total received to allow for the fact that, instead of having 250 shares, you will have some unknown quantity of shares?

Here's another rather more substantial example involving the use of algebraic expressions.

Krunchy Plc manufactures breakfast cereal. Like most food manufacturers, the company needs to plan its purchasing of raw materials quite a long time in advance. But the price it will have to pay for oats next year is uncertain, and the amount it will decide to buy probably depends on the price, so that's unknown too. How, then, can we write down anything that will be helpful to Krunchy about the total it will have to spend on oats next year?

One good way to start, if we don't have any definite numbers to begin with, is to invent some. Let's assume that the company buys 20 tonnes of oats at £600 per tonne; then it's easy to see that the total cost will be £12,000. But this answer only applies for these particular figures – it doesn't help us to say what the cost will be for *any* number of tonnes, at *any* price.

However, we can use the numerical calculation to help us see what's going on. In order to find the cost in £, we multiplied the price in £ per tonne by the number of tonnes bought. (Notice that we're being careful to specify the units again.) That process will be the same irrespective of the particular numbers involved.

Now what algebra does is to use letters – often known as *variables*, because their values can vary – to represent unknown numbers. Thus, if £P is the price per tonne paid for oats, and Q is the quantity in tonnes purchased by Krunchy, then the cost will be £C, where

$$C = P \times Q$$

We've done exactly the same calculation here as when we used the specific values £600 and 20 tonnes – that's to say, we've used the fact that total cost = number of tonnes purchased × cost per tonne. We have just written the operation using letters instead of numbers.

Once the price of the oats and the number of tonnes bought are known, next year, we can use the formula to work out the total cost. But in case you are thinking that this is rather a long-winded way of arriving at that figure, notice that we now have a representation of the cost for any price and quantity – a *formula*, in fact, for the cost – which we can use in thinking about other aspects of the situation. For example, if the supplier offers a discount of 5% of the total price for payment on delivery, then we can say that the discount will be 5% of C = 5% of $P \times Q$ = $0.05 \times P \times Q$ (remember from Chapter 1 that 5% as a decimal is 0.05).

There are a few important ideas here:

- We're using letters or variables to represent numerical quantities.
- We need to be careful to include the units when we are defining what the variables mean.
- These variables are combined into algebraic expressions using the operations of ordinary arithmetic.
- We can get some insight into how to put together the algebraic expression by asking ourselves how we would do the calculation with numerical values if we had them.

Test your understanding

1. Use the formula above to work out the cost if 12 tonnes are purchased at £450 per tonne.
2. Use the formula to work out how many tonnes should be purchased if the cost per tonne is £400 and the budgeted amount to be spent on potatoes is £8000.

The two examples we have looked at so far have been very simple. Before we can apply the ideas of algebra to more complex practical problems, we need to look in more detail at the rules and the terminology of algebra.

Pause for reflection

Your 11-year-old nephew has just started to learn algebra, and doesn't like it much! Write a short note explaining to him why it is useful in solving practical problems.

3.2 Writing and simplifying algebraic expressions

Some basic principles

In the last section we used the expression

$$C = P \times Q$$

which represented the cost in £ of buying Q tonnes of potatoes at £P per tonne. Usually we don't bother to write the multiplication sign between the letters – the expression PQ is taken to mean $P \times Q$. Likewise, if we wanted to double this quantity, we would write $2PQ$ rather than $2 \times P \times Q$. In other words, two quantities written next to each other with no sign in between are assumed to be multiplied.

With numerical expressions, we are accustomed to reducing answers to a single number by using the rules of arithmetic: so, for example, we'd reduce the expression $2 + 3 \times 7 - 4$ to the single figure 19 (in working this out, you need to remember the rules about priority of operations explained in Chapter 1). With algebraic expressions, this isn't always possible; we can only combine terms if they involve the same variables.

Thus with the expression $2a + 3b - a$, we can change the order to get

$$2a - a + 3b \qquad\qquad 3.1$$

and then combine the $2a$ and the $-a$ to obtain

$$a + 3b$$

but that's as far as we can go. The term in a and the one in b can't be combined in any way, because they involve different variables. A bit of terminology helps here: the numbers in front of the variables are called *coefficients*. The coefficient of a in the first term of Equation 3.1 above is 2, and the coefficient of a in the second term is -1. So when we combine the terms, we are really just operating with the coefficients according to the usual rules of arithmetic.

Here's another example; check that you can follow the logic of the steps by which the expression is simplified:

$$4pq - 6p + 11q + 2\,pq = 6pq - 6p + 11q$$

Test your understanding

Simplify the following expressions:

1. $2xy - x + y - 3x$ 2. $7s + 2t - st + t$
3. $2x - 4x + 3y - 11$ 4. $3ab + a - 2b - 4ab$

Powers and roots

The idea of a power

In the last section we used expressions involving the product of two variables, such as ab, or $2xy$. But sometimes we want to multiply a variable by itself, as the following example illustrates.

Suppose the managing director of ABC Mobile Phones sets the rather demanding target that the total sales volume of a new model of phone must be doubled every month during its first year on the market. If the sales volume in the first month is 100 units, then in the second month it should be 200 units, in the third month 400 units, and so on. Each month the previous month's figure is multiplied by 2.

So to find the target level for month 6, we need to work out

$$100 \times 2 \times 2 \times 2 \times 2 \times 2$$

(Can you see why there are only five 2's and not six?) This is clearly a clumsy expression, and so a shorthand has been devised to represent '2 multiplied by itself 5 times'. We write $2 \times 2 \times 2 \times 2 \times 2$ as 2^5, reading it as 'two to the power five'. Sometimes the whole process of doing this calculation is called 'raising 2 to the power 5'.

More generally, if the managing director sets the less precise target that sales volume should be multiplied by a factor k each month, then in month 6 the target would be

$$100 \times k \times k \times k \times k \times k$$

and we would write this as $100 \times k^5$ or simply $100k^5$, and read it as '100 times k to the power 5'.

Two things are worth noticing at this point:

- When we write $100k^5$, only the k is raised to the power of 5 – not the 100. So in carrying out the calculation, you would need to work out the k^5 first, and then multiply this by 100. We'll be returning to this question of the order in which calculations should be carried out shortly.
- We have some special terms for powers 2 and 3, as you may already know. Raising a quantity to the power 2 is called *squaring* it, so x^2 is read as 'x squared'. Raising it to the power 3 is referred to as *cubing*: x^3 is thus x cubed.

Pause for reflection

Can you see why we use the terms squared and cubed in this context?

In general, then, we define a power as follows:

k^n means k multiplied by itself n times

There are some further bits of terminology sometimes used in connection with powers. In the expression k^n, n is known as the *exponent* (remember this term from Section 2.5?) or the *index* (plural *indices*), though it's often referred to more loosely as the *power*.

Test your understanding

Simplify the following expressions:

1. 3^5 2. The square of 7   3. The cube of 0.1   4. $(2a)^4$

Rules for operating with powers

(a) Priority: We saw in Chapter 1 that there are rules for the order in which arithmetical operations are carried out – multiplication and division before addition and subtraction. We now need to extend those rules to the new operation of raising a variable to a power.

If we write $2a^2$, the interpretation is that the squaring of a takes place before the multiplication by 2. More generally:

● Raising a number to a power takes precedence over multiplication and division, which take precedence over addition and subtraction.

(b) Addition and subtraction: There is really nothing new here – what we said previously about combining terms involving different variables applies also to powers. So for example, we can say $a^2 + a^2 = 2a^2$, but we cannot simplify $a^2 + a^3$ because the two terms involve different powers. We can sum this up by saying:

● To add or subtract like powers of a variable, just add or subtract their coefficients.

Example: $ab^2 + 2ab + a^2 - ab + 3ab^2 = 4ab^2 + ab + a^2$

Here the ab terms can be combined, as can the ab^2 terms, but they can't be combined with each other or with the a^2 term because these involve different powers.

(c) Multiplication: If we are multiplying powers of different variables, then there is little we can do by way of simplification. For example, the expression x^2y^3 can't be simplified because the powers involve different variables.

If, however, the powers being multiplied involve the same variable, then we can simplify products. For example, if we want to multiply a^2 by a^3 then we note that:

$$a^2 \times a^3 = (a \times a) \times (a \times a \times a) \text{ (using the definition of a power)}$$
$$= a \times a \times a \times a \times a \text{ (taking the brackets away)}$$
$$= a^5 \text{ (using the definition again).}$$

We seem to have added the indices here, since $2 + 3 = 5$. This rule will work for any powers, so we can say

● To multiply powers, add their indices.

In symbols, this can be expressed as $a^m \times a^n = a^{m+n}$.

Some further examples of this rule in action:

$a^3 \times ab^4 = a^3 \times a \times b^4 = a^4\, b^4$ (remembering that when we write x this is really shorthand for x^1).

$5 \times 2^4 \times 2^4 = 5 \times 2^8 = 5 \times 256 = 1280.$

(d) Division: As with products, we can't simplify a quotient involving powers of different variables. So b^4/a^3 has to be left as it is.

When we are dividing powers of the same variable, we can do as we did with products and go back to the definition of a power to get some insight into how the process works. For instance, to evaluate b^4/b^2, write out the powers in full:

$(b \times b \times b \times b)/(b \times b) = b \times b$ (the other two bs on the top cancelling)
$= b^2$

It looks as though we have subtracted the powers here: b^4 divided by b^2 gives $b^{4-2} = b^2$. More generally we can say

● To divide powers, subtract the index in the denominator from that in the numerator.

or symbolically, $a^m/a^n = a^{m-n}$.

(e) Raising a power to another power: This isn't something you would need to do very often in practical applications, but we include it here for completeness. Suppose you want to find $(a^2)^3$. Writing this out in full gives $(a \times a) \times (a \times a) \times (a \times a) = a \times a \times a \times a \times a \times a = a^6$. It seems that here we have multiplied the two original powers to get the final power: $2 \times 3 = 6$. More generally the rule is:

- To raise a power to another power, multiply the two indices.

or symbolically $(a^m)^n = a^{mn}$.

Here's an example showing all these rules in action:

$$(ab^2)^4/(a^2b) = (a^4b^8)/(a^2b) = a^{4-2}b^{8-1} = a^3b^7.$$

Test your understanding

1. Explain in your own words to a friend on your course how the rules for working with powers operate, and the logic behind them. Then listen to your friend's explanation. Compare the different ways you've expressed the ideas, and the different aspects of the method that you've emphasised. Doing this can often help to clarify your thinking.
2. Simplify the following:

   (a) $(p^3q^4) \times (qp^2)$ (b) $(xy)^3/y^2$ (c) $(2t^2)^4/4$

Fractional powers

All the examples above involved positive integer powers (look back at page 12 if you don't remember what an integer is). Having defined what they mean, the logical next step is to ask whether we can attach any meaning to a power which isn't a whole number. So let's take a simple case and begin by asking what $4^{1/2}$ might mean.

The rules for multiplying powers tell us that $4^{1/2} \times 4^{1/2} = 4^{1/2 + 1/2} = 4^1 = 4$.

In other words, $4^{1/2}$ is the quantity which, when multiplied by itself, gives us 4. But you are probably already familiar with another name for that quantity – it's the *square root* of 4. In other words, $4^{1/2} = \sqrt{4} = 2$ (or –2, since $(-2) \times (-2) = +4$).

So it looks as though we can identify a fractional power with a root. This is in fact true more generally, and we can say that

- $a^{1/n} = \sqrt[n]{a}$

where the *n*th root of a means the quantity which multiplied by itself *n* times gives us *a*.

Negative powers

Now we are really getting into the swing! If a fractional power can have a meaning, why not a negative one? Here we can see what's going on by returning to the rule for dividing powers. Consider $3^2/3^3$; before you knew much about the rules you would probably have worked this out as $9/27 = 1/3$ (cancelling by 9). However, according to the division rule it is also equal to $3^{2-3} = 3^{-1}$. So 3^{-1} and $1/3$ must mean the same thing.

Try the same approach to get an interpretation for 3^{-2}; you should find that this is equal to $1/9$ or $1/3^2$. The shape of the rule is now emerging; generally we can say that

- $a^{-n} = 1/a^n$

This explains the use of the minus sign in 'scientific notation', discussed in Section 2.5.

The power zero ...

To complete the picture, what meaning can we give to x^0? Again, the division rule gives us some ideas: applying this rule to the quotient $3^3/3^3$ gives $3^{3-3} = 3^0$, while the ordinary rules of arithmetic give $3^3/3^3 = 27/27 = 1$. Thus for consistency we must say that $3^0 = 1$. We could apply the same argument for any variable raised to the power zero, so we have the general rule:

- $a^0 = 1$ for any value of a.

... and some nonexistent values!

Not all fractional powers exist within the ordinary number system. For example, a negative number does not have a square root. This is because there is no number which, when multiplied by itself, gives a negative result. The square of a negative quantity is positive because 'minus times minus is plus'. So if you've been carrying out a complex calculation (maybe one of the statistical calculations we'll learn about later in the book) and you find yourself trying to calculate, say, $\sqrt{(-16)}$, you must have gone wrong somewhere! (The same is actually true for all even roots of negative numbers, such as $\sqrt[4]{(-81)}$.) If you study more advanced mathematics later in your career, you might come across the *complex number* system, in which all negative numbers do have roots.

Test your understanding

Evaluate the following:

1. 14^2
2. $\sqrt{625}$
3. 6^4
4. $\sqrt[3]{125}$
5. $\sqrt[3]{(-343)}$
6. $\sqrt[4]{(-256)}$
7. $\sqrt[2]{(a-2)^2}$
8. $\sqrt[3]{(-2x)^6}$
9. 5^{-1}
10. 1234^0

3.3 | Brackets

What are brackets for?

We have already seen the use of brackets in expressions such as $(a + b)^2$, where they show that everything in the bracket is to be raised to the power 2, and in expressions like $2 \times (-3)$ where they serve to separate two arithmetical symbols. In this section we shall discuss in more detail the 'how' and 'why' of using brackets in algebra.

The basic rule for the use of brackets is

- Operations within brackets are performed before operations outside them.

This shows why brackets are so useful – we can use them to change the usual priorities of operations. You can see from the following example why we might want to do this.

Example

A group of four friends goes on a picnic. They purchase six packs of sandwiches at £1.95 each, three packs of crisps at 32p each, and a fruit cake at £1.70. How much will each pay if they share the cost equally among them?

Solution

You could probably work out the answer to this quite easily without the use of brackets, but for the sake of illustration, think about it like this (all the costs are given in £):

Cost of sandwiches = 6×1.95
Cost of crisps = 3×0.32
Cost of cake = 1.70.
Total cost = $6 \times 1.95 + 3 \times 0.32 + 1.70$.

To find each person's share, we need to divide this by 4. But if we write simply

$6 \times 1.95 + 3 \times 0.32 + 1.70 \div 4$

then according to our priority rules, only the 1.70 will be divided by 4, giving the answer 13.085, which is clearly not correct. So instead we insert brackets thus:

$(6 \times 1.95 + 3 \times 0.32 + 1.70) \div 4$

to indicate that the calculation in the brackets has to be done first. This will give

$14.36 \div 4 = 3.59$

which is the correct answer, because we have now divided the *total* cost by 4.

So brackets are used to ensure that operations are carried out in the desired order. If you are uncertain whether or not you need brackets in order to obtain the correct result from a calculation, put them in! It's never wrong to have too many, even if they aren't strictly necessary. Sometimes we may even need several sets of brackets one inside the other (*nested*, as it's sometimes described) to get the correct result, as we shall see in later examples.

Test your understanding

You want to show that the cost of four loaves at 80 pence each and two packs of ham at £1.50 each is to be shared between five people. Which of the following correctly represents this calculation?

(a) $4 \times 80 + 2 \times 1.5 \div 5$

(c) $(4 \times 80) + (2 \times 1.5) \div 5$

(b) $4 \times 80/5 + 2 \times 1.5/5$

(d) $(4 \times 80 + 2 \times 1.5) \div 5$

Removing brackets

Sometimes, instead of putting brackets into an expression, we want to get rid of them. Then a few rules are helpful. First:

- Simplify expressions within the brackets as far as possible.

Example: before removing the brackets from the expression $2x(6x + 3y - 2x)$, we can combine the two terms in x within the bracket, to get $2x(4x + 3y)$.
    Second:

- When the brackets are removed, each term within the brackets is multiplied by anything in front of the brackets.

Example: carrying on with simplification of the expression above, we have

$$2x(4x + 3y) = 2x \times 4x + 2x \times 3y = 8x^2 + 6xy$$

Note that when we apply this rule, we must remember that the *sign* is also part of the term in front of the brackets; so $-3a(2a - 4b)$ becomes $-6a^2 + 12ab$ when the brackets are removed; we multiply both the terms in the bracket by $-3a$.
    Note also that a minus sign on its own in front of a bracket can always be thought of as -1. For example, if we want to simplify $11 - (x - 6)$, we need to multiply the terms in the bracket by -1 when we take the brackets away. This gives $11 - x + 6$ or $17 - x$.
    Third:

- When multiplying one bracketed expression by another, remove the brackets one pair at a time.

Example: to simplify $(x + y)(2x - y)$, multiply everything in the first bracket by the second bracketed expression:

$$(x + y)(2x - y) = x(2x - y) + y(2x - y) = 2x^2 - xy + 2xy - y^2$$
$$= 2x^2 + xy - y^2$$

Finally:

- If you have nested brackets, remove the brackets from the inside outwards.

Example: to simplify $11[3x - (y - x)]$, remove the inner brackets first to get $11[3x - y + x] = 11[4x - y]$, and then remove the outer brackets to obtain $44x - 11y$.

Test your understanding

Remove the brackets from the following expressions and simplify as far as possible:

1. $2(10 - 4)$ 2. $-(6 - 8)$ 3. $a - 2(4 - b)$ 4. $4(b - a)$ 5. $-a(2a - b)$
6. $(a - b)(a + b)$ 7. $b(c - b(cd + b))$ 8. $2(x + y) - 3(x - y)$
9. A hospital trust is working out how many nurses it requires to staff its wards. The management has decided that there should be one nurse to every ten patients classed as 'routine' or 'minor', and one to every five classed as 'serious'. If the numbers of routine, minor and serious patients are denoted by R, M and S respectively, write an expression using brackets to give the total number of nurses required by the hospital.
10. A company operates the following policy for reimbursement of car travel expenses to its employees: for journeys of up to 80 miles, a rate of 25p per mile is paid; after this, the rate is 12p per mile. Write down an expression using brackets to give the amount (in £) which can be claimed for a journey of x miles, where $x > 80$. Check that your expression is correct by working out the cost of travelling 100 miles.

3.4 Putting it all together

Much of the material in this chapter has been fairly technical, and you need plenty of practice with routine examples in order to feel comfortable with the handling of algebraic expressions. However, it's easy while getting that practice to lose sight of why we are covering all this material – that is, to assist in solving practical problems. Here's an example drawn from real life to show an algebraic formula in action.

The New You Health Club wants to offer its clients some advice on healthy living, and one of the measures to be used is the client's body mass index – a measure which can be used to give a rough idea whether she or he is overweight. The manager of the club does a web search and comes across the following information on a webpage at: www.thusness.com/bmi.t.html.

Calculate your Body-mass Index
Your body-mass index ('BMI') measures your height/weight ratio. It is your weight in kilograms divided by the square of your height in meters.
...

People with BMIs between 19 and 22 live longest. Death rates are noticeably higher for people with indexes 25 and above.

...

The U.S. government recently changed these ranges to a minimum of 20 and a maximum of 24. (I encourage you to take these numbers with a grain of salt; they are not as accurate as they sound.)

The web page provides a 'one-click' version of the calculation, but the manager decides to work out from scratch what the formula would be in symbols. (Incidentally, there is a misleading statement in the first paragraph quoted above – can you spot it? Answer at the end of this section!)

The problem is complicated by the fact that many British people still give their weight in stones and pounds and their height in feet and inches. So the manager decides to derive two versions of the formula – one for these so-called imperial measurements, and one for European clients who use metric measurements.

The metric version is easy. Suppose your height is h metres, your weight is w kilograms, and your body mass index is denoted by BMI. Then translating the verbal explanation given in the quote into symbols, we have

$$BMI = w/h^2$$

Remember that the square takes precedence over the division. So someone whose height is 170 cm – that's 1.70 m – and weight 60 kg will have a BMI of $60/1.7^2 = 60/2.89 = 20.76$, well within the healthy range.

Now let's see how the formula gets modified if we have a height in feet and inches and a weight in stones and pounds. First the height needs to be converted to inches, and the weight to pounds (formulae can't cope with mixtures of units – one of the many problems with a non-decimal measurement system). Let's call the height in inches H and the weight in pounds W.

I happen to know that there are 2.54 cm in one inch. So to convert the height in inches, H, to a height in metres, h, we need to multiply by 2.54 and then divide by 100 – or equivalently, multiply by 0.0254. In symbols this gives:

$$h = 0.0254H$$

Can you see why this is? If you find it hard to follow, try doing the conversion with some specific numbers first, and remember that we expect the height in metres to be considerably less than that in inches – after all, a metre is more than a yard!

I also know that one kilogram is 2.2 pounds. So to convert the weight in pounds to kilograms, we need to divide by 2.2 – that is:

$$w = W/2.2$$

Again we expect the weight in kilograms to be smaller, since a kilogram is a lot heavier than a pound.

Now we can substitute these expressions for h and w in the BMI formula to get

$$\text{BMI} = (W/2.2)/(0.0254H)^2$$

This can be simplified to

$$\text{BMI} = W/(2.2 \times 0.0254^2 \times H^2) = W/(0.0014H^2)$$

(Make sure you can follow the steps of this calculation.)

By using one or other of these formulae, the manager can calculate the BMI for any client, whether they express their weight and height in imperial or metric units.

Try finding your BMI with this formula. If you have web access you can then check your result with the version given by the website.

Here's a further point to think about: the site mentions a BMI of 19 as the lowest limit for a longer life expectancy. Can you use the formula to work out, given your height, what your weight would need to be to give the BMI a value of 19?

Everyone's answer will vary, but the calculation involves swapping the formula around as follows:

BMI = $W/(0.0014H^2)$, so for a BMI of 19 we have $19 = W/(0.0014H^2)$.
Thus $W = 19 \times 0.0014H^2$.

This means that a person with height 5 ft 3 inches or 63 inches would need to weigh about 105.6 pounds in order to have a BMI of 19.

One final question: why do you think the BMI uses the square of the height, and not just the height itself, as the divisor?

(Did you spot the misleading statement in the website quote? It says that the BMI measures height/weight ratio, but in fact it's weight/height – or to be strictly accurate, weight/square of height. Keep an eye out for this kind of sloppy use of mathematical ideas – there is plenty of it about!)

3.5 For Excel users

The rules of algebra, which we've been examining in this chapter, are at the heart of the way in which spreadsheets work. You can enter a formula – essentially an algebraic expression – into a cell of the spreadsheet, and have its value automatically updated as the values of the variables in the formula change. This is what makes spreadsheets such a powerful tool, and essentially different from any other kind of computational aid.

To see how the process works, let's go back to the example in the first section of this chapter, where we wanted to work out the amount which Krunchy Plc would have to pay for oats next year, given the price per tonne they were charged and the number of tonnes they purchased. We will use Excel to explore the equation we developed. You should follow this through having opened a new sheet in Excel.

Suppose that possible amounts to be purchased range from 2 tonnes to 20 tonnes, in steps of 2 tonnes. Enter the name 'tonnes' at the top of column A Then enter the possible amounts 2, 4, ..., 20 tonnes into the column. The quick way to do this is to enter the first two amounts into cells A2 and A3, highlight these, then take hold of the handle at the lower-right corner of the highlighted area (the cursor will change to a cross) and 'pull' the column down until you get to the value of 20 in cell A11.

Now we'll put the price per tonne into cell B13. In cell A13, write 'Price' and then enter the initial price you'd like to explore – let's say £200 per tonne – into cell B13. What we want to do next is to put the formula for total cost into the cells of column B, so that we can see the range of costs associated with the different tonnages purchased. With that in mind, let's put the label 'cost' into cell B1.

This is where the algebra bit comes in. The formula we need is precisely the one we derived in Section 3.1 – only instead of using letters to represent variables, the spreadsheet uses cell addresses. In terms of letters the formula for total cost was just $T \times C$ (the number of tonnes purchased times the cost per tonne). We replace the letters by the addresses of the relevant cells. So into cell B2 we put the formula =B2*B13. The = sign here signals that it's a formula, and the * is Excel's way of writing a multiplication sign (look back at the 'For Excel users' section of Chapter 1 if you've forgotten about these special symbols). The $ signs indicate that we want the address of the price per tonne figure – cell B13 – to stay fixed even when we move the formula around.

You should now have a figure of 400 in cell B2 – the cost of 2 tonnes at £200 a tonne. Now comes the clever part. Click on cell B2, take hold of the bottom right-hand corner of the cell, and 'pull' the formula down to cell B11. The column will fill up with the values of the total cost for the various different amounts purchased. If you place the cursor in cell B5, for example, you can see from the formula bar at the top of the screen that the formula in that particular cell is =A5*B13, so the number of tonnes used in the calculation is the value in cell A5 – that's 8 tonnes.

Now try changing the value of the price per tonne in cell B13 to another value – say, £400 per tonne – and notice how all the cost values change to correspond.

All of this is much more complicated to explain than to see on the screen. The point is that the algebraic formula underlies the way in which Excel carries out the calculations – so you need to be able to write the formula correctly in order to get Excel to do the calculations you need.

Test your understanding

What formula would you put into the relevant cell to get Excel to do each of the following calculations?

1. To calculate a column of values for the discount to be given to wholesale customers, who make orders ranging in value from £100 to £1000 in steps of £100. The discount is calculated as 10% of the value of the order. The order values are in column A, and the discounts are to be put into column B.

2. Column A of the spreadsheet contains the number of full-time staff employed by a company in each of the 12 months of 2001; column B contains the numbers of part-time staff over the same period. You want to calculate the total wage-bill for each month, given that full-time staff are paid £1200 per month and part-time staff are paid £800 per month. The wage bills are to be put into column C.

What have I learned?

At the start of the chapter, you wrote down some of the ideas that the word 'algebra' brought into your mind. Have another look at them. Has the work you've done in the chapter changed the way you feel about algebra? If so, how?

Think too about the two quotes from students given in Section 3.1. Jane, you'll recall, said 'Algebra always seemed like something mysterious – these minus signs kept appearing...'. Now that you've reviewed your understanding of algebra, can you suggest what sort of calculation she might have been thinking of, and why in fact the 'appearance' of minus signs in a calculation may not be at all mysterious?

Asha's problem was 'When we learned a new method, I could do the exercises just after the lesson, but then I just forgot it all.' It sounds as though she might have been trying to deal with exercises using rote learning of a 'method', rather than by really understanding the principles of the calculation. Is this something that you sometimes do?

Exercises

Simplify the following expressions as much as possible:

1. $16^{-0.5}$
2. $x(x+2y) - y(3x - y)$
3. $(6x^2y) \times (2xy^3)$
4. $(2x - y)(3x + y)$
5. $7pq^2/14p^2q$
6. $a + ab - abc$
7. Find the value of $100xy^2$ when $x = 4$ and $y = 3$.
8. For what values of b would the expression $12 - 3b^2$ have a negative value?
9. A friend asks you to check his working of the following example. Point out where, if at all, he has gone wrong, and suggest a correct version:

   $3(x + 2y) - (x - y) = 3x + 2y - x - y = 2x + y.$

10. Explain as if to someone who only knows about positive powers what a negative integer power means, using 4^{-2} as an example.

Case Study: Grossman Pharmaceuticals

Grossman Pharmaceuticals is a company that manufactures a number of leading over-the-counter drugs for the treatment of digestive problems. It is currently researching a new product which incorporates 'good' bacteria to promote effective digestion.

These bacteria have to be grown in the laboratory, and company scientists have developed the following formula to show the number of bacteria N (in millions) present in a culture vessel after a time t hours:

$$N = At/(t^2 + 1)$$

where A is a constant related to the concentration of nutrients in the culture.

1. Use the formula to find how many bacteria will be present after 2 hours, 4 hours and 10 hours when $A = 16$. Give your answers in millions correct to 2 decimal places.
2. What do you think seems to be happening to the size of the population as time goes on? How does this relate to the formula?
3. (If you have access to Excel.) Set up a column of values of t running in 1-hour intervals from 1 to 20. Use the formula above to generate a column showing the numbers of bacteria present at that time. At what time will the number of bacteria fall below 1 million? Does this calculation confirm your conclusion in part 2?

For further exercises and multiple choice revision questions visit the companion website: www.palgrave.com/business/morris

CHAPTER 4

Graphs

Intended learning outcomes

By the end of your work on this chapter you should:

- appreciate the reasons for using graphical methods
- be able to plot graphs using numerical information
- be able to plot graphs of simple algebraic relationships
- be able to interpret information presented graphically
- know how to recognise a linear equation and to interpret the numerical constants in such an equation
- be aware of some important types of non-linear relationship.

Prerequisites

Before starting work on this chapter you need to feel confident about the use of algebraic expressions as discussed in Chapter 2.

4.1 The importance of relationships

Many of the applications of mathematics in business are concerned with the question of relationships. How do levels of customer satisfaction relate to the number of staff on duty in a call centre? Is there any relationship between the length of time an accounts assistant has been employed and the number of minor errors she makes in a week? Some big questions about the economic environment in which business operates are of a similar kind. For example, what is the relationship between the £ to $ exchange rate and the value of exports to the USA? Relationships of this kind can be expressed, and further insight into them can be obtained, with the assistance of algebra. In fact, this is the main reason why we revised the basics of algebra in the last chapter.

We've actually already been formulating expressions of this kind in Chapter 3. One example is the Krunchy Plc situation, which involved developing an expression for the relationship between the number of tonnes of oats purchased and the cost of the purchase. Glance back at Chapter 3 and see how many other examples involving the relationship between variables you can spot.

A very powerful way of examining the relationship between two quantities is provided by graphs. A graph is simply a visual representation of a relationship, which exploits the fact that on a two-dimensional sheet of paper, one dimension can be used to represent each of the quantities. In this chapter, you will be reminded of the basic ideas about graph plotting, before we go on to examine some important standard types of graph that are useful in dealing with business problems.

Pause for reflection

Graphs and various other kinds of visual representation of information are now widely used in the media. Think about some examples of this kind of visual presentation that you have seen recently. What relationships were those who produced the graphs trying to show, and do you think they succeeded?

4.2 The basics of graph plotting

As we've just mentioned, a graph shows a relationship between two quantities or variables (if you've forgotten what this term means, have a look back at Section 3.1). You may be most familiar with the use of x and y to represent the two variables, but as we'll see, it's often better to use more meaningful letters when you're dealing with a practical problem.

Let's take a very simple example to see how graph plotting works. A sandwich-making company regularly purchases different amounts of tomatoes from a wholesaler, and has a contract with the wholesaler for a standard price of £2.20 a kilo. If the number of kilos purchased is represented by x, and the cost of the purchase (in £) by y, then we can say that $y = 2.2x$, since each kilo costs £2.20. If we want to show this relationship in graphical form, then we use two scales or *axes* to represent the variables x and y.

You're probably familiar with the convention that the y-variable is plotted using the vertical axis, and the x-variable along the horizontal axis. While there is nothing special about the letters x and y, there is an underlying reason why we choose to put y (the cost) vertically and x (the number of kilos purchased) horizontally. We say that x is the *independent* variable, because the company can choose to give x any value it likes. Then y, the cost of the purchase, depends on the choice of x, and so is called the *dependent* variable. It's a pretty standard convention in mathematics that independent variables are plotted horizontally, and dependent ones vertically, so when you are deciding which way round to put the axes of a graph, ask yourself what depends on what in your problem.

The x and y axes divide the plane of the paper into four regions, and cross at a point called the *origin*, where both x and y are zero. Figure 4.1 shows the general picture – for x, positive values are to the right of the origin and negative ones to the left, while for y, the positive values are above the origin and the negatives are below. The four regions into which the axes divide the page are known as *quadrants*.

One very important point to notice is that, on both axes, the scales are such that an equal distance represents an equal amount of change in the variable; thus the distance from $x = 2$ to $x = 4$ is the same as that from $x = 4$ to $x = 6$, and so on. This is what's known

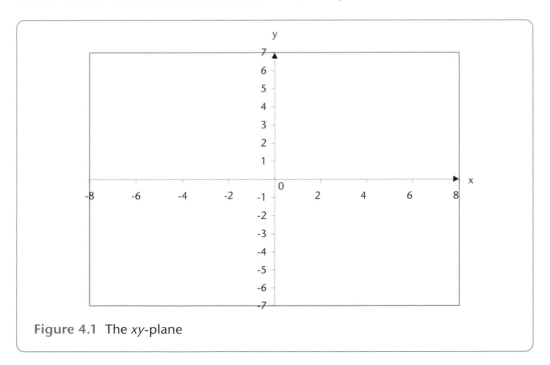

Figure 4.1 The *xy*-plane

as a *linear* scale (for reasons we'll come to later in this chapter), and it's by far the most common type of graph scale. Notice too that while both *x* and *y* have linear scales, there is no requirement for the two scales to be the same; the distance which represents an increase of 2 in the *x*-scale could represent an increase of 10 in the *y*-scale.

To decide exactly what scales to adopt for each axis, ask yourself what range of values of the variable you need to accommodate. In our example, it may be that the company knows it has never purchased more than 10 kilos of tomatoes at a time, and so the *x*-scale could run from 0 to 10. Now 10 kilos will cost $10 \times £2.20 = £22$, and thus the *y*-scale needs to go from 0 to at least 22; it might however be more convenient to use a scale in multiples of 5, and thus take the upper limit as 25. If you are plotting a graph by hand using graph paper, which has squares arranged in sets of 10, then it's generally a good idea to use scales which increase by a 'nice' amount like 2, 5, 10, 20, 100, and so on, and not by 'awkward' amounts like 3 or 7, which can make it difficult to read off intermediate points accurately.

Note that neither of the variables we are using here can take negative values. The company can't buy –2 kilos of tomatoes ,and so the graph only needs to show the positive quadrant. To actually plot the graph, one possibility is to draw up a table showing a range of values of *x* and the corresponding values of *y*, thus:

x	2	4	6	8	10
y	4.4	8.8	13.2	17.6	22

The pairs of values of *x* and *y* are sometimes shown as (2, 4.4), (4, 8.8) and so on – the *x*-values are always shown first. These pairs of values define unique points on the graph, and are called the *coordinates* of that point. To actually plot the point (2, 4.4), we proceed as follows. Go along the *x*-axis until you reach the point *x* = 2, and draw a line vertically through this point. Go up the *y*-axis to the value 4.4, and draw a line horizontally through that point. The point (2, 4.4) is at the intersection of these two lines. Figure 4.2 illustrates this construction. Of course, in practice there is no need to actually plot the vertical and horizontal lines – a short-hand version of the process could be expressed as 'go along the *x*-axis to *x* = 2 and then vertically upwards until you're opposite 4.4 on the *y*-axis'.

We can reverse this process to find the coordinates of any point on the graph. Dropping a perpendicular from the point to the *x*-axis enables us to read off the *x*-coordinate, while the *y*-coordinate is given by the value at which a horizontal line through the point meets the *y*-axis.

The situation once we have plotted all the points in the table above is shown in Figure 4.2. It's pretty clear that the points lie on a straight line, and if we were to work out the costs for intermediate values of *x* – whether whole numbers of kilos or not – those points would also lie on the line. (Try this for *x* = 1 and for *x* = 5.5.) This is of course no coincidence – each additional kilo costs an extra £2.20, so the line goes up with a constant slope. It also passes through the origin, which is sensible since if no tomatoes are purchased, then there will be no cost.

This is in fact an example of a linear relationship – so called because its graph is a straight line. We shall discuss linear relationships in more detail in the next section.

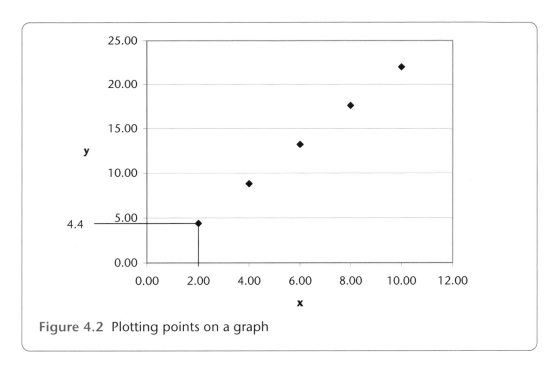

Figure 4.2 Plotting points on a graph

Test your understanding

1. On a sheet of graph paper, draw a horizontal axis with a scale running from –5 to 5, and a vertical axis with a scale running from –200 to +500. Use these axes to plot the following points:
   (–1, –100); (4, 400); (–4, 400); (–2, –200); (0, 500); (5, 0).
2. Decide what scale you would use if you wanted to plot a variable whose values run from 0 to £463 using your standard graph paper. Compare your choice with that of other people in your group. Can you see examples of 'better' and 'less good' scales?

4.3 Linear relationships and their graphs

An example of a linear relationship

Many relationships encountered in business applications are linear – that is, they give rise to straight-line graphs, like the one illustrated in the previous section. As we shall see, it is also the case that the equations corresponding to such graphs have the simplest algebraic form. For both these reasons, we shall spend some time looking at the features of linear relationships.

To see what the general form of a linear relationship might look like, it is probably easiest to start with an example. Suppose that the manager of a city ambulance service wants to develop a graph which will enable him to predict how long it will take to respond to an emergency call. By studying past data, he has worked out that, on average, every mile that has to be covered to the site of the emergency takes the ambulance 1.5 minutes. On top of this, the paramedics take an average of 7 minutes to respond to the call, collect the necessary equipment and staff the ambulance.

Let's call the distance to the emergency site x miles, and the time taken y minutes. Note that this is in line with our definitions of dependent and independent variables above, since y, the time, depends on x, the distance. Note too how important it is to specify the units in which each of the variables is measured.

Then we can say that the total time taken to reach an emergency x miles away will be 1.5 multiplied by x (the distance) plus the extra 7 minutes on top of this. Symbolically, this can be expressed as $y = 1.5x + 7$. (If you can't see why this 'works', try doing the calculation with some specific numbers first – finding the time for emergencies at distances of, say, 5 miles and 10 miles.)

Now we shall plot the graph from this equation. Using values of x from 1 to 10 miles, we get the table below for the corresponding values of y.

x	1	2	3	4	5	6	7	8	9	10
y	8.5	10	11.5	13	14.5	16	17.5	19	20.5	22

This in turn gives the graph shown in Figure 4.3.

This is clearly a straight line, for the same reason as in our earlier example about the cost of tomatoes – for every additional mile travelled, an extra time of 1.5 minutes is added. This causes the graph to rise at a constant rate, hence its linear form.

However, there is a difference between this graph and the one in Section 4.2: it does not pass through the origin. This is in line with common sense, since even if the distance

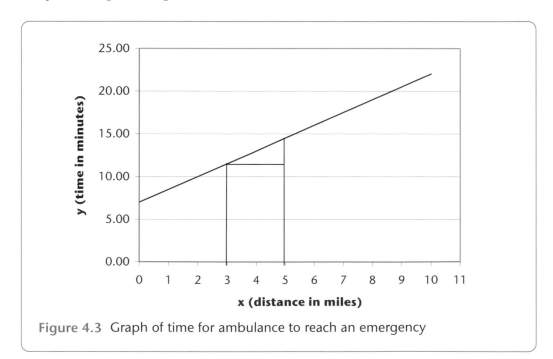

Figure 4.3 Graph of time for ambulance to reach an emergency

to be travelled were zero miles (not a very likely scenario, admittedly), there would still be the 'fixed' time element of 7 minutes to add into the equation. So the graph passes through the point $y = 7$ when $x = 0$.

The general equation of a straight line

The equation $y = 1.5x + 7$ has a couple of features worth noting. It contains just one x and one y, no x^2 terms, no $\sqrt{y}$ terms. It also contains two fixed numbers, the 1.5 and the 7.

In fact, the equation of any straight line will have an equation which is the same 'shape' as this one. We might express it in words as 'y equals a number times x plus another number'. And conversely, any equation that has that form will give a straight line when plotted. If we use m to represent the number multiplying x, and c for the number on its own, then the equation can be written as $y = mx + c$ (other letters can be used for the fixed numbers, but this version is fairly standard). So we have the important result:

The general equation of a straight line is $y = mx + c$

We can actually go further and attach a meaning to the m and the c. The c is the value of y when $x = 0$. This is called the *intercept* of the graph, and it is often loosely described as 'where the graph cuts the y-axis'. However, you need to be a bit careful about this – that will only be the case if the x-scale starts from zero. (Note that the word we use here is intercePt, not interseCt, even though it is where the graph intersects the y-axis!)

As for the m, it's the amount by which y increases every time x increases by one unit (the time for one extra mile in our example). This is called the *slope* or the *gradient* of the line. Another way of defining it is:

slope = increase in y/corresponding increase in x

and this can be calculated by using a triangle as shown in Figure 4.3. For the triangle shown, the increase in y is $14.5 - 11.5 = 3$, and the corresponding increase in x is $5 - 3 = 2$, so the slope is $3/2 = 1.5$, which is indeed equal to the value of m in the equation. You can try using different triangles. Because the slope of the straight line is constant, you will of course always get the same answer.

In more practical terms, you can think of c as the fixed element of the equation and m as the part which varies with x.

By giving m and c different values, we can obtain various different straight lines. Here are a few examples:

When $m = 2$ and $c = -7$, the equation is $y = 2x - 7$, and looks like line A in Figure 4.4.
When $m = 6$ and $c = 0$, the equation is $y = 6x$, and looks like line B in Figure 4.4.
When $m = -3$ and $c = 2$, the value of y decreases by 3 units for each 1 unit increase in x. This gives us a graph that slopes downwards from left to right, and is said to have a negative slope. This would be represented by line C in Figure 4.4. When $m = -3$ and $c = 4$, we get another line with slope -3, but with a different intercept (line D). In fact we can say that all linear equations with the same value of m will have graphs that are parallel.

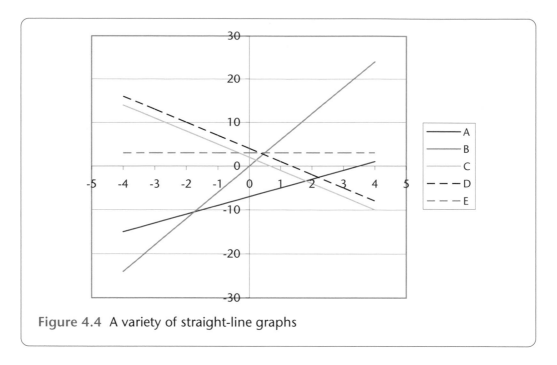

Figure 4.4 A variety of straight-line graphs

When $m = 0$ and $c = 3$, we get the horizontal line, line E in Figure 4.4. So a graph with a zero slope is 'flat'.

Test your understanding

1. For each of these equations, identify the slope and the intercept of the corresponding graph:

   (a) $y = 4x + 11$ (b) $3y = 6x - 6$ (c) $2(x + y) = 3$
   (d) $y/5 - 3 = 2x$ (e) $y = 4x$ (f) $y = 7$

   Are there any pairs of parallel lines represented here?
2. Sketch the graphs of the following:

   (a) $y = 6 + 2x$ for x from 0 to 5   (b) $y = 2 - 3x$ for x between −2 and 2

More about linear graphs

It's worth noting that as Figure 4.4 shows, the bigger the value of m – whether positive or negative – the steeper the slope of the line. However, the appearance of the slope depends on the scales we are using for x and y. So, for example, students sometimes say that a line with a slope of 1 – one unit increase in y for every one unit increase in x – will be 'at 45°', but that will only be the case if we use the same scale on both axes.

Another point to beware of is that, while the general equation of a straight line can, as we've stated, always be written as $y = mx + c$, it can be rearranged so that it looks rather different. For instance, $x + y = 7$ represents a straight line, but it needs to be rearranged (by subtracting x from both sides) into the form $y = 7 - x$ or $y = -x + 7$ before we can recognise it as having the form $y = mx + c$ with $m = -1$ and $c = 7$. Similarly, $y/x = 2$ doesn't look much like the standard equation, until you realise that it can be rearranged as $y = 2x$, which has $m = 2$ and $c = 0$.

Finally, a word about sketching, as distinct from plotting, graphs. Because we only need to know the position of two points on a straight line graph in order to be able to plot the graph, it is possible to get a good idea of the appearance of the graph without actually using graph paper or drawing up an extensive table of values as we did above. It's a good idea to get used to doing this. Very often what we need is an overall picture of the shape of a relationship, rather than an accurate plot from which precise values can be read. And of course, it is very much quicker to sketch than to plot accurately, which can be useful when it comes to examinations!

Some business applications of linear graphs

Example 1: A demand graph.

You don't need to have a PhD in management to realise that, with many commodities, the more you charge, the less you sell. Economists, and people concerned with setting pricing policies, are interested in exploring the relationship between price charged and quantity sold. For example, the manager of a corner shop might notice that when she charges 80p for a small pack of biscuits, she sells 200 packs per month, but when she puts the price up to 90p, sales go down to 160 packs per month.

If we are prepared to accept that the relationship between the price and the quantity sold can be represented with reasonable accuracy by a straight line, then we can use this information to work out an equation for that relationship. If we let x represent the price charged, and y represent the amount sold (choosing x and y this way round because sales depend on price), then we want to find the equation of a line that passes through the two points (80, 200) and (90, 160). (Can you see why those two points will be sufficient to define a unique line?)

Looking at the information we've got, we can see that when the price goes up by 10p, sales go down by 40 units per month. So each increase of 1p produces a drop in sales of four units, by a simple proportion calculation. But this is exactly what we mean by the slope of the graph, the 'm' in the standard equation. We can therefore say that $m = -4$ in this case, the minus sign being there to show that *increasing x reduces y*.

The equation must therefore be of the form $y = -4x + c$. To find the value of c, the intercept, is now easy, we just use the fact that the graph has to pass through (80, 200). That means that when $x = 80$, $y = 200$, and putting these values into the equation gives $200 = -4 \times 80 + c$, so that $200 = -320 + c$, and thus c must be 520. The full equation is therefore $y = -4x + 520$, which looks better written as $y = 520 - 4x$. You can check that this is correct by making sure that the point (90, 160) also lies on the line.

The line is plotted in Figure 4.5. You can see that when the price rises to 130p, sales will fall to zero, while at the other end of the scale, if the biscuits are given away (that is, the price is zero), then 520 packs per month will be demanded. Neither of these extremes is actually very realistic. In practice what would probably happen at the top end is that demand will level off at a small but positive value as the price goes up, rather than decreasing to zero; and if word got round that the shop was giving away biscuits then the demand would probably shoot up well above 520 packs! The true demand graph might thus look more like the curve in Figure 4.5 than the straight line.

This illustrates an important point: while the linear graph may give a good representation of the relationship between price and quantity sold in the middle of the range (where the shopkeeper had collected her data), its reliability is much less at the extremes. This is often the case when we try to apply a mathematical model – which is what the graph is – to a practical situation: the model may fit well within a certain range, but be a less good model outside that range. It's partly because many curves include a region that looks almost like a straight line that linear models are so widespread.

One final observation: it might have been better, in this case, to use more meaningful letters to represent the variables, so that it is easier to remember which letter represents which quantity. So instead of x we could use p for the price in pence of a pack of biscuits, and instead of y we could represent the number of packs sold by n. Then the equation would become $n = 520 - 4p$. There is nothing special about the letters x and y, and you should be able to recognise a straight line equation even when other letters are being used.

Example 2: Direct proportion

We are often told that one quantity is *directly proportional* to another. For example, a company that manufactures high-quality chocolate may know that the weight of cocoa solids required per week is directly proportional to the weight of chocolate made during

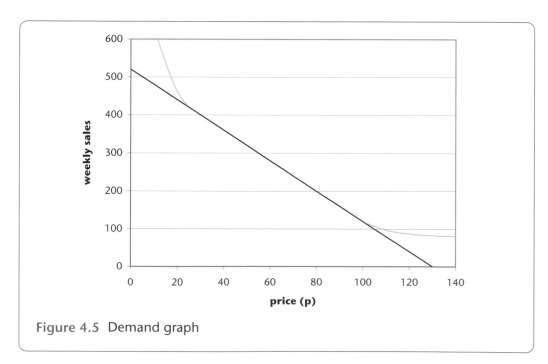

Figure 4.5 Demand graph

that week, since each kilo of chocolate contains 700 g of cocoa solids. Then if the weight of cocoa solids required is denoted by S kg per week, and the weight of chocolate manufactured during the week is C kg, we can say that $S = 0.7\,C$ (remember that we are working in kilos, so 700 g becomes 0.7).

You should be able to spot that this equation represents a line through the origin with slope 0.7, as shown in Figure 4.6. Any direct proportion relationship of this kind will be represented by a similar line, but the slope will vary depending on the constant term in the equation – what is sometimes called the *constant of proportionality*.

Example 3: Linear growth

A recently-launched web-based company is monitoring the numbers of visitors to its site over its first few weeks in operation. It finds that in the first week, it had 120 visitors, and that the number increases by a steady 20 visitors per week. Can we represent this growth graphically, and use it to predict the number of visitors in, say, week 10 of operation?

There is an interesting issue here which we haven't come across before. How are we to denote the weeks, which are not a 'measurement' in the same way as the number of kilos of chocolate manufactured? One way is to number the weeks off, so that the first week of operation might be called week 0, and so on. Then we can say

number of visitors in week $k = 120 + 20 \times k$

That is, we start with sales of 120 when $k = 0$, and then an extra 20 is added with each passing week. If we denote the number of visitors by n, and leave out the unnecessary multiplication sign, then the equation becomes $n = 120 + 20k$.

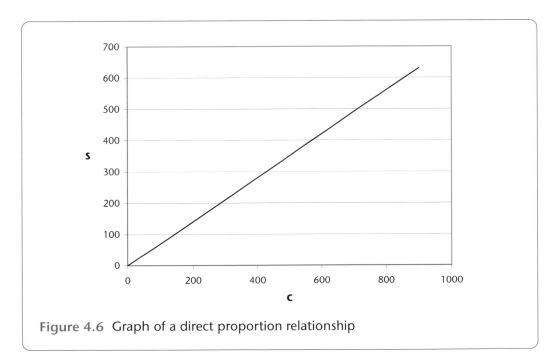

Figure 4.6 Graph of a direct proportion relationship

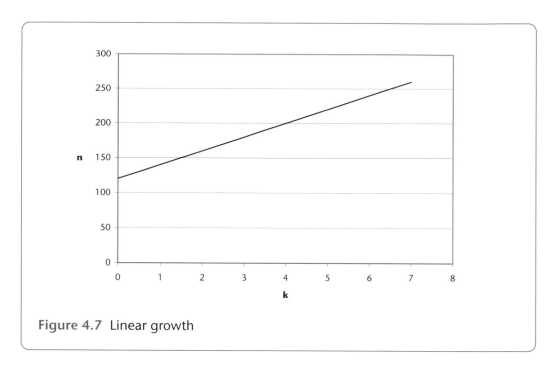

Figure 4.7 Linear growth

The graph plotted from this equation is shown in Figure 4.7. The intercept is 120, the initial level of visits, and the slope is 20, representing 20 extra visits for each additional week that the site is open. We say that the number of visitors to the site shows a linear growth – each extra week produces a constant number of extra visitors, thus giving a constant slope. We can identify the rate of growth – 20 visitors per week – with the coefficient 20 in the linear equation. More generally, the same would be true for any linear equation $y = mx + c$, where the constant rate of growth is m.

It would be easy to extend the line to $k = 9$ to read off the number of visitors in week 10. (Can you see why we use $k = 9$ here and not $k = 10$?) Of course, by doing so we would be making the assumption that the growth will continue to be linear, which may or may not be correct – this is one of the problems with trying to forecast data into the future.

Test your understanding

1. The price of a taxi journey is made up of two elements: a fixed charge of £1.50, plus a charge of 75p per mile travelled. Write down an expression to show the price of a journey, £P, in terms of the distance travelled, d miles, and plot or sketch the corresponding graph for journeys up to 20 miles in length. Use your graph to determine the distance that can be travelled for a cost of £7.50.

2. The costs of running the purchasing department in an engineering company are twofold: there is a fixed cost of £1500 per week (associated with staff wages plus the cost of maintaining the building where the department is located, heating,

lighting and so on) together with a variable cost depending on the number of orders placed during the week. Each order placed is reckoned to have an associated cost of £25. Write down an expression linking the total weekly cost of running the department, £C, with the number of orders placed during the week, n, assuming that n may run from 0 to 100. Plot the corresponding graph, and use it to find the total cost in a week when 50 orders are placed.

4.4 Some important nonlinear relationships

Pause for reflection

Can you think of variables that are related in a way that is unlikely to give a straight-line graph? For example, what would be an example of a variable which increases over time for a while, and then starts to decrease? What would the graph of such a variable against time look like?

And we have talked about direct proportion relationships, but what about an inverse proportion, the situation where one quantity decreases as another increases? Can you think of an example of two variables that might be related in this way? Would their graph be a straight line?

Many real-life variables, as we've seen in the last section, are related in ways that either give an exact linear graph, or which can be approximated by a straight line over part of their range. But there are practical situations for which a *nonlinear* – that is, curved – graph is needed to give an adequate model. Unfortunately, while everyone can recognise a straight line, there are infinitely many different shapes of curve, and it is not easy to recognise simply by looking at a curved plot exactly what its equation might be.

Parabolas and quadratic expressions

We shall take a look at a few of the simplest types of curve. We've seen that a linear graph contains only an x term – in other words, a term in x^1. The next simplest algebraic expression is one containing both an x and an x^2 term, such as $y = x^2 + 3x - 28$. Such an expression is known as a *quadratic*, a term which may be familiar to you from school-level maths.

Let's think first about what the graph of such a relationship will look like, and then examine what practical problems might give rise to such a graph. To plot $y = x^2 + 3x - 28$ accurately, we need to draw up a table of values as we did for the linear plot in Section 4.3:

x	–10	–8	–6	–4	–2	0	2	4	6	8	10
y	42	12	–10	–24	–30	–28	–18	0	26	60	102

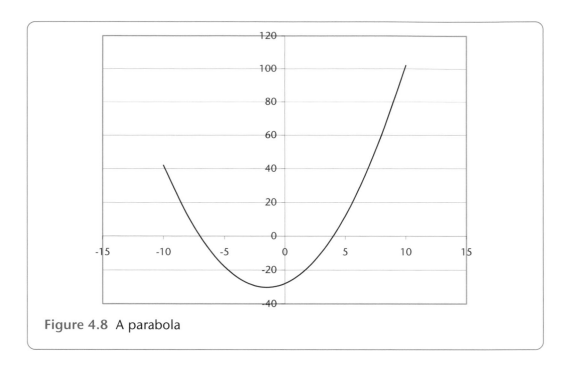

Figure 4.8 A parabola

This gives rise to the graph shown in Figure 4.8.

This graph has a shape known as a *parabola*: it changes direction only once, in this case with a minimum value when *x* is just less than zero. As *x* gets bigger in both the positive and negative directions, *y* also increases without limit.

The general equation of a *parabolic* curve (parabolic is the adjective from parabola) is *y* = ax^2 + b*x* + c, which is like the linear equation but with the addition of the extra term ax^2. We can obtain different versions of the parabola by giving the constants *a*, *b* and *c* different values. For certain values of the constants, the curve will be the other way up, with a maximum value instead of the minimum we see in Figure 4.8. Figure 4.9 shows a number of different parabolas.

Probably the most familiar example of a parabola is the trajectory of a ball when it is thrown; the way gravity works means that the path of the ball is always parabolic. For a business-related application, let's return to the retailer introduced in Section 4.3, who has developed the relationship *n* = 520 – 4*p* to represent the way the number of packs of biscuits sold per week (*n*) depends on the price in pence charged per pack (*p*). We're going to use this equation to work out what weekly revenue the retailer can expect.

The revenue generated by the sale of the biscuits is, of course, just *n* × *p* (*n* packs sold at *p* pence). However, we need to take into account the relationship *n* = 520 – 4*p*. We can change this equation around to find p in terms of n, as follows:

n = 520 – 4*p*
n + 4*p* = 520 (adding 4*p* to both sides)
4*p* = 520 – *n* (subtracting *n* from both sides)
p = (520 – *n*)/4 or 130 – 0.25*n* (remembering that the 4 divides everything in the numerator)

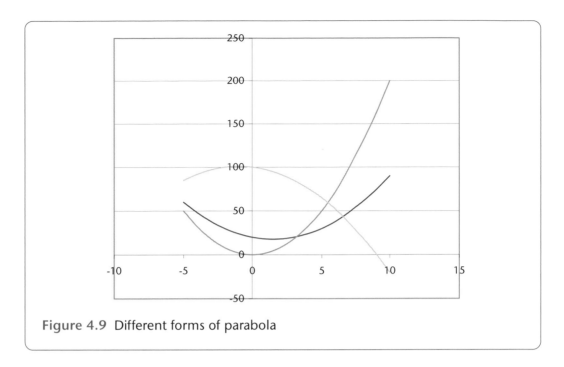

Figure 4.9 Different forms of parabola

This means that we can replace the *p* in the expression revenue = $n \times p$ by 130 – 0.25*n*, to get revenue = $n(130 – 0.25n) = 130n – 0.25n^2$ (the *n* multiplies everything inside the brackets). If we call the revenue *R* pence per week (the units have to be pence to match those used for the price) then the final equation is

$$R = 130n – 0.25n^2$$

which you should recognise as a quadratic relationship.

In order to plot the graph, we need to set up the usual table of values of *n* and *R*. You might ask 'How do we know what range of values of *n* to use?' To answer this question, we need to look again at the equation. It's clear that *R* will be 0 when *n* is 0, which makes sense – no sales, no revenue. It's also clear, if you look at the relationship in the form $R = n(130 – 0.25n)$, that *R* will be zero when *n* = 520. So there is no point in tabulating values outside this range. A sensible table is therefore:

n	0	50	100	150	200	250	300	350	400	450	500
R	0	5875	10,500	13,875	16,000	16,875	16,500	14,875	12,000	7875	2500

From this, we can construct the graph in Figure 4.10.

You can see how the revenue rises to a maximum at about *n* = 260, and then falls back to zero. This reflects the fact that at first, as the price is lowered to generate more sales, the total revenue increases, but eventually the price has to be reduced so much that the increased sales don't compensate, and so the revenue starts to decrease.

This has been quite a complex example, so don't worry if you haven't followed every

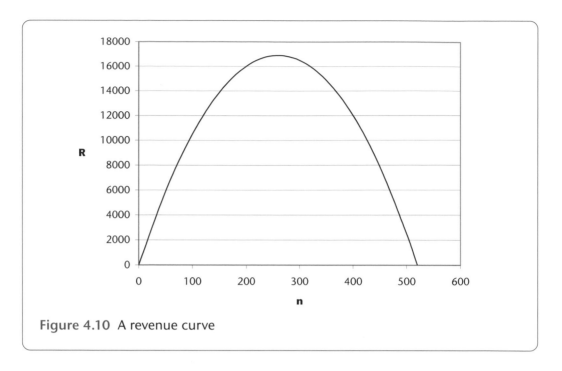

Figure 4.10 A revenue curve

step in detail You will have a chance to get more practice later, and we'll be returning to this example in Section 4.5.

Inverse proportion and hyperbolas

In a directly proportional relationship, as we saw earlier, two quantities increase together, in a manner which can be represented by an equation of the type $y = kx$, where k is any number. An inverse proportion relationship, on the other hand, exists where one variable decreases as the other increases, the corresponding equation being $y = k/x$. You can see here that the bigger x becomes, the smaller y will be, whatever the value of k.

To examine the graph of such a relationship, consider the case of a catering company that orders large quantities of paper plates from a wholesaler. These come in boxes of 1000, and the wholesaler charges £16 for a delivery, irrespective of how many boxes are ordered. How does the delivery charge per box vary with the number of boxes ordered?

If 4 boxes are ordered, the charge per box will work out at £16/4 = £4; if 8 boxes are ordered, the charge per box will be £2, and so on. In general, if n boxes are ordered, we can find the charge per box by dividing the £16 by n, so we get the equation

$$C = 16/n$$

where C is the charge per box in £. As usual, we can now draw up a table of values of n and C which will enable us to plot the graph of their relationship. For values of n from 1 to 16, the table looks like this:

n	1	2	4	6	8	10	12	14	16
C	16	8	4	2.67	2	1.60	1.33	1.14	1

giving the graph shown in Figure 4.11.

You can see that as the number of boxes, n, increases, the charge per box, C, gets smaller, which makes sense since the fixed delivery charge is being 'spread' over a greater number of boxes – or, to put it another way, since the charge is fixed, we get better value by ordering a larger number of boxes. You'll notice that we've started the values of n from 1, and not from zero, and there's a good reason for this: if you try to divide 16 by zero, your calculator will give you an error, because as we noted in Chapter 2, division by zero gives an infinitely large answer. Likewise, as n gets bigger and bigger, the value of C gets closer and closer to zero, but never quite gets there – even if we order 1000 boxes, the charge per box will still be the small but finite quantity £0.016. So the graph gets closer and closer to the horizontal axis without ever actually meeting it.

We call the type of graph shown in Figure 4.11 a *hyperbola*, and we say that it approaches the x-axis *asymptotically*, which is a technical term meaning 'getting closer and closer without actually meeting'. Any relationship of the form $y = k/x$ will give a similar-looking graph.

Other types of graph

We could go on to discuss a range of other relationships and their graphs: for example, the relationship $y = ax^3 + bx^2 + cx + d$ is called a cubic equation, a quartic equation would include a term in x^4, and so on. However, such equations have few applications

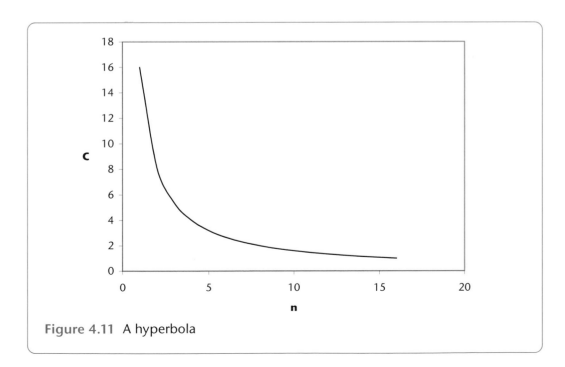

Figure 4.11 A hyperbola

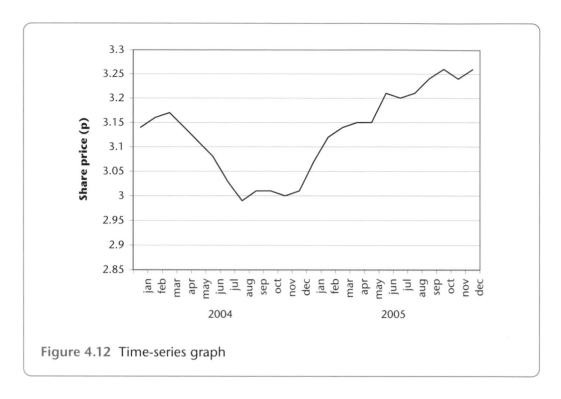

Figure 4.12 Time-series graph

in business situations, and so you are unlikely to encounter them. The three types of relationship we've examined – quadratic, inverse proportion of the type $y = k/x$, and above all linear – are by far the most important.

There are a couple of additional points that are worth noting in relation to graphs. First, you may have spotted in the hyperbola example above that, although the number of boxes, n, has to be a whole number, we have plotted the graph as if n could take on any value. Thus, strictly speaking, only the points on the graph corresponding to whole-number values of n have any meaning. You'll find that this happens quite often – the points are joined so that we can see the general trend of the graph, but you need to remember that not all values that you might read off from the graph actually make sense in practical terms.

Second, not all graphs represent relationships that have a neat algebraic form. Very often, we use a graph just to give a pictorial representation of numerical information. This type of graph is particularly common when we want to show how a set of figures has moved over time. So, for example, a company that wishes to show how its share price, averaged out over a month, has varied over a two-year period, might choose to display the information in a graph like Figure 4.12. This is called a time-series graph.

This plot shows very clearly the way that the share price has dropped and then picked up again to more than recover its value. It would be quite misleading (as well as almost impossible) to try to plot any kind of smooth curve through this set of points – the best way to show the overall trend is simply to join the individual points by straight lines. Nor do the values in between the monthly points have any meaning – the line joining them is merely there to emphasise the movement of the figures.

Some terminology and notation

Throughout this chapter we've been referring to graphs as showing relationships – the relationship between number of items sold and revenue, the relationship between x and y, and so on. An alternative and more technical term that you may come across is *function*. Instead of saying that there is a relationship between x and y, we could say that y is a *function* of x. (The term actually has a rather more tightly defined meaning than this, which we shan't go into here.)

We can extend this terminology to refer to a linear function, a quadratic function, and so on. For example, if $y = 3x + 5$, then y is a linear function of x.

Sometimes we want simply to express the fact that y is related to x in some general way, but we don't know the precise form of the function linking the two variables. Then a handy notation is to write $y = f(x)$, read as 'y is a function of x' or just 'y equals f of x'. This enables us to show the link between y and x without needing to represent that link by a particular algebraic expression.

Test your understanding

1. Plot the graphs of the following, and name the type of curve which results:

   (a) $y = 2x^2 - 5x + 7$ for x between -5 and 5
   (b) $s = t^2 - 6t$ for t between 0 and 10
   (c) $C = 11 + 2/n$ for positive values of n

2. An advertising agency has discovered that the percentage P of people surveyed who show awareness of a product varies with the number of days since the broadcast of the last TV advertisement for the product according to the formula

   $$P = 80 + 15/t$$

   Plot the graph of this relationship, and use it to find when awareness falls to less than 83%.

3. The publisher of a local daily paper estimates that 500,000 copies of his paper will be sold daily if it is priced at £0.65 a copy. If the price charged is £$(0.65 + P)$, then the number of copies sold will be $(500 - 600P)$ thousands.

   (a) Write down an expression showing the relationship between the publisher's revenue from the sale of the paper and the change £P in the price. (Remember that revenue = price × quantity sold.)
   (b) Plot the expression you wrote down in (a) for values of P between 0 and 0.65. What is the name of the curve you obtain?
   (c) What happens to revenue as the price charged per copy rises from £0.65 to £1.30?

4.5 Putting it all together

To consolidate the ideas introduced in this chapter, let's return once more to the retailer of Section 4.3 and her biscuits. We've already constructed a graph to represent the weekly revenue from the sales of biscuits. We're now going to extend that graph to give us a break-even graph – a very important tool in accounting. The break-even point is the number of units which need to be sold before a company starts to make a profit on a product, so you can see that the break-even graph provides key information which could make the difference between success or failure for an organisation.

In order to look at the profit generated by the biscuit sales, we need to know not just about the price at which they're sold, but also what they cost to the retailer when she buys them wholesale. Let's suppose that the cost is made up of two elements: the wholesaler makes a fixed delivery charge of £40 irrespective of the size of the order, and then there is a charge of 30p per packet. The total cost of purchasing n packets from the wholesaler and having them delivered will then be given by C pence, where

$$C = 4000 + 30n$$

We've chosen to work in pence here, since that was the unit we used in plotting the revenue graph in Figure 4.10, so we need to turn the £40 into 4000 pence.

You should recognise this equation as being a linear relationship, which starts at 4000 when $n = 0$, and rises with a slope of 30. If we tabulate some values across the same range as we used for the revenue graph, we get the following:

n	0	100	200	300	400	500
C	4000	7000	10,000	13,000	16,000	19,000

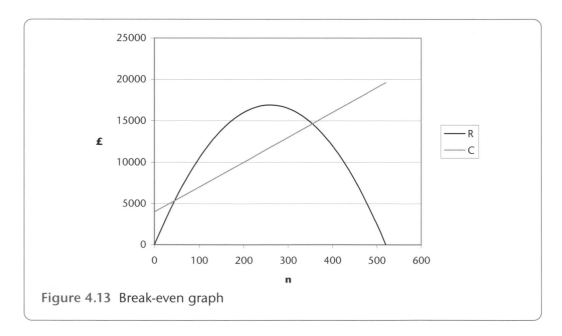

Figure 4.13 Break-even graph

Figure 4.13 shows this line plotted together with the revenue graph. At values of *n* for which the cost line is above the revenue curve, a loss will be made; if the revenue curve is above the cost line, the retailer will be making a profit. The vertical distance between the two graphs represents the profit in pence for that number of packets.

You can see that for small values of *n*, the retailer makes a loss; the break-even point is at A, and a profit is then made up to a value of n somewhere between 300 and 400 packets, at which point the profit falls to zero, and beyond which a loss is once again made. On an accurate plot of the graph, you could read off these values of *n* accurately; however, in Chapter 5 we shall look at a way of calculating precisely what they are.

4.6 For Excel users

Excel offers the possibility of plotting a wide range of charts and graphs, with the aid of the Chart Wizard. However, there are a number of potential pitfalls for the unwary in using these.

To plot a graph from an algebraic expression using Excel

Suppose we wish to plot the graph of the quadratic relationship $y = x^2 + 3x - 28$, which was plotted 'by hand' in Section 4.4. The first step is to set up a table of values, much as we did when doing the hand plotting. This can be done within Excel in the following way:

1. If we want to plot the graph for a range of *x*-values running from –10 to +10, as we did before, then enter the figures –10 and –9 into the top two cells of column A. Then select these two cells, and use the cursor to 'take hold' of the bottom right-hand corner of the selection box; you'll notice that at this point the cursor symbol changes from its usual symbol to a cross sign. Holding down the left mouse button, move down to row 21; you'll see a little box which shows the value in the current cell. Every time you move down a cell, the value is increased by 1, so by the time you've moved down to row 21, you should have a set of values running from –10 to +10.

2. Now move to cell B1. We're going to put the values of y into column B, using the quadratic expression to work them out. So into this cell you should type =A1^2+3*A1-28. This formula references the value of x in cell A1, and should give you a value of 42. You can now copy this cell down the column to row 21; you'll see the value A1 changing to A2, A3 and so on as you move down, and the values given by the formula will change correspondingly. The screenshot in Figure 4.14 shows what your worksheet should look like at this point.

3. Highlight the whole of both columns, and then click on the Chart Wizard in the toolbar. You'll be offered a long list of chart types; the one you want is rather confusingly called XY (Scatter). When you select this, you'll be shown a set of five formats for the plot; choose either of the ones in the second row. Both of these have the points connected by a curve; the difference between them is that one shows the individual points as blobs on the curve, whereas the other does not.

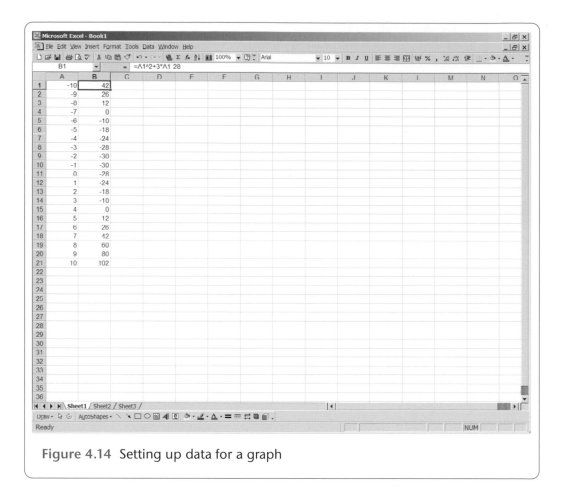

Figure 4.14 Setting up data for a graph

4. If you press the button labelled 'Press and Hold to view sample' at this stage, you'll be able to see what your graph is going to look like, and you can check that it appears reasonable.

5. Clicking 'Next' gives you the chance to say if your data is in rows rather than columns; as it isn't, you can click 'Next' again immediately, at which point you have the opportunity to put labels on the axes, to give the whole graph a title, to add or remove a 'legend' (that's a label telling you what the curve represents; only really useful if you're plotting several curves on one diagram), to change the scales, and to add or remove 'gridlines' (horizontal and vertical lines) on the plot.

6. Finally, clicking 'Finish' will give you your graph, which should look like Figure 4.8 (this figure was actually drawn using Excel).

This same process can be used to plot a straight line, or any other type of curve for which we have the formula. One source of some confusion to beginners is the fact that in its list of types of graph, Excel also includes 'Line', which you might imagine would be the appropriate tool for plotting a straight line. However, this format does not give you a properly scaled x-axis (it is only designed for plotting data against an equally spaced timescale) and so it will give you a very odd graph if you try to use it for general algebraic plots.

What have I learned?

1. Name three different kinds of graph which you've learned about in this chapter. Give a sketch of each type. Can you suggest a business-related use for each?
2. Explain, as if you were teaching an intelligent person who knows nothing about graphs, how you would go about deciding what scale to use in plotting a graph.
3. List some things that you now know/understand about graphs, but did not know when you started on the work of this chapter.

Exercises

1. Sketch (don't plot accurately) the graphs of

   (a) $y = 2x - 3$ (b) $2y = 5x$ (c) $2x + 5y = 20$
   (d) $x^2 - 8x = y$ (e) $y = 1/x^3$

2. A marketing expert has suggested that the percentage, P, of people in a series of towns who are likely to visit a nearby retail park varies in relation to the distance of the particular town (d km) from the park according to the following relationship:

   $$P = 2 + 18/\sqrt{(1 + d)}.$$

   Plot the graph of this relationship for values of d between 0 and 20. What seems to be happening to the graph as d increases? Do you think this pattern will, in reality, continue for larger values of d? (If you have used Excel to plot the graph, you can try extending your plot to $d = 40$ or $d = 60$ and then think about how useful this is.)

Case Study: C21 Graphic Design

C21 Graphic Design is an agency which was set up by its three partners some 15 years ago, immediately after they graduated together from a Graphic Arts programme. It has been very successful, and has grown to employ some 50 permanent staff plus a further 20 to 50 contracted staff, split between offices in Manchester and Liverpool. This includes about 20 administrative staff as well as designers; the contracted staff are typically on short contracts of 3 to 6 months.

The company uses a number of highly specialised graphics software packages, and is about to purchase some new photo-processing software. Three products, which are essentially indistinguishable in function, are under consideration, and information about the associated costs is as follows (all figures refer to use for one year):

TrifPix   fixed charge of £750 for numbers of users up to and including 50, then an additional £10 for each extra user

FotOps   standard rate of £20 per user, applies to any number of users

Pictidy   fixed charge of £200 plus £12 per user.

You are on a placement with C21 as part of your Media and Management degree, and have been asked to write a short report summarising the pros and cons of the three products. Draft this report, addressed to the IT manager Shona McFarlane, and including the following:

(a) a graph showing the costs for the three products for numbers of users ranging between 0 and 100 (use Excel to produce this if possible)
(b) a table showing over what range of users each product is cheapest
(c) a discussion of the best option for C21 given the likely numbers of staff who will need access to the software in the course of the year.

For further exercises and multiple choice revision questions visit the companion website: www.palgrave.com/business/morris

CHAPTER 5

Solving equations

Intended learning outcomes

By the end of your work on this chapter you should:

- understand what is meant by an equation and its solution
- be able to recognise and solve linear equations
- be able to recognise and solve quadratic equations using the formula method
- be able to solve two simultaneous linear equations
- feel confident in manipulating formulae
- understand inequalities and be able to manipulate them correctly
- be able to build equations to represent practical situations, and to interpret their solutions appropriately.

Prerequisites

Before you start work on this chapter, you should be confident in your understanding of the material of Chapters 3 and 4.

5.1 Equations in practice

> ### Before you start
>
> What do you understand by the expression 'an equation'? What do you think 'solving an equation' means? See if your ideas on these two questions are the same as those of other people in your group or class.

In Chapter 4, we've seen a number of examples showing how algebraic expressions can be used to represent practical relationships. Very often, we wish to go further and, rather than just looking at the general relationship, ask what value a variable will have in particular circumstances. Here are two examples, based on problems we've already come across in the preceding chapter.

Example 1: How much should we charge?

In Section 4.3, we developed the relationship $n = 520 - 4p$ which linked the price in pence of a packet of biscuits with the number of packets sold per week. If the retailer decides that she wishes to sell 200 packets a week, how much should she charge per packet?

When 200 packets are sold, $n = 200$, and so we can replace n in the general relationship by 200, to get $200 = 520 - 4p$. This is an equation which, as we will see, can be solved to tell us the specific value of p required.

Example 2: How long will we have to wait?

Also in Section 4.3, we built up the expression $n = 120 + 20k$ to show how the number of visitors per week to a website, n, increases with the number of weeks it's been operating, k. How can the website owner use this expression to find out how long he/she will have to wait before the number of visitors per week exceeds 500?

To answer the question, we need to replace the general n in the expression by 500, obtaining $500 = 120 + 20k$. Again, we'll see shortly how this can be solved to give us the required value of k.

Before we start to look at methods for solving equations, however, we need to define our terms a bit more specifically, and clear away some potential misconceptions.

> ### Pause for reflection
>
> How would you define an equation? What kinds of methods have you used to solve equations in your previous mathematical experience? (For example, you may recall the

formula for solving quadratic equations.) Were there aspects of the equation-solving process that you didn't fully understand, and if so, what were they?

There are several features of the two equations we've just derived which are worth noting. First, obviously, they involve = signs; the word 'equation' is of course related to 'equals'. So a bunch of symbols such as $8a^2/b$ is not an equation; it's simply an *algebraic expression*.

Second, the two equations $200 = 520 - 4p$ and $500 = 120 + 20k$ both involve just one unknown quantity, p in the first example and k in the second. What we mean by *solving* the equation is finding the numerical value or values of the unknown quantity that makes the two sides of the equation equal – that 'makes the equation true', if you like. We sometimes say that such values *satisfy* the equation.

Generally speaking a single equation can only be solved, in this sense, if it contains just one unknown. So the relationship $n = 520 - 4p$ with which we started in the first example cannot be solved to find numerical values for n and p. An infinite number of combinations of n and p exist for which the relationship holds true; this is exactly the set of values shown by the graph of the relationship in Figure 4.5.

Finally, do we call $n = 520 - 4p$ an equation, or not? It certainly contains an = sign, but it's got more than one variable, so it can't be solved in the sense of finding a finite set of values for n and p that satisfy the equation. It could however be regarded as an equation that gives the value of n in terms of p. Such an expression would be called a *function* by mathematicians, but many people would refer to it as a *formula* – the formula for obtaining the value of n when we know the value of p.

It's important to keep the concepts of a formula, an equation containing a single variable that can be solved, and an algebraic expression separate and clear in your mind to avoid confusion.

Test your understanding

Which of the following are equations that could be solved, which are formulae (the plural of formula), and which are just algebraic expressions?

1. $2x + 3 = 11$ 2. $6x - 4$ 3. $15/x = 3$ 4. $v = u + ft$ 5. $4x^2$
6. $5x - 4 = 3x + 6$ 7. $1/x$ 8. $x + y = 7$ 9. $3z - 4 = 18$ 10. $3z$

5.2 Solving linear equations

Some general principles

Let's return to the equation $200 = 520 - 4p$, which we need to solve to find the price at which the retailer will sell 200 packets of biscuits. We call this a linear equation, because it contains only a term in p – no p^2, $1/p$, etc. This is consistent with the way we defined a linear relationship in Chapter 4.

We can solve linear equations of this kind by performing algebraic manipulations with the objective of getting the unknown quantity – p in this case – on its own on one side of the equation (usually the left, but there's nothing magic about that), and everything else on the other side. To achieve this, we can perform any legitimate algebraic operations on the equation, as long as we remember one key rule:

Whatever we do to one side of the equation, we must do the same to the other.

You can think of the two sides of the equation as being like the two pans of an old-fashioned balance scale – if you add something to one side, you must add the same amount to the other, in order to keep the scale in balance.

It will also be helpful to remind ourselves of two points which we noted in Chapter 2:

To undo the effect of an addition, subtract, and vice versa.
To undo the effect of a multiplication, divide, and vice versa.

Armed with these principles, let's attack the equation.

Solving the equation

$$200 = 520 - 4p$$

To get the $-4p$ on to the left-hand side of the equation, we need to undo the subtraction of $4p$ by adding $4p$, and we must do so to both sides. This gives us:

$$200 + 4p = 520 - 4p + 4p$$

We can simplify the right-hand side, since there are two terms involving p:

$$200 + 4p = 520$$

So adding $4p$ to both sides has 'got rid of' the $-4p$ on the right-hand side, as intended.

Now to eliminate the 200 on the left-hand side, we need to subtract 200 from both sides:

$$200 + 4p - 200 = 520 - 200$$

which simplifies to

$$4p = 320$$

Finally, to undo the multiplication of p by 4, we need to divide both sides by 4:

$$4p/4 = 320/4$$

or more simply

$p = 80$

This is the solution of the equation. In practical terms, it tells us that to sell 200 packets of biscuits per week, the retailer should be charging 80p per packet.

You can always check whether you've got the correct solution to an equation by putting the value you've found back into the equation. This is called *substituting*. This if we substitute 80 for p in the equation, we should find that the two sides become equal. With $200 = 520 - 4p$, putting 80 instead of p gives $200 = 520 - 4 \times 80 = 520 - 320 = 200$, so the two sides are indeed equal.

Good and bad practice

We have made rather a meal of solving this first equation, so that you can follow every step. Normally you would probably not write the argument out in such detail; the following steps would probably be sufficient:

$200 = 520 - 4p$
$200 + 4p = 520$ (adding $4p$ to each side)
$4p = 520 - 200$ (subtracting 200 from each side)
$4p = 320$
$p = 320/4 = 80$ (dividing both sides by 4)

Get into the habit of noting what you've done at each stage, and don't try to do too many steps in your head. If in doubt, write it down!

It's perfectly OK to combine two steps of this argument by writing $4p = 520 - 200 = 320$. However, do be careful not to put = signs between things that aren't really equal. For example, I often see things like this:

$5x + 6 = 21$
$5x = 21 - 6 = 15 = x = 3$

Now although this does end up with the correct value of x, as you can check by substitution, it contains some statements which are patently not correct, such as $15 = 3$! Students, when criticised for writing this kind of thing, often protest that 'you know what I mean'. While that may be true, it isn't always the case that *they* will know what they meant when they come to revise the work – and in any case, it is bad (and confusing) mathematical practice to say that things are equal when they aren't.

Test your understanding

1. The following illustrates the process of solving a linear equation. Write comments next to each line (as has been done with the solution above) explaining what is being done at that stage:

$5x - 4 = 16$
$5x = 16 + 4 = 20$
$x = 4$

2. What is wrong with the following process of 'solution' given by a student? Identify the point at which she went wrong. How could you tell without examining the solution in detail that the solution is not correct? Provide a correct solution.

$10 - 2x = 7$
$10 - x = 7/2 = 3.5$ (dividing by 2)
$10 = 3.5 + x$
$10 - 3.5 = x$
$6.5 = x$

3. Do the same as in Question 2 for the following 'solution':

$3x + 2 = 20$
$3x = 20 - 2 = 18$
$x = 18 - 3 = 15$

Not every linear equation is recognisable at first glance. You might think that $4/x = 10$ is not a linear equation, because it seems to contain an x^{-1} term. However, if we multiply both sides by x we get $4 = 10x$, which is clearly linear and gives the solution $x = 4/10 = 0.4$.

The link with graphs

Recall that in Chapter 4 we plotted the graph of $n = 520 - 4p$; it's shown again in Figure 5.1.

There is a connection between this graph and our solution of the equation $200 = 520 - 4p$. Can you spot what it is?

If we read across from the value $n = 200$ on the vertical axis, and then down to the corresponding value of p, we find $p = 80$; precisely the value that we got from solving the equation $200 = 520 - 4p$. Of course, this is no coincidence, because we obtained the equation in the first place by putting $n = 200$ in the relationship between n and p. So the equation could have been solved graphically in this way; however, unless you have already plotted the graph for some other purpose, it's a great deal quicker to use the algebraic method.

A further example

We'll finish this section by solving the equation $500 = 120 + 20k$, the solution of which tells us when the weekly number of visitors to the website will reach 500.

$500 = 120 + 20k$
$500 - 120 = 20k$ (subtracting 120 from each side)

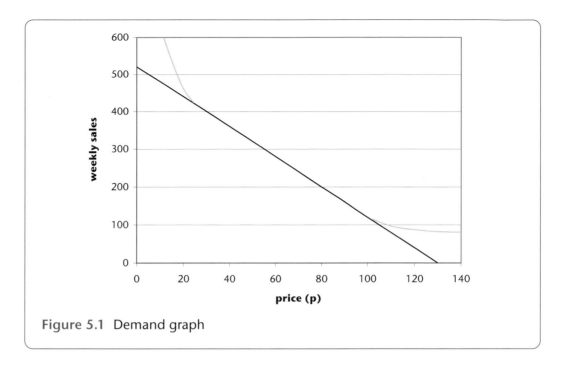

Figure 5.1 Demand graph

$380 = 20k$
$380/20 = k$ (dividing by 20)
$19 = k$

We have to be a bit careful when translating this back into the practical context. Recall from Chapter 4 that the first week of operation of the website was coded as $k = 0$, so k = 19 in fact represents the 20th week of operation.

Test your understanding

Solve the following equations:

1. $x + 4 = 16$ 2. $3x + 20 = 11$ 3. $21 - 5x = 11$ 4. $x/3 = 6$
5. $5z - 9 = 21$ 6. $12/p = 4$ 7. $2 = 8/(m + 1)$ 8. $3x + 8 = 1$
9. $4x + 3 = 2x + 6$ 10. $3a - 12 = 4 - a$

5.3 Solving quadratic equations

Using the formula

The relationship we used in Section 4.4 to introduce the idea of a quadratic relationship was $y = x^2 + 3x - 28$. Let's now see how we can solve the related *quadratic equation* $x^2 + 3x - 28 = 0$.

We recognise this equation as a quadratic because it contains a term in x^2 as well as an x term $(+3x)$ and a constant (-28). We also recognise it as an equation that can be solved, because it contains only terms in x; there are no other unknown quantities. Actually, it would be more correct here to say that it *may* be able to be solved – we shall see shortly that not every quadratic has a solution in the real number system.

If you have studied quadratic equations before, then you may have learned various methods for solving equations of this kind. For example, some equations can be *factorised*, giving a simple route to a solution. (If that doesn't mean anything to you, don't worry – we're not going to use that method.)

However, we are going to concentrate on a method that will enable you to solve any quadratic equation – or to say definitely that it doesn't have a solution. The method involves using a *formula* to find the solutions, and this will be one of the few times in this book when I ask you to accept a result based on a demonstration that it 'works', rather than explain the rationale behind the method. There *is* a rationale, but it is a little complicated and would not be particularly helpful in enabling you to understand the application of the method.

To see how the formula works, we need to go back to our sample equation:

$$x^2 + 3x - 28 = 0$$

In line with the notation you met in Section 4.4, we can regard this as a special case of the general quadratic equation

$$ax^2 + bx + c = 0$$

with $a = 1$, $b = 3$ and $c = -28$ (note that c is negative in this case, and the minus sign must be included).

The formula we use for solving a general quadratic equation is

$$x = \frac{-b \pm \sqrt{b^2 - 4ac}}{2a}$$

where a, b and c are as defined above. Substituting the values of a, b and c from our equation, we get:

$$x = \frac{-3 \pm \sqrt{3^2 - 4 \times 1 \times (-28)}}{2 \times 1}$$

or $\quad x = \dfrac{-3 \pm \sqrt{9 + 112}}{2} = \dfrac{-3 \pm \sqrt{121}}{2} = \dfrac{-3 \pm 11}{2}$

You may have noticed an unfamiliar symbol here. The sign $\pm$ is read as 'plus or minus', and it means that we shall in fact obtain two solutions to the equation: one from using the $+$ sign and the other from using the $-$ sign. It's probably easier to deal with each sign separately, so we can say that

either $x = (-3-11)/2 = -14/2 = -7$
or $x = (-3+11)/2 = 8/2 = 4$.

The two solutions to the equation are therefore $x = -7$ and $x = 4$. You should verify that these are indeed solutions by putting each of them in turn back into the original equation.

The link with the graph

In Section 4.8, we plotted the graph of the equation $y = x^2 + 3x - 28$. For convenience, the graph is shown again as (a) in Figure 5.2.

The solutions of the equation $x^2 + 3x - 28 = 0$ correspond to the points on the graph where $y = 0$; that is, where the graph crosses the x-axis. Figure 5.2 confirms that these points are $x = -7$ and $x = 4$, confirming the solution obtained by using the formula.

In general, a quadratic equation will have two solutions, since a parabolic curve (whether it has a maximum or a minimum) will cross the x-axis twice. There are, however, some special cases which we need to examine.

Imagine the parabola (a) in Figure 5.2 being moved upwards. The two points where it crosses the x-axis will get closer and closer together, until they eventually merge into a single point, as in curve (b). After that, if we move the graph up any further, there will be no intersections at all; this is shown in curve (c). So it follows that there will be some quadratic equations that have two solutions, some that have only one, and some that don't have any real solutions at all.

We can see why this is if we look back at the formula for the solutions. It contains the term $\sqrt{(b^2 - 4ac)}$. Now we know from our work in Chapter 3 that only positive numbers have square roots – the root of a negative number does not exist in the real number system. The expression inside the square root sign, $b^2 - 4ac$, will only be positive if b^2 is bigger than $4ac$. If b^2 is less than $4ac$, then the expression is negative and there are no solutions to the equation. This corresponds to the graph (c) in Figure 5.2, where there are

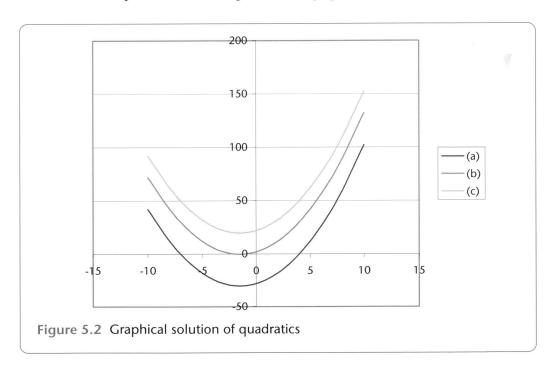

Figure 5.2 Graphical solution of quadratics

no intersections with the *x*-axis. The intermediate case, where the graph just touches the axis and there is one solution, corresponds to the position when $b^2 = 4ac$, so that the expression under the square root sign is zero. You'll sometimes see the statement that in such a case there are two *coincident* roots, reflecting the view that the two roots have at this point merged into one.

We can sum all this up as follows:

When b^2 is bigger than $4ac$, there are two real solutions to the equation.
When b^2 is equal to $4ac$, there is one real solution to the equation.
When b^2 is smaller than $4ac$, there are no real solutions.

Some more examples

The equation $2x^2 + 3x + 2 = 0$ gives us values $a = 2$, $b = 3$, $c = 2$, so the formula gives

$$x = \frac{-3 \pm \sqrt{3^2 - 4 \times 2 \times 2}}{2 \times 2}$$

Here the quantity under the square root works out to $9 - 16 = -7$, so there are no real solutions of the equation. (Try plotting the equation, either by hand or using Excel, to see a confirmation of this fact.)

In the equation $2x^2 + 3x - 2 = 0$, $a = 2$, $b = 3$, and $c = -2$ (remember that we must include the sign), so

$$x = \frac{-3 \pm \sqrt{3^2 - 4 \times 2 \times (-2)}}{2 \times 2} = \frac{-3 \pm \sqrt{9 + 16}}{4}$$

so either $x = (-3 + \sqrt{25})/4 = (-3 + 5)/4 = 2/4 = 0.5$
or $x = (-3 - 5)/4 = -8/4 = -2$.

Verify that these two values are indeed solutions of the equation.

Finally, the equation $x^2 - 6x + 9 = 0$ gives $a = 1$, $b = -6$, $c = 9$, and thus

$$x = \frac{-(-6) \pm \sqrt{(-6)^2 - 4 \times 1 \times 9}}{2 \times 1} = \frac{6 \pm \sqrt{36 - 36}}{2} = 6/2 = 3$$

So there is just one solution, $x = 3$, in this case. Again, sketching the graph will help you to see why this is.

Test your understanding

Without solving the equations, say which of the following will have two solutions, which one, and which no solutions:

1. $x^2 - 4x + 11 = 0$ 2. $3x^2 + 6x - 11 = 0$ 3. $5x^2 - 6x = 0$
4. $x^2 + 10x + 25 = 0$

Higher order equations, and some terminology

As we've said before, you are unlikely to encounter anything more complicated that a quadratic equation in your study of management. However, it's interesting to note that:

a linear equation has 1 as the highest power of x, and has just one solution
a quadratic equation has 2 as the highest power of x, and has at most two solutions.

You might surmise that an equation with an x^3 term (a cubic equation) would have no more than three solutions – and you would be quite correct. This 'rule' can be extended to any power of x. However, it's a remarkable fact, the proof of which involves some difficult mathematics, that there is no 'formula' for solving equations involving x to the power 5 or higher. It's just as well that we don't need to do so very often in solving practical problems!

We've been referring to the solutions of an equation, but an alternative term which you may come across is the *roots* of the equation. So we could say that a quadratic equation has at most two real roots.

Another technical term that you may encounter is the word *coefficient*. This is used to refer to the numbers that appear in the equation – the a, b and c, for example, in our general quadratic. Thus we would say that the coefficient of x^2 in the equation $2x^2 + 3x + 2 = 0$ is 2 (or +2 if you want to emphasise the sign); the coefficient of x in the equation $6x - 4 = 7$ is 6, and so on.

A final reminder: we say that the solution *satisfies* the equation – that is, makes the two sides of the equation equal. So the process of solution can be viewed as finding the value or values of the variable that satisfy the equation.

Applying the theory

To conclude our discussion of quadratic equations, we're going to return one final time to the biscuit sales situation of Chapter 4. Remember that when we plotted the cost and revenue graphs in Figure 4.13, we were able to see roughly where the profit-making region started and finished. We are now going to solve a quadratic equation to find those values more precisely.

The equation for the cost of obtaining the packets of biscuits was

$$C = 4000 + 30n$$

while the revenue R pence from sales of n packets was given by

$$R = 130n - 0.25n^2$$

Now the profit is the difference between revenue and costs, so if we denote the profit per week in pence by P, then

$$P = R - C = (130n - 0.25n^2) - (4000 + 30n)$$

We can remove the brackets from this to get:

$$P = 130n - 0.25n^2 - 4000 - 30n = 100n - 0.25n^2 - 4000$$

and rearrange this into the more usual order:

$$P = -0.25n^2 + 100n - 4000$$

which is of course a quadratic relationship.

How is this going to help us to find the break-even points? Well, those are the points at which the revenue and costs are exactly equal, so that the profit, P, is zero. If we put $P = 0$ into the equation above, we get

$$-0.25n^2 + 100n - 4000 = 0$$

which looks rather more familiar if we multiply all the way through by –1, thus changing all the signs, so the coefficient (remember that term?) of n^2 becomes positive:

$$0.25n^2 - 100n + 4000 = 0$$

We can now see that $a = 0.25$, $b = -100$, and $c = 4000$, so the formula gives:

$$n = \frac{-(-100) \pm \sqrt{(-100)^2 - 4 \times 0.25 \times 4000}}{2 \times 0.25} = \frac{100 \pm \sqrt{10000 - 4000}}{0.5}$$

$$= \frac{100 \pm \sqrt{6000}}{0.5} = \frac{100 \pm 77.5}{0.5}$$

Dealing with the two roots separately, we have either $n = 177.5/0.5 = 355$, or $n = 22.5/0.5 = 45$. So the retailer begins to make a profit at 45 packets of biscuits, and stops doing so at 355 packets. If you look back at Figure 4.13, you will see that this agrees with the points where the two graphs cross. However, using the algebraic method – that is, by solving the quadratic equation – we get a more accurate value than could be obtained simply by reading a value from a graph.

Test your understanding

1. Solve   (a) $x^2 - 6x + 8 = 0$ (b) $5x - x^2 = 0$ (c) $3x^2 + 4x + 8 = 0$

   Sketch or plot graphs to help explain your results.

2. A chemical manufacturer has worked out that the relationship between the yield in tonnes of a product (y) and the length of time in hours for which the chemical production process is allowed to run (t) is given by the following equation:

$$y = 80t - 2t^2$$

Find the values of t for which the yield is zero, and interpret your answer with the aid of a graph.

3. A manufacturer of frozen foods has developed the equation $R = 400n - 2n^2$ to represent the relationship between the number of frozen chickens packaged per hour (n) and the amount of revenue generated (R pence). It is also known that the packaging operation has a fixed cost of £50 per hour plus a variable cost of 50p per chicken.

(a) Write down an equation to give the total cost per hour of the operation, in pence, in terms of n.

(b) Use this equation and the revenue equation given above to find the profit generated per hour.

(c) Hence determine the values of n for which the operation makes a profit.

Pause for reflection

We've covered quite a lot of ground in this chapter already. Before going any further, write down, on one side of A4, a summary of what you think are the main points covered so far. You might want to cover the following:

- What kinds of equations have we discussed?
- What general principles have been established about solving equations?
- What specific methods have been used to obtain solutions to different types of equations?
- What practical applications can the solution of equations have?

Compare your summaries with those of others in your group to see if you have mentioned similar points.

5.4 Solving simultaneous equations

What are simultaneous equations?

When in Section 5.3 we found the points where the revenue and cost graphs intersect, what we were really doing was finding points that satisfied the revenue and the cost equations *simultaneously*, because they are on the graphs of both. This leads us to a general definition of simultaneous equations: two or more equations that have to be satisfied *at the same time*, by the same value(s) of the variables.

Many practical problems lead to sets of equations rather than to a single equation. For example, if you have algebraic expressions for the rate of growth over time of your company and a competitor, you might be interested in seeing when both companies will be the same size – which, looked at in another way, is the point at which one overtakes the other. A more domestic example would be the problem of making a decision between the multiplicity of different tariffs operated by mobile phone companies. By plotting graphs of the various charging regimes and finding where the graphs intersect, you could work out what volume of calls would make it cheaper for you to switch to a different provider.

More generally, it's clear that in the complex world of organisations and management, very few problems will be able to be represented by just a single equation with one unknown quantity. It's much more likely that sets of equations, representing groups of interacting factors, will be required to give a true model of reality. So simultaneous equations, and more advanced topics relating to sets of equations, have an important part to play in the modelling of business problems.

Solving simultaneous linear equations

If you have come across the idea of simultaneous equations before, then it was probably in relation to pairs of simultaneous linear equations, like the following:

$$x + 2y = 5$$
$$3x + 5y = 11$$

These are linear equations, because they contain no powers of x or y higher than the first, no xy terms, and so on. However, there are now two unknown variables – x and y – whereas up to now we've only dealt with equations with one variable. Will we be able to solve for both x and y?

The answer is yes – because we have not one, but two equations linking our two variables. Just as we could solve one equation with one unknown variable, so in general we need two equations to give us a numerical solution for two variables (and so on, although we won't be dealing with more than two).

There are two methods for solving pairs of equations of this kind, and we are going to cover both of them, because you might have come across either if you've met this topic before. We'll illustrate both with the pair of equations above.

(a) The elimination method

This method gets its name because we eliminate one variable from the equations and solve for the one that's left. With our example

$$x + 2y = 5 \qquad\qquad 5.1$$
$$3x + 5y = 11 \qquad\qquad 5.2$$

The first step is to multiply one or both of the equations by a constant, so that we have the same coefficient (remember that's the number multiplying a variable) of either x or y in both equations. Here, if we multiply throughout Equation 5.1 by 3, we'll get

$3x + 6y = 15$ 5.3
$3x + 5y = 11$ 5.4

so that we have $3x$ in each equation. Now we are going to subtract Equation 5.4 from Equation 5.3, which will eliminate x, thus:

$(3x + 6y) - (3x + 5y) = 15 - 11$

Removing the brackets:

$3x + 6y - 3x - 5y = 15 - 11$ (remember that the – sign in front of the second bracket multiplies everything inside that bracket)

so $y = 4$ (collecting up the x and y terms).

We haven't quite finished – we need a value for x as well. To find this, we substitute the numerical value of y into either of the original equations – we'll choose 5.1, since it makes no difference to the solution.

$x + 2 \times 4 = 5$
$x + 8 = 5$
$x = 5 - 8 = -3.$

Thus the full solution is $x = -3$, $y = 4$. We can use Equation 5.2 to check this (it's no good using Equation 5.1, since we already used that to find x). If we substitute the values of x and y into 5.2, we have $3 \times (-3) + 5 \times 4 = -9 + 20 = 11$, which is correct.

To summarise this method:

- Multiply one or both equations throughout by a constant in order to equalise the coefficients of either x or y.
- Subtract or add the two equations to eliminate one variable.
- Solve to find the value of the remaining variable.
- Substitute this value back into one of the original equations to find the value of the other variable.

Here's another example:

$4x + 5y = 42$
$3x - 4y = 16$

This time we shall equalise the coefficients of y by multiplying the top equation by 4 and the bottom one by 5:

$$16x + 20y = 168$$
$$15x - 20y = 80$$

Now we add the two equations (can you see why we need to add rather than subtract in this case?):

$$(16x + 20y) + (15x - 20y) = 168 + 80$$
$$16x + 20y + 15x - 20y = 248$$
$$31x = 248$$
$$x = 8$$

Substitution in the first of the original equations gives:

$$4 \times 8 + 20y = 42$$
$$\text{so } 32 + 20y = 42$$
$$20y = 42 - 32$$
$$20y = 10$$
$$\text{and } y = 2.$$

Checking with the second original equation: $3 \times 8 - 4 \times 2 = 24 - 8 = 16$, which is correct.

No examples for you to practise on just yet – first we need to examine the second method.

(b) The substitution method

We'll use the two equations

$$x + 2y = 5 \qquad\qquad\qquad 5.1$$
$$3x + 5y = 11 \qquad\qquad\qquad 5.2$$

again. The method here is to use Equation 5.1 to express x in terms of y, and then replace the x term in Equation 5.2 by this expression.

From 5.1, $x = 5 - 2y$ (subtracting $2y$ from each side).
Replacing x in Equation 5.2 by $5 - 2y$ gives $3(5 - 2y) + 5y = 11$.
This simplifies to $15 - 6y + 5y = 11$, whence $15 - y = 11$.
Adding y to both sides: $15 = 11 + y$.
So finally $15 - 11 = 4 = y$.

That is, $y = 4$ as before. The final stage is the same as for method (a) – substitute this value of y into either of the original equations to find x. I'll leave you to check that this leads correctly to $x = -3$.

If you have learned either of these methods before, I recommend that you stick with the one that is familiar. If the whole topic is new to you, then method (a) is probably more widely used, and you should concentrate on that. I have written out the solution process in these examples in detail to show each stage of the argument. When you become more familiar with the methods, you might be able to combine some of the steps, but as with all mathematical arguments, if you are in any doubt, it's better to write things down!

Test your understanding

1. Here is the solution of a pair of simultaneous equations using method (a). Annotate the argument to show what is going on at each step.

$2x - y = 7$
$x + 4y = 17$
$2x - y = 7$
$2x + 8y = 34$
$(2x - y) - (2x + 8y) = 7 - 34$
$2x - y - 2x - 8y = -27$
$-9y = -27$
$9y = 27$
$y = 3$

$2x - 3 = 7$
$2x = 7 + 3 = 10$
$x = 5$

2. Solve the following pairs of simultaneous equations, where possible:

(a) $x - 3y = 10$
$2x + 5y = 42$

(b) $3x + 5y = 15$
$x + y = 3$

(c) $2s - 3t = 2$
$3s + 2t = 16$

(d) $2x + 5y = 13$
$4x + 10y = 15$

(e) $3a + 4b = 1$
$8a - b = 1$

(f) $x + y = 4$
$2x + 2y = 8$

3. Find a pair of numbers whose sum is 7 and whose difference is 15.
4. You regularly purchase office stationery supplies. On one occasion, two small and one large note pads cost £6.60, while on another occasion you buy two large and three small pads for £11.40. What is the price of each size of pad?

The graphical interpretation

Figure 5.3 shows the graphs of the two equations $x + 2y = 5$ and $3x + 5y = 11$ which we solved earlier.

You can see that the intersection of the two lines is precisely at the point $x = -3$, $y = 4$, which is the solution we found for the pair of equations. So the solution of a pair of simultaneous linear equations represents the point of intersection of their graphs – the point that lies on both lines and therefore satisfies both equations.

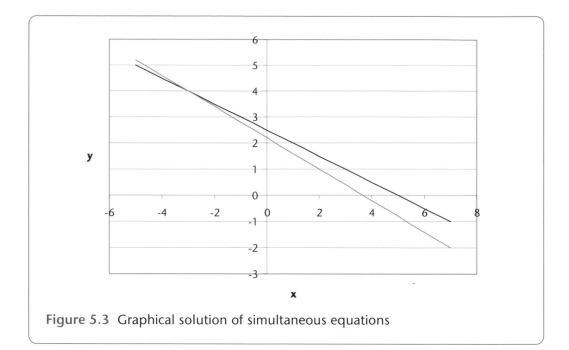

Figure 5.3 Graphical solution of simultaneous equations

Some odd cases

The equations

$$2x + y = 11$$
$$4x + 2y = 24$$

look quite innocent, but if you try to solve them you will soon come across a problem. Using method (a), we multiply the top equation by 2 to get $4x + 2y = 22$. But the second equations says that $4x + 2y = 24$, and it's impossible to have two quantities that add up simultaneously to 22 and 24. We say that the equations are *inconsistent*, and they therefore don't have a solution. If you look at the graphs in Figure 5.4 you will soon see why this is: the lines representing the equations are parallel, and so there is no point of intersection, hence no solution. (Question 2(d) on page 93 was an example of this situation.)

A different problem arises with the equations

$$x + 3y = 4$$
$$3x + 9y = 12$$

If you set out to solve these using method (a), you might choose to multiply the first equation by 3, to equalise the coefficients of x. But if you do so, you will get $3x + 9y = 12$, exactly the same as the second equation. So we don't really have two independent equations here – they are really both the same equation, and thus there is no unique solution. The pair of equations is sometimes referred to as *degenerate*. (Question 2(f) on page 93 was an example of this situation.)

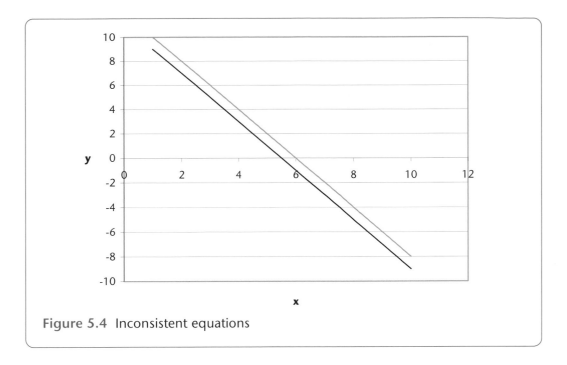

Figure 5.4 Inconsistent equations

You're unlikely to encounter either of these odd cases in relation to practical problems, but I mention them to show that it can't always be taken for granted that a mathematical method will 'work' in every situation.

More complex simultaneous equations

It is possible to solve larger sets of simultaneous equations – for example, three equations involving three unknowns, and so on. Such sets of equations, often with large numbers of variables, do arise in dealing with real-life problems: for example, in certain optimisation problems where a company is trying to discover its best strategy subject to a number of constraints.

It is also possible to solve two equations, one of which is linear and one quadratic. We did actually do this, albeit graphically, when we considered the intersections of the revenue and cost graphs in Figure 4.13, and there is another example for you to try in the exercises that follow.

Simultaneous quadratics, and sets of equations involving higher powers, can be difficult or even impossible to solve, and it's unlikely that you will come across them in your study of management, or in your working life.

5.5 | Working with formulae

We've seen that in order to solve for two variables, you need to have two independent equations, and so on. So what can you do when faced by a single expression involving more than one variable, such as $C = F + Vn$? This is what, in Section 5.1, we called a formula. This one is the formula for the total cost in £ of manufacturing n items per time period (week, month, etc.), where there is a fixed cost of £F per time period and a variable cost of £V per item.

We certainly can't determine a numerical value for any of the variables here – nor would it be sensible to try to do so, since the formula represents a general relationship, rather than something that is only true for specific numerical values. What we can do, though, is to manipulate the formula so that, for example, instead of giving us C in terms of F, V and n, it gives n in terms of C, F and V. To achieve this, we proceed in exactly the same way, and following the same rules, as we did with our solution of equations – whatever you do to one side, do the same to the other to maintain the balance. The only difference is that we are now working with letters instead of numbers.

If we are aiming to get a formula for n in terms of the other variables, then we might proceed as follows:

$C = V + Fn$
$C - V = Fn$ (subtracting V from both sides)
$(C - V)/F = n$ (dividing both sides by F)

You'll sometimes see this process described in textbooks as 'transformation of formulae', an expression I don't like, since it makes the process sound slightly like magic! Another instruction that is sometimes seen is 'make n the subject of the formula': in other words, get it into the form $n = ...$

It's worth noting that often there are several different ways of arriving at a correct result, both when solving equations and when swapping formulae around, depending on the order in which the steps are carried out. For instance, in the example above we could have proceeded like this:

$C = V + Fn$
$C/F = V/F + n$ (dividing throughout by F)
$C/F - V/F = n$ (subtracting V/F from each side)
$(C-V)/F = n$ (putting the two terms C/F and V/F over a common denominator)

which is the same answer as before.

Here's another example, this time based on the formula $q = \sqrt{(2CD/H)}$, which gives the best (cheapest) size of order for a company to place (q) in terms of the cost of holding an item in stock for a given time-period (H), the cost of getting an order delivered (C) and the demand for the items per time period (D). To use this formula to express D in terms of the other variables, we proceed as follows:

$q = \sqrt{(2CD/H)}$
$q^2 = 2CD/H$ (squaring to get rid of the square root sign)
$Hq^2 = 2CD$ (multiplying both sides by H)
$Hq^2 /2C = D$ (dividing both sides by $2C$)

Test your understanding

1. Rearrange the formula $q = \sqrt{(2CD/H)}$ (explained above) into the form $H = \ldots$
2. The formula $A = P(1+r/100)^n$ shows the amount A in a savings account when an initial investment P is left for n years earning compound interest at a rate of $r\%$ per annum. Rearrange the formula to give $P = \ldots$ What question would this version of the formula enable you to answer?

5.6 Handling inequalities

What are inequalities?

An equation, as we've seen, expresses the fact that two algebraic expressions are equal to each other, and in solving the equation we seek the values of the variable for which that equality holds true.

In many business problems, however, the reality of the situation is not that things are equal to each other, but that one must be less than or more than the other. For example, we might wish to express the fact that a coffee shop can't serve coffee to more customers than the number of servings of coffee it has in stock; or that a hospital can't accommodate more patients than it has beds; or that the number of people voting in an election must be no greater than the number of people registered to vote.

Pause for reflection

Think of three more business situations that involve statements like 'no greater than', 'less than' or 'at least'.

Take the first example above, and suppose that on a particular day the coffee shop has 360 servings of coffee available. If we use n to denote the number of customers buying a coffee, then clearly that number must be less than, or at most equal to, 360. We write this as $n \leq 360$, where the symbol $\leq$ is read as 'less than or equal to'.

$\leq$ belongs to a family of symbols known collectively as inequality signs. Its partner is $\geq$, read as 'greater than or equal to'. If you have difficulty remembering which way round the signs work, recall that the 'big end' of the sign points to the bigger quantity.

There are two more such signs, not quite so widely encountered: these are $<$ ('strictly less than') and $>$ ('strictly greater than'). You can see that the $\leq$ is a combination of the $<$ with an $=$ sign, and similarly for $\geq$.

A couple more examples of the use of these signs: if a mail-order clothing company has advance orders for 60 of a particular design of T-shirt, then it must obtain at least 60 from its supplier. This can be expressed as number ordered from supplier ≥ 60. Another way to express this would be to say that number ordered > 59.

And if a company has 80 employees, and needs to set all hands to work on an important project, then number of people on the project ≤ 80, or equivalently number < 81.

The signs can also be combined when we wish to specify that a quantity lies within a certain range. Thus if a human resources department wants to advertise a job at a salary of between £22,000 and £25,000 per year, it could say £22,000 ≤ salary ≤ £25,000.

These signs come in handy when we want to indicate the range within which a relationship holds. For example, many of the relationships we have looked at only make sense for positive values of the variables, because they represent real quantities such as numbers of items manufactured, which can't take on negative values. If the number of items is n, then $n \geq 0$ indicates that n must be positive (or strictly speaking non-negative, since it could have a value of zero).

Test your understanding

Use inequality signs to express the following statements:

1. x is non-negative and can take any value up to and including 10.
2. y may have any value between (and including) -4 and 4.
3. The sum of s and t must be strictly greater than 5.

Linear inequalities and their graphs

Inequalities may be manipulated and solved by similar methods to those we have used with equations. For example, suppose that a company manufacturing men's jackets knows that it needs six buttons for each jacket, and that only 480 buttons are available for use next week. Then if x is the number of jackets which can be made, we can say that the total number of buttons needed will be $6x$. Given the limited number of buttons, we then have $6x \leq 480$. This is a linear algebraic inequality, and we can solve it using the same rules and operations as we used for a linear equation (with one important exception which we'll look at in a moment).

Here, if we divide both sides of the inequality by 6, then $x \leq 480/6 = 80$, and so no more than 80 jackets can be made next week.

The exception arises if we multiply or divide both sides of an inequality by a negative quantity. For example, we can certainly say that 3 < 5. However, if we multiply the two sides of this inequality separately by –1, we get –3 and –5, and it would not be true to say that –3 < –5; actually –3 > –5. So multiplying the two sides of the inequality by a negative number seems to have reversed the direction of the inequality – and this is in fact a general rule – when both sides of an inequality are multiplied or divided by a negative number, the sign of the inequality is reversed.

Thus if we had the algebraic inequality $-6x \leq 12$, the solution would be $x \geq -2$, not

$x \leq -2$. Once again, we find that not all the 'rules' of ordinary arithmetic work in every context.

Inequalities can also involve algebraic expressions as well as single quantities. Staying with the buttons example, suppose now that as well as the jackets with six buttons, the company makes waistcoats which use four of the same buttons. Then if we denote the number of jackets made per week by x, as before, and the number of waistcoats by y, the total number of buttons needed in the week will be $6x + 4y$. The upper limit of 480 still applies, and so we have $6x + 4y \leq 480$. There will be an infinite number of pairs of values of x and y that satisfy this inequality, though only positive integer values make sense in the context of the practical problem. For example, the origin $(0, 0)$ is clearly one such point; $x = 20$, $y = 20$ is another (using 200 buttons), and so on.

Test your understanding

1. Health and Safety regulations permit no more than 40 adults to ride on a fairground roller-coaster at any one time; for the purposes of the regulation, two children under 10 count as one adult. If the number of adults is denoted by A, and the number of children under 10 by C, write down an inequality to show the Health and Safety requirement. Use the inequality to tell you, if 25 adults have already boarded the ride, how many children could then be allowed to board.

2. A hospital consultant's outpatient appointments are divided into routine (R) and complex (C). Her schedule allows 10 minutes for each routine case, and 15 for each complex one. Her regular morning clinic lasts three hours, including a 20-minute break for coffee. Write down an inequality to show how many routine and complex cases she can deal with within this constraint. If there are already seven routine cases on her list, how many complex cases can be added?

Just as algebraic relationships between two variables involving the equals sign can be represented by graphs, as we saw in Chapter 4, so we can represent inequalities graphically, as an example will show.

Consider the inequality $6x + 4y \leq 480$ developed above for the button problem. We begin by plotting what you might call the limiting line for this inequality; that is, the linear equation we get by taking the = part of the $\leq$ sign, This is $6x + 4y = 480$. To plot the line, one simple way is to look at what happens when $x = 0$ and when $y = 0$. When $x = 0$, $4y = 480$, so $y = 120$; when $y = 0$, $6x = 480$, so $x = 80$. Thus the line will pass through the points $(0, 120)$ and $(80, 0)$. These two points are sufficient to define the line, which is shown in Figure 5.5.

Points on the line satisfy the equation. However, any point to the left of and below the line will satisfy the inequality $6x + 4y \leq 480$, as you can see by trying some values – the origin, for example. In practice, x and y cannot be negative, since they represent numbers of items manufactured, and so the final area representing the practical solution of the equality is the triangular area in Figure 5.5.

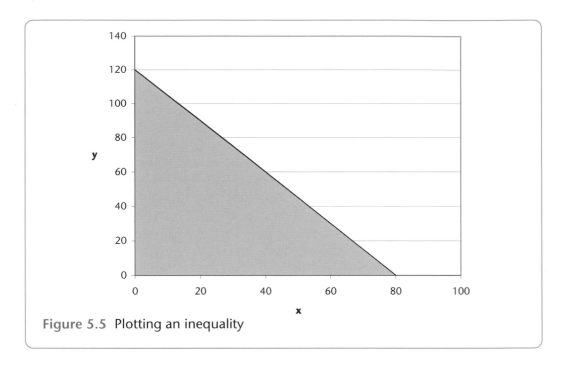

Figure 5.5 Plotting an inequality

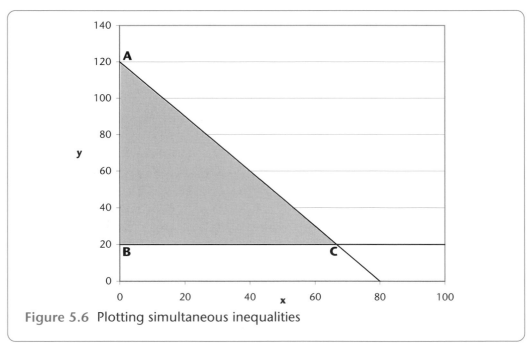

Figure 5.6 Plotting simultaneous inequalities

Nor are we limited to plotting a single inequality per graph; there is no reason why we should not show simultaneous inequalities. For instance, if the manufacturer in the button problem knows that he must meet a standing order from a retailer for 20 waist-coats per week, then $y \geq 20$, and we could add that fact to the graph in Figure 5.5, to get

Figure 5.6. Notice that the line is horizontal, since it applies regardless of the value of x. The triangular area ABC then represents the set of values of x and y that satisfy both inequalities simultaneously (and where x and y are non-negative).

You can see how useful sets of simultaneous inequalities like this can be in enabling companies to identify what levels of output of various items are feasible. A region like ABC in Figure 5.6 is often called a *feasible region*. The idea can then be extended to enable the company to identify, out of the whole set of points in the region, the one that gives the best values to a measure such as profit or use of machinery.

We are really touching here on the beginnings of a large and important area of application of mathematics known as *linear programming*, or more generally as mathematical programming. You may well study this topic in more depth later in your course.

Test your understanding

1. Plot a graph to show the inequality which you developed in Question 1 on page 99 for the fairground ride health and safety constraint. Use your graph to identify three possible combinations of numbers of adults and children which use the maximum capacity of the ride. Write down a further inequality to show that there must be at least one adult per four children on the ride, and add this inequality to your graph.
2. Plot a graph to show the hospital consultant inequality which you developed in Question 2 on page 99. Identify all the feasible solutions which lie on the limiting line of the constraint.

5.7 Putting it all together

You may recall that in 2004, the supermarket group Morrisons took over Safeway supermarkets. When deals of this kind, with very big implications for shareholders, are being discussed, firms of business advisers produce reports that review the prospects of the companies involved, and attempt to predict what might happen to profits, share prices, and other financial indicators in the future as a consequence of the deal.

In one such report, from Charles Stanley Equity Research (available via that organisation's website at www.charles-stanley.co.uk), the following figures were given for year-end values of annual sales in £m:

2004	2005	2006	2007	2008
12,274	13,171	14,265	15,087	15,776

Now since this report was produced in 2004, only the 2004 figure is based on actual sales; the remaining figures are projections. Being curious as to how such projections are made, I worked out that they were probably based on an equation which says the sales, £S

(millions), in year n are given by the equation $S = 11,439 + 892n$. (The technique I used to arrive at this equation is called *regression*, and is beyond the scope of this book, though you may study it later in your course.)

As an investor who wishes to decide whether or not to invest in the company, you might well be interested in the question, 'How long will sales take to reach a value of £20,000m at this rate?' In order to answer that question, we need to solve the equation:

$$20,000 = 11,439 + 829n$$

This gives

$$20,000 - 11,439 = 829n \text{ (subtracting 11,439 from each side)}$$
so
$$8561 = 829n$$
whence
$$8561/829 = n \text{ (dividing both sides by 829).}$$

This gives the value of n as 10.33 to two decimal places. However, this is not a practical answer. The years are counted off in integer values of n, starting with the end of 2004 when $n = 1$, so $n = 10$ corresponds to the end of 2013, and $n = 11$ to the end of 2014. Thus we can say that the £20,000m figure will be reached during 2014.

A plot of the figures, with the line $S = 11,439 + 829n$, is given in Figure 5.7. This confirms the approximate value of our answer.

You can see from this problem that in real life, the numbers involved in calculations

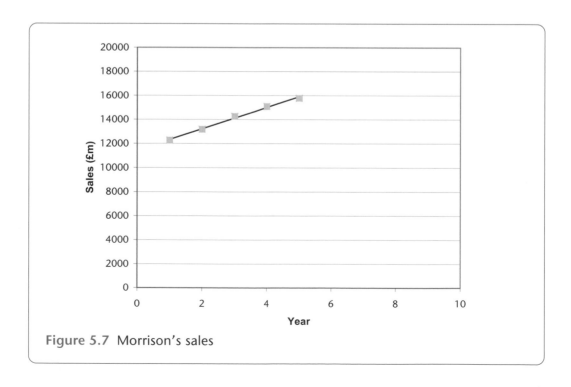

Figure 5.7 Morrison's sales

are not always 'nice'. However, don't be fazed by large numbers. Just work with them in exactly the same way, following the same rules, as we have done in simpler examples.

One point that arises here is worth a little reflection. We were told that the sales figures were in millions of GB pounds, or £m for short. The figure of 12,274 for 2004 thus represents sales of £12,274,000,000 – a rather mind-boggling figure, but not incredible when you reflect that this represents the takings of all the supermarkets, nationwide, over a full year. So when we come to seek the value of n for which sales will be £20,000 million, we need to put $S = 20,000$, not $S = 20$ or $S = 20,000,000,000$. If you did fall into the trap of using either of these values, you should soon realise your error, since you would get a 'silly' value of n in each case. Financial data for large companies are often given using units of thousands or millions of pounds, so you need to get used to handling these large numbers, and noting carefully, if you use data from newspapers or other sources, what units are being employed.

You will notice that there is no 'For Excel users' section in this chapter. Solution of equations is a process best carried out by hand, though you might use Excel to plot graphs to confirm your algebraic solutions of linear, quadratic or simultaneous linear equations, as we've done in earlier sections.

What have I learned?

Look back at what you wrote under the heading 'Before you start' at the beginning of the chapter. Is there anything you would now want to change in your definition of what 'an equation' and 'solving an equation' mean?

Exercises

Solve the following equations:

1. $3x + 4 = 12$ 2. $0.4a - 1 = 1.6$ 3. $3x - 4y = 25$ and $2x + y = 24$.
4. $3p^2 - 6p + 2 = 0$ 5. $2s^2 - 1 = 0$
6. Supermarket branches receive deliveries from a central depot. The time taken to load a delivery lorry is a fixed 20 minutes, while the time to reach the branch depends on its distance from the depot, at an average speed of 40 km/hour. Write down an equation linking the time taken for a lorry to load and reach its destination, t minutes, with the distance to the branch, d km. Use your equation to find the distance to a branch which could be reached in 1 hour and 40 minutes.
7. A market analyst has been studying the rate of growth of two recent technology start-up companies, as measured by their monthly turnover, and has found that the turnover T of XX Technologies, in thousands of dollars, follows the model $T = 17 + 1.5n$, where n is the number of months since start-up, while that of Infitech is best

modelled by the equation $T = 8 + 1.8n$. Use these equations to find: (a) when Infitech's turnover will reach \$44,000 per month; (b) at what point Infitech will overtake XX Technologies. What have you assumed in solving these problems?

8. What range of values of x satisfies simultaneously the inequalities $3x - 4 = 2$, $-4x - 6 = -14$, and $4x - 2 = 1$?

Case Study: The Voice Friend Trust

The Voice Friend Trust is a small charity which provides intensive speech therapy for children with various speech difficulties. Recently it has hired a consultant to examine the patterns of giving among its supporters, and in particular the effectiveness of its telephone contact campaigns.

Only a small amount of data is available; it is known that in a week when 250 potential donors were contacted by telephone, the resulting donations totalled £1320, whereas when only 120 donors were contacted, £800 was donated.

(a) The consultant initially suggests using a linear model based on these two points. Find the equation of the straight line which passes through the two points. On the basis of this model, what would be the base level of giving per week with no telephone contact at all? How many calls would need to be made in order to generate £2000 per week? What is the interpretation of the slope of the equation in this case?

(b) A representative of the trust then points out that giving may level off after a certain number of calls (because the less likely donors are being contacted), so that a curved model might fit the data better. She cites the fact that, in one week where 300 calls were made, only £1400 was generated in donations. Using the three points now available, the consultant derives the equation $D = -80 + 8.9333n - 0.0133n^2$ to model the data. (Figures are quoted to 4 decimal places.) Show that this equation does indeed pass through the three known points. What kind of equation is this? Can you see any problems in using this equation to try to forecast the donations generated by larger numbers of phone calls?

For further exercises and multiple choice revision questions visit the companion website: www.palgrave.com/business/morris

CHAPTER 6

Introducing calculus

Intended learning outcomes

By the end of your work on this chapter you should:

- be able to define what is meant by the slope of a curve at a point
- know what is meant by differentiation, derivative and rate of change
- be able to find the derivative of algebraic expressions involving powers of x
- understand the significance of second derivatives, and be able to use them to find maximum/minimum values of a function
- be able to apply the processes of calculus to the solution of practical problems.

Prerequisites

Before starting work on this chapter you should feel confident with the content covered in Chapters 3 to 5.

6.1 Growth, decline and rates of change

Questions about the rates at which quantities (profits, sales, numbers of customers and so on) are growing or declining are crucial in business. How often do we hear phrases such as 'sales are growing exponentially' or 'the rate of growth of the economy is slowing down'?

One famous example of very rapid growth was the so-called 'dotcom bubble' which occurred with the expansion of the new Internet business sector in the late 1990s. As a consequence of rapidly increasing share prices and a good deal of 'hype' in relation to many of the new companies, stock markets experienced very rapid growth. Figure 6.1 (taken from a Wikipedia article on the dotcom bubble) shows the value of the NASDAQ index, an American share index which is heavily biased towards the technology sector, over this period. You can see the expansion up to 2000, followed by the equally rapid collapse and stabilisation as many of the new companies failed to deliver and went out of business, causing the 'bubble' to burst.

Concentrate on the general trend over the years from 1994 to 2000; you can see that each year the absolute size of the increase in the value of the index gets bigger. This is in contrast to the linear growth behaviour we examined in Chapter 4, where the increase in a quantity from one period to the next remains constant.

Where linear growth was concerned, we were able to identify the constant rate of growth with the slope of the line, and hence with the coefficient m in the general linear equation $y = mx + c$. So the question naturally arises: is there any way we can identify a rate of growth when it is non-constant, as in Figure 6.1 – in other words, when the underlying relationship is not linear but represented by a curve of some kind?

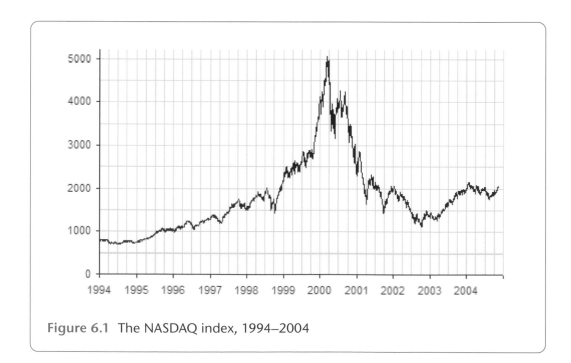

Figure 6.1 The NASDAQ index, 1994–2004

The problem of determining rates of growth – or equivalently, slopes – for nonlinear relationships requires the use of a branch of mathematics known as *calculus*, and that's what we'll be addressing in the remainder of this chapter.

Pause for reflection

Look at the graph in Figure 6.2, which represents the growth of an initial amount of £100 invested for 25 years at 7% per annum compound interest (you might want to look back at Section 2.9 of Chapter 2 to remind yourself how compound interest works). If you were asked to define the slope of this curve at any point, what do you think would be a sensible definition?

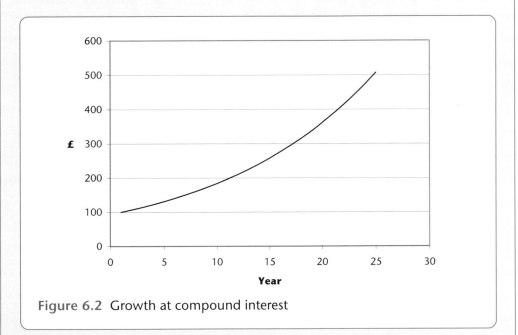

Figure 6.2 Growth at compound interest

We've introduced the concept of the slope of a curve in relation to growth over time. How would the situation differ if we were considering a quantity which declined rather than growing? We use the general term *rate of change* to cover both growth and decline.

6.2 Finding the slope of a graph

Before we can talk about finding the slope of a curve (representing a nonlinear relationship of some kind), we need to define 'slope' in this context. Recall our definition of slope in Chapter 4, as 'increase in *y*/corresponding increase in *x*'. This definition only 'works' for a straight line – don't try to use it with a curve! The point about the curve, of course, is that its slope is always changing.

However, we can construct a *tangent* to the curve at any point – that's a straight line which touches the curve at a single point, like the line AB in Figure 6.3.

The tangent then has a slope defined just as for any other straight line. So we define the slope of the curve at any point as being equal to the slope of the tangent to the curve at that point. You can see that the two tangents AB and CD in Figure 6.3 have different slopes, confirming that the slope of the curve, unlike that of a straight line, is different at each and every point.

This would seem to present a rather daunting prospect if we want to find the general slope of a curve. Do we really need to draw tangents at a whole series of points, and then compute the slope of each of them? That would be one way to proceed, but fortunately if we have an algebraic equation for the curve, then there is a much simpler method, using a process called *differentiation*.

6.3 | The idea of differentiation

A specific example

To see how the process of differentiation works, suppose that we want to determine the slope of the graph of $y = x^2$ at the point where $x = 1$. That means that we need the slope of the tangent to the curve at this point. How are we to find that, without actually doing a geometrical construction?

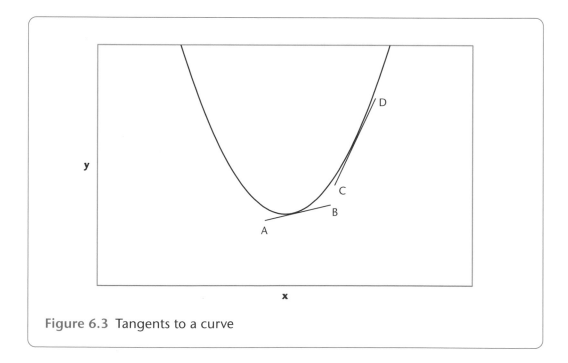

Figure 6.3 Tangents to a curve

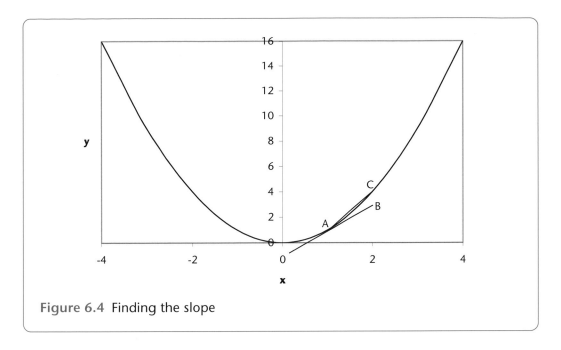

Figure 6.4 Finding the slope

Figure 6.4 shows the curve $y = x^2$. Look at the line AC. Point A corresponds to $x = 1$, and point C to $x = 2$. Because both these points are on the curve, and we know its equation, we can work out the corresponding y values using the equation $y = x^2$; when $x = 1$, $y = 1$ too, and when $x = 2$, $y = 4$. So the slope of the line AC is, using the usual definition for slope of a straight line:

slope = change in y/change in x = $(4 – 1)/(2 – 1) = 3$.

Now of course AC is not the tangent at A, so this is certainly not a good representation of the slope at A. However, if we let the point C slide down the curve towards A, then the line AC will get closer and closer to the slope of the tangent AB. For example, if C moves to a new position C' where $x = 1.1$, then the corresponding value of y is $1.1^2 = 1.21$, and the slope of the line AC' is $(1.21 – 1)/(1.1 – 1) = 0.21/0.1 = 2.1$.

Test your understanding

1. Try calculating the slope of the line AC for other positions of C; for example, use $x = 1.01$ and 1.001. Where do you think the slope is going to end up as C moves towards A?
2. Now go through the same process to try to estimate the slope at $x = 2$. Begin with the slope of the line from the point on the curve where $x = 2$ to the point where $x = 3$, then try $x = 2.1$, $x = 2.01$, and so on. Where does the value of the slope seem to end up this time?

You should have noticed that for the point A where $x = 1$, the slope looks as though it's going to be 2. Here's a table of some positions of C and corresponding values of the slope:

x value at C	2	1.1	1.01	1.001
slope of AC	3	2.1	2.01	2.001

This does not by any means constitute a mathematical proof, but it does strongly suggest that the slope of $y = x^2$ at $x = 1$ is 2.

Similarly, if you put your calculations for $x = 2$ into a table like this, you should get:

x value at C	3	2.1	2.01	2.001
slope of AC	5	4.1	4.01	4.001

So the slope at $x = 2$ seems to be 4. These two results would suggest that the slope at any point on the curve is twice the x value at that point – in other words, that the slope of $y = x^2$ is $2x$.

The general rule

It's possible to go through the same kind of argument as we've just used, but using general points on the line rather than specific values. You'll find the argument in any textbook on introductory calculus, though there is no need to understand it in order to follow the rest of this chapter. What that argument establishes is that the slope of the curve $y = x^2$ at any point is indeed $2x$, and more generally that:

the slope of a curve with equation $y = x^n$ for any value of x is given by nx^{n-1}.

So the slope of the curve whose equation is $y = x^4$ at a general value of x is obtained by using the result above with $n = 4$. This gives the slope as $4x^{(4-1)}$ or $4x^3$. If we want the slope at the specific point where $x = 3$, we then substitute this value:

slope at $x = 3$ is $4 \times 3^3 = 4 \times 27 = 108$.

Test your understanding

Use the formula for the slope of $y = x^n$ to find the following slopes:

1. $y = x^5$ 2. $y = x^{11}$ 3. $y = x^{-3}$ 4. $y = 1/x$ 5. $y = \sqrt{x}$.
   (for the last two, you may need to remind yourself of the use of negative and fractional powers by looking back at Chapter 3.)
6. Find the slope of $y = x^6$ at $x = 2$ at $x = -1$.
7. Find the slope of $y = 1/x^2$ at $x = 1$. Try to find the slope at $x = 0$; what do you notice? Sketch (or use Excel to plot) the curve and see what happens at $x = 0$.

Notation and terminology

As we've already mentioned, the technical term for the process 'find the slope of' is 'differentiate'. For instance, instead of saying in the first exercise above 'find the slope of $y = x^5$' we could say 'differentiate x^5 with respect to x'. The 'with respect to x' part of the statement indicates to which variable we are applying the rule – in our examples, there will only be one possible variable, but in more advanced applications there might be several, hence the need to specify which one we are using.

We also need a notation to represent 'the slope' or 'the derivative', and here it's useful to recall the general notation for 'y is related to x' or 'y is a function of x' which we introduced at the end of Chapter 4. There we wrote $y = f(x)$ to indicate a general relationship between y and x without specifying in detail what algebraic form that relationship takes. Now we can say that if $y = f(x)$, then the slope of the graph of this relationship at any point = the derivative of y with respect to x = dy/dx (read as 'dee y by dee x'). So if $y = x^5$, then dy/d$x = 5x^4$, using the rule established above.

There are a number of points to note about the expression dy/dx. The convention of writing the derivative in this form arose from the process (outlined above) of finding the slope from the tangent to the curve as (change in y)/(change in x). Then the notation dy came into use to represent 'change in y', and similarly for x. It follows from this that the dy and the dx are indivisible – they do *not* mean 'd times y' and 'd times x'. So the d can't be separated from the x or y which follows it – and certainly not cancelled out!

We also sometimes write an expression such as d(x^5)/dx to mean 'differentiate x^5 with respect to x'.

We've now encountered quite a range of ways of describing the differentiation process, so let's summarise them:

> **the slope of the graph of $y = f(x)$ at any point**
> = **the derivative of y with respect to x**
> = **the rate of change of y with respect to x**
> = **dy/dx.**

Students coming to this subject for the first time often wonder why we need so many different ways of writing the same thing. It's really a question of context: if we are thinking in terms of graphs, then the concept of the slope makes sense; if we are discussing a practical problem, such as the relationship between number of units manufactured and cost of production, then it's useful to talk about the rate of change of cost with units; the term derivative is generally used in more abstract mathematical applications, and dy/dx is just a convenient shorthand notation.

Note also that there is nothing special about the notation using x and y. If we had the linear equation $C = 500 + 4n$, representing the relationship between the weekly costs incurred by a manufacturer in £ and the number of items n which are made, then we could find dC/dn, which would give us the slope of the line, or equivalently the rate of change of the cost with respect to the number of items made. Before we can actually work out this slope, however, we need some rules for differentiating an expression of this kind.

6.4 | Some rules for differentiation

So far, we only have a rule for differentiating a power of x. What happens if we want to differentiate a more complex expression – for instance, a quadratic such as $y = 3x^2 + 2x - 11$?

There are a number of fairly obvious rules for building up the derivative of such an expression.

- The derivative of the product of a number and a power of x is the product of the number and the derivative of the power of x. This is easier to express symbolically:

$$d(kx^n)/dx = kd(x^n)/dx = knx^{n-1}$$

where k represents a constant number.

So $d(3x^2)/dx = 3d(x^2)/dx = 3 \times 2x = 6x$

- The derivative of the sum of terms is the sum of the derivatives of the separate terms.

So $d(x^2 + x^3)/dx = d(x^2)/dx + d(x^3)/dx = 2x + 3x^2$

- The derivative of a constant number is zero.

This follows from the general rule for differentiation: if we want to differentiate 7, we can always write this as $7x^0$. Now $d(7x^0)/dx = 7d(x^0)/dx = 7 \times 0 \times x^{0-1} = 0$.

If you think of the derivative as a slope, you can see why this result makes sense. The graph of the equation $y = 7$ will just be a horizontal (flat) line through $y = 7$, so its slope will be zero, and the same will hold for any other constant value.

There are further more complex rules, dealing with the differentiation of products, quotients, and more complicated expressions, but we will stick with these three.

We are now in a position to differentiate the expression $y = 3x^2 + 2x - 11$. We can say:

$$dy/dx = d(3x^2 + 2x - 11)/dx = d(3x^2)/dx + d(2x)/dx + d(-11)/dx$$
$$= 6x^1 + 2x^0 - 0 = 6x + 2$$

It's interesting in particular to think about the slope of a straight line. We already know from our work in Chapter 4 that straight lines have constant slopes, so the use of differentiation should confirm this.

Consider the equation $y = 6x + 4$. We know from earlier work that the slope of this line is 6 (the intercept is 4, but that won't concern us here). Now if we find the slope dy/dx, using the rules above, we have $dy/dx = d(6x + 4)/dx = d(6x)/dx + d(4)/dx = 6x^0 + 0 = 6$. So this way of calculating the slope agrees with our previous definition, and confirms that the slope of the straight line is indeed constant.

Finally in this section, let's return to the question of the rate of change of costs with number of items made, when the two are linked by the equation $C = 500 + 4n$ (this is the problem mentioned at the end of the previous section). We can now say that

$$dC/dn = d(500)/dn + d(4n)/dn = 0 + 4 = 4$$

So the rate of change of C with n is 4, indicating that as n increases by 1 unit, C increases by £4. This is a very simple example but it should give you a flavour of the way in which the differentiation idea can be used in a practical context.

Test your understanding

Differentiate the following with respect to x:

1. $x^2 + 2x$ 2. $3x(x + 2)$ 3. $x + 1/x$ 4. $x^2 - 4x + 2$ 5. $2\sqrt{x} - 2x$

Find the slope of the curves with the following equations (6–9) at the points indicated:

6. $y = 3x^2 - 7x$ at $x = 0$ 7. $y = x(x + 1)$ at $x = -1$
8. $v = 6 + 8t$ at $t = 5$ 9. $y = 75x - x^3$ at $x = 2$
10. Find the point on the curve $y = x^2 + 6x + 3$ where the slope is zero. What is special about the curve at this point?

6.5 Differentiating more than once

There is no reason why we should not apply the differentiation process to a function more than once. For example, if $y = x^4$ then $dy/dx = 4x^3$. We could go on to say that $d(dy/dx)/dx = d(4x^3)/dx = 12x^2$. We use the notation d^2y/dx^2 (read as 'dee two y by dee x squared') to represent the process of differentiating twice; the resulting expression is called the *second derivative* (by implication, dy/dx is the first derivative). In a similar way, we could define third and higher derivatives, though we will not be using those in the rest of this chapter.

You might be wondering whether this process is of purely theoretical interest. The answer is that second derivatives in particular have some important practical applications, as we'll see in the next section. One example to which we can all relate is that of distance, velocity and acceleration: if we have an expression linking the distance s km travelled by a car to the time t hours for which it has been travelling, then the first derivative ds/dt will represent the rate of change of distance with time – that's what we generally call the velocity of the car. Now if we differentiate again to find the second derivative $d^2s/dt^2 = d(ds/dt)/dt = d(\text{velocity})/dt$, we have the rate of change of velocity with time, which is of course the acceleration.

For example, if the distance travelled, s km, is given by $s = 8t^2 + 7t$, then velocity $= ds/dt = 16t + 7$, and so acceleration $= d(16t + 7)/dt = 16$. Thus if the distance is a quadratic function of the time, then the acceleration is constant.

Test your understanding

Find d^2y/dx^2 in the following cases:

1. $y = 3x^2 - 4x + 11$ 2. $y = 27x - 12$ 3. $y = x^6$ 4. $y = \sqrt{x}$
5. $y = 1/x - 1/x^2$ 6. $y = 2x(3 - x)$ 7. $y = 4x^3 - 3x^2 + 2x - 1$

6.6 Finding maximum and minimum values

Pause for reflection

Take a look back to Exercise 10 in Section 6.4, where you were asked to find the point on the curve $y = x^2 + 6x + 3$ where the slope is zero. If you answered this question correctly, you should have found that the zero slope occurs where $x = -3$, and you may have worked out that at such a point, the tangent to the curve is horizontal ('flat' in colloquial terms). Try sketching some curves and identifying the points at which they have zero slope; what seems to be special about those points?

Defining local maximum and minimum points

If you examine the graph in Figure 6.5, you will see that the points where the curve has zero slope – that is, a flat tangent – are of three kinds.

At point A, we have what is called a local maximum point – the value of y at this point is bigger than at the neighbouring points on either side. Notice that it isn't what we'd mean in ordinary speech by a 'maximum' – it's not the biggest value y ever reaches, since there are many larger values of y elsewhere on the graph. That's why we can only say that the point is a *local* maximum.

At point B, the reverse happens and we have a local minimum – the value of y at this point is less than at the neighbouring points on either side.

And at point C, we have a rather odd point called a *point of inflection* – the graph flattens out, but then instead of changing direction, as at a maximum or minimum, it starts to get steeper again in the same direction.

So we have a general rule:

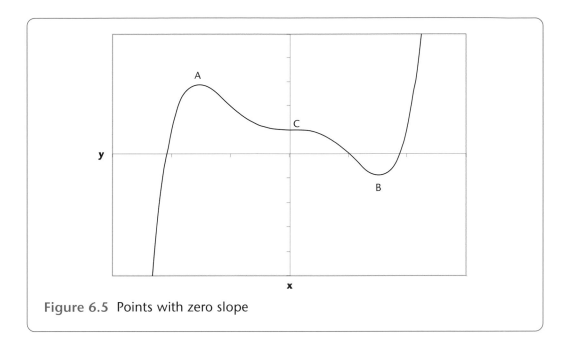

Figure 6.5 Points with zero slope

where dy/dx = 0, the graph of $y = f(x)$ has either a local maximum, a local minimum or a point of inflection.

The plural of maximum is maxima (because the word is derived from Latin), and the plural of minimum is minima; the generic term 'turning points' is often used to cover both types of point, because the curve 'turns round' at such points. Maxima and minima may have important practical implications – for example, business are very interested in knowing what price they should charge for goods and services in order to achieve maximum profits. Now we know that, once an expression for the profit function has been obtained, we can determine where it will have either a maximum or a minimum by looking for the points at which the slope is zero. But it would be unfortunate if the business found itself minimising profits rather than maximising them! So is there a way to determine, without plotting a graph, whether a point is a maximum, a minimum, or a point of inflection?

Distinguishing between maxima and minima

Figure 6.6 shows the graph of the function $y = x^2 + 6x + 3$ which you were asked to consider at the start of this section. You can see that, just as your calculations showed, the function has a zero slope at $x = -3$, but the graph enables us to go further and identify this point as a local minimum.

Now look at the slope of the graph to the left of $x = -3$. You can see that the slope in that region is negative, getting smaller and smaller until at $x = -3$ the slope reaches zero. In contrast, if we look to the right of $x = -3$ we see that the slope is positive, and getting bigger. So in summary, at the minimum value the slope changes from being negative to being positive – in other words, dy/dx is increasing.

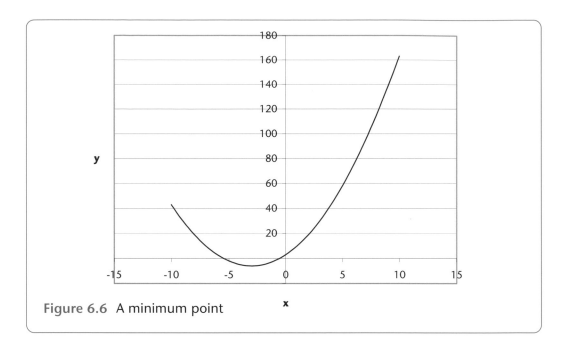

Figure 6.6 A minimum point

Pause for reflection

Try calculating the slope of $y = x^2 + 6x + 3$ for $x = -5$, $x = -4$, $x = -2$ and $x = -1$ to confirm what has just been stated.

The reverse is true when we have a maximum point, as you can see by sketching a curve with a maximum. You should see that at the maximum the slope changes from being positive to being negative – that is, dy/dx is decreasing.

And finally, for a point of inflection, the sign of the slope doesn't change at all. Around the point C in Figure 6.5, the slope is positive, becomes zero but then becomes positive again.

We can show what's been demonstrated thus far in the form of a table:

Minimum	dy/dx changes from negative to positive – increasing
Maximum	dy/dx changes from positive to negative – decreasing
Point of inflection	dy/dx does not change sign

However, although we now have a way to distinguish the three types of point where $dy/dx = 0$, it isn't a very efficient method, since it would seem to involve calculating the value of dy/dx at a whole set of points along the curve.

Fortunately, there is a much neater way. Remember that d^2y/dx^2 tells us the rate of change of dy/dx with x. So if dy/dx is increasing, then d^2y/dx^2 will be positive; if dy/dx is decreasing, then d^2y/dx^2 will be negative. We can therefore add a column to the table above:

Minimum $\quad$ dy/dx changes from negative to positive – increasing $\quad$ d^2y/dx^2 is ≥ 0
Maximum $\quad$ dy/dx changes from positive to negative – decreasing $\quad$ d^2y/dx^2 is ≤ 0
Point of $\quad$ dy/dx does not change sign $\quad$ d^2y/dx^2 is zero
inflection

This in turn leads to the following procedure for finding the turning points of a function $y = f(x)$:

- Find dy/dx.
- Find the value(s) of x for which $dy/dx = 0$.
- For each of these values, find the corresponding value of d^2y/dx^2.
- If d^2y/dx^2 is positive, the point is a minimum; if negative, it's a maximum, and if zero, it is (probably) a point of inflection. (We have to say 'probably' because there are odd cases where d^2y/dx^2 can be zero at a maximum or minimum point, but you don't really need to worry about that.)

Let's see how this works with the function $y = x^2 + 6x + 3$. We've already established that this function has $dy/dx = 2x + 6$, and that this is zero at $x = -3$. Now we can go on and calculate that $d^2y/dx^2 = 2$; that is, it's positive for all values of x, including $x = -3$. Thus the turning point at $x = -3$ must be a minimum, and the graph in Figure 6.6 confirms this.

We shall finish this section by applying the procedure to a number of further examples.

Example (a) $\quad$ $y = 11 - 2x + 5x^2$
Find dy/dx: $\quad$ $dy/dx = -2 + 10x$
Solve $dy/dx = 0$: $\quad$ $-2 + 10x = 0$, so $10x = 2$, whence $x = 0.2$
Find d^2y/dx^2: $\quad$ $d^2y/dx^2 = 10$
This is positive, so the function has a minimum at $x = 0.2$.
(You might like to check this by sketching the graph or plotting it with Excel.)

Example (b) $\quad$ $y = 2x^3 - 3x^2 - 36x + 11$
Find dy/dx: $\quad$ $dy/dx = 6x^2 - 6x - 36$
Solve $dy/dx = 0$: $\quad$ $6x^2 - 6x - 36 = 0$
$\quad$ Using the formula to solve this quadratic gives

$$x = \frac{6 \pm \sqrt{36+864}}{12} = \frac{6 \pm 30}{12} = 3 \text{ or } -2$$

$\quad$ Thus the graph has turning points at $x = 3$ and $x = -2$.
Find d^2y/dx^2: $\quad$ $d^2y/dx^2 = 12x - 6$.
When $x = 3$, $d^2y/dx^2 = 30$, and when $x = -2$, $d^2y/dx^2 = -30$.
So there is a minimum at $x = 3$ and a maximum at $x = -2$.
(Again, it would be good to sketch the graph to confirm this.)

Example (c) $y = x^3$
Find dy/dx: $dy/dx = 3x^2$
Solve $dy/dx = 0$:   clearly $dy/dx = 0$ when $x = 0$.
Find d^2y/dx^2: $d^2y/dx^2 = 6x$.
When $x = 0$, $d^2y/dx^2 = 0$ also.
So there is a point of inflection at $x = 0$.

Pause for reflection

Look back at the examples we have just considered. Can you begin to draw any conclusions about the numbers of turning points which you would expect to find with a quadratic function, a cubic function, and so on? Are there any exceptions to the 'rule' you have formulated?

As you've probably realised, generally speaking a quadratic function will have just one turning point, which is either a maximum or a minimum; a cubic function will have one maximum and one minimum (though sometimes these merge into a single point of inflection), and a function whose highest power of x is x^n will have $n - 1$ turning points.

Test your understanding

Find the turning points of the following functions, and in each case determine whether they are local maxima, minima or neither.

1. $y = 0.5x^2 + 2x + 20$
2. $y = x^3 - 6x^2 + 12x - 7$
3. $y = x^3 - 6x^2 - 5$
4. $y = x^2 - 8x + 3$
5. $y = x + 1/x$

6.7 Putting it all together

In the last section we determined the location of maxima and minima of various algebraic functions, without considering the practical implications of the process. However, as we indicated earlier in the chapter, the determination of maximum and minimum values in fact has very important applications in dealing with business problems. We therefore conclude the chapter by returning to an example which we first encountered in Chapter 4, to see how the techniques of calculus can be used to help a company maximise its profits.

To save you looking back to Chapter 4, here's a reminder of the problem: a retailer selling packets of biscuits has determined that the weekly profit in pence from sales of n packets is given by the formula $R = n(130 - 0.25n)$. The cost of obtaining the biscuits from the wholesaler, also in pence, is $C = 4000 + 30n$.

We can now use these two equations to obtain a formula for the profit in terms of n. Profit = revenue – cost, so if we call the weekly profit in pence P, then

$$P = n(130 - 0.25n) - (4000 + 30n)$$

Removing the brackets gives

$$P = 130n - 0.25n^2 - 4000 - 30n$$

which simplifies to

$$P = 100n - 0.25n^2 - 4000.$$

To find where the profit is a maximum (or possibly a minimum) we need to find dP/dn (since P replaces y and n replaces x here). Using the usual rules:

$$dP/dn = 100 - 0.50n.$$

At a maximum or minimum point, this will be zero, so $100 - 0.50n = 0$, whence $n = 100/0.50 = 200$.

To find whether this is a maximum or a minimum, we need $d^2P/dn^2 = -0.50$. As this is negative, the turning point at $n = 200$ is a maximum – good news for the retailer! So sales of 200 packets per week will result in maximum profits. You can confirm that this agrees with the information plotted as a graph in Figure 4.13 – the profit is represented by the vertical distance between the cost line and the revenue curve.

You will find more examples of practical problems which require the determination of maximum or minimum values of functions in the Exercises at the end of the chapter.

6.8 For Excel users

Excel does not provide any assistance with the material of this chapter – spreadsheets essentially work with numerical data, whereas calculus is concerned with the behaviour of algebraic functions. There are dedicated mathematical software packages – and indeed, some hand-held calculators – which will carry out operations such as finding the derivative of a function, but it is unlikely that you would come across them in a course at this level.

What have I learned?

There has been quite a lot of material to get to grips with in this chapter, most of which was probably quite unfamiliar. To see how your understanding of the concepts introduced in the chapter has developed, consider the following questions:

How can we define the slope of a curve?
What is special about the slope of a straight line?
What is special about the slope of a curve at a local maximum or minimum point?
Have we come across any examples of curves which don't have a slope defined at every point?

Compare your answers with those of others in your group.

Exercises

1. Differentiate the following functions:

    (a) $y = x^2 - 2x + 3$ (b) $s = 1/t + 2t^3$ (c) $y = x(x+1)$

2. Find the turning points of the following functions, and identify whether each point is a maximum, minimum, or point of inflection:

    (a) $y = x^3/3 - x^2/2 - 6x + 5$ (b) $y = x^4 + x^3 + x^2$ (c) $P = 6x(1-x)$

3. The daily cost of producing t tonnes of paint at a factory has been found to be satisfactorily modelled by the equation $C = t^3/3 - 6t^2 + 32t + 25$, where C is in thousands of £.

    (a) Find the production level at which the daily cost of production is a minimum.
    (b) Find the production level at which the daily cost of production is a maximum.
    (c) If constraints on equipment mean that production must lie between 5 and 10 tonnes per day, does this change either of your answers above? (Hint: a sketch of the graph may help here.)

4. The proprietor of a hairdressing salon has found that the relationship between the price she charges for a basic haircut and the number of customers per week having such haircuts is of the form $C = 200 - 20P$, where C is the number of customers and P if the price charged in £.

(a) Use this expression to derive a formula for the weekly revenue, £R, in terms of P. (Hint: remember that revenue = price x number of customers.)

(b) Determine what price should be charged to maximise revenue. How many customers will be attracted at this price?

(c) The *marginal revenue* at a given price is the rate at which the revenue will rise when the price is increased from its current level – in other words, the marginal revenue is the rate of change of revenue with price, or dR/dP. Find the marginal revenue at a price of £4.50 and at £5.50, and comment on your results.

5. The speed in metres per second of a conveyor belt on a section of a car-assembly line is given by $s = 0.001t(80 - t)$, where t is the number of seconds since the belt was switched on.

(a) At what time will the belt return to rest?

(b) What is the maximum speed of the belt, and at what time is it attained?

Case Study: ToysisUS

ToysisUs, a large toy retailer, has been offered the chance to be the sole European retailer of a new toy which has become a craze in Japan, a puzzle called Frustrato. The management of ToysisUs knows that the span of time over which such items can achieve high sales volumes is usually short, and so wishes to apply a model which has been used successfully to predict the sales of such items in the past.

This model suggests that if t is the number of months for which the product has been on the market, and n is the number of units sold during the month (in tens of thousands), then the relationship between t and n is as follows:

$n = t^2$ for $0 \leq t \leq 3$
$n = 12t - t^2 - 18$ for $3 \leq t \leq 9$
$n = 18/(3t - 25)$ for $t \geq 9$

As a sales analyst for ToysisUs, you have been asked to comment on the likely sales in the light of this model.

(a) Sketch, draw accurately or plot using Excel the graph of the predicted sales over the year after launch of the product. (Hint: remember you should only plot each equation over the range for which it is valid – so, for example, only draw from $t = 0$ to $t = 3$.)

(b) Use calculus to find when the sales will be a maximum. What maximum sales level will be achieved?

(c) Show that the slope of $n = t^2$ and of $n = 12t - t^2 - 18$ are the same at the point $t = 3$. What does this imply about the graph?

(d) According to the model, what will eventually happen to the sales in the long term? (look at your graph.)

(e) What reservations about the model might you wish to voice to the management of ToysisUs?

For further exercises and multiple choice revision questions visit the companion website: www.palgrave.com/business/morris

Solving practical problems with mathematics

7.1 Introduction

This chapter does not introduce any new mathematical concepts or methods. Instead, it sets out to demonstrate how the mathematical ideas you have encountered in the previous five chapters of this book may be used to obtain useful information about practical business situations, and to solve business problems. So the format of the chapter is rather different – there are no 'Test your understanding' boxes, though there are Exercises at the end of the chapter.

We have, of course, already encountered many practical applications of the techniques introduced in the earlier chapters.

Before you start

Go back over your work on Chapters 2 to 6 and identify at least three practical situations which you have investigated with the aid of arithmetical and algebraic methods. To start you thinking, one example would be the use of graphs to solve break-even problems in Chapter 4.

However, the emphasis in this chapter will be placed not so much on the actual techniques being used as on the process of applying them in the context of a specific business problem. So if possible, you should try to concentrate on that aspect in each of the examples we examine, and not get too involved in the details of the mathematics.

Many people who are starting to use mathematics to help them solve real-life problems, whether in the area of business and management or in other fields such as social science or engineering, experience the same initial difficulties. These difficulties tend to be not so much with the mathematical methods themselves, which may be quite simple when viewed from a purely technical standpoint, but with the process of translating the original problem into a form which can be expressed mathematically, and then interpreting the mathematical solution back into useful practical information. The situation is shown diagrammatically in Figure 7.1: the tricky steps are the transitions between what we might call the 'real world' and the 'model world' of mathematics, represented by the two sides of the diagram.

A closer inspection of the process represented in Figure 7.1 reveals that there are three major steps involved:

1. The practical problem, usually expressed in words, has to be translated into arithmetical or algebraic terms, usually expressed in symbols. The translation process may require us to make some assumptions about, or simplifications to, the real-world problem.
2. We need to choose a suitable mathematical technique to help us get the information we require (should we plot a graph, solve an equation …?)
3. Having applied our chosen technique, we must then interpret the solution in terms which make sense in the context of the original problem. Because of the assumptions

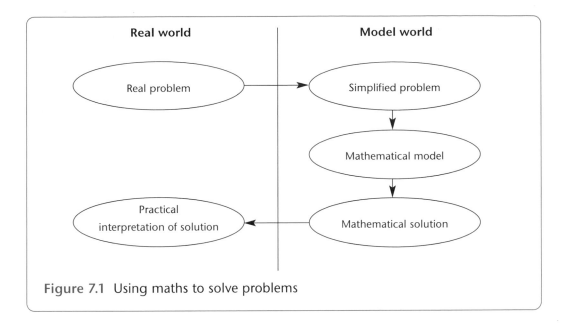

Figure 7.1 Using maths to solve problems

and simplifications which we may have made at Stage 1, this interpretation may require us to identify the limitations on the solution.

It's not possible to set out a 'method' for tackling these steps in relation to a particular problem – that's one of the reasons why the process often seems tricky at first. Instead, we shall examine three typical problems which can be dealt with using the mathematics we have studied in Chapters 1 to 6, and draw out from these some general principles which you can use as guidance. We shall stick to problems which are relatively simple to solve, so that you can focus on the problem-solving process and not be distracted by complex calculations or formulae.

7.2 A financial question

The problem

The first problem we shall examine is in fact an extension of one which we encountered in Section 2.9. There, we examined how an investor's savings would mount up in an interest-bearing account over a number of years. Here, we look at the related problem which asks how much needs to be invested per annum in order to achieve a given total after a set number of years.

The Stuff of Life bakery company knows that it will need to replace a large commercial oven in three years' time, and wishes to make provision for the purchase of the replacement by building up a special investment account. In order to decide on an investment policy, the company needs to answer the following question: how much should be invested per year in order to provide for the purchase, taking into account the interest which will be earned on the investment account?

What do we know?

Our first step is to *identify what information we can obtain (or have been given) about the problem*. We already know that the oven will need to be replaced in three years' time. We shall suppose that 'three years' means precisely that – exactly three years from today. In practice this is unlikely to be the case, but it's a good starting point – we often have to make *assumptions* of this kind in solving real-life problems, in order to make progress with a solution.

Next we need to know what the replacement oven is likely to cost. Enquiries among manufacturers suggest that the figure will be in the region of £60,000. Again, this isn't likely to be the exact figure, but as long as we are confident that the estimate is above rather than below the exact figure, the lack of accuracy should not be a concern.

Now we need to make another, and more significant, assumption – that we know what the interest rate earned by the investment account will be over the three-year period, and that it will not change in that time. This is probably a pretty unlikely scenario, but it is the best that we can do since we don't have perfect knowledge about the future. So let's suppose that the account will earn a guaranteed fixed rate of 4.5% per annum.

Our final assumption is that the payments into the account will be made annually, the first being made today, and the last exactly one year before the purchase of the oven. So there will be three payments altogether.

It should be clear by now that you need to think through a problem carefully in order to extract the information needed to reach a mathematical solution – and that, if you are doing this in a real-life situation, you may need to go around asking quite a few questions before you have the full picture.

Formulating the problem

We can now start to express the problem in mathematical terms. We begin by *identifying the unknown quantities involved and giving them names*. In this case the single unknown quantity which we are trying to determine is the amount of the annual payment into the investment account. We might say, as we often do with unknown quantities, 'let's call it y', but we need to be a bit more careful about the exact definition. To begin with, it's a good idea, as we've already pointed out in Chapter 3, to represent variables by letters which are related to the name of the variable, so P rather than y for the annual payment into the account would be a good idea. Secondly, as this is an amount of money, we need to specify the units in which it's measured. So we should say: let P = annual investment in £. (The amounts involved are going to be large, so £ rather than pence is the sensible unit to use.)

In general, when defining variables, we should *specify units clearly and make sure they are used consistently* – we could not, for example, express P in £ and then decide to express the total to be saved, £60,000, in units of thousands of pounds as 60, since this would be inconsistent.

Now that we have a name for the unknown variable, we can start to build up a mathematical expression for the problem. Begin by asking yourself '*What basic relationship do I wish to express here?*' In the present problem, the answer is:

Total of three annual investments plus interest earned = cost of replacement oven.

The right-hand side of this equation is simply the £60,000 cost. The left-hand side, however, requires a bit more thought. The first payment will be in the account for three years, the second for two, and the third for just one year, so we shall deal with the three payments separately for the moment.

Consider payment 1: its history over the three-year period looks like this:

Date	Amount in account
start of year 1,	P
end of year 1,	$P + P \times 4.5\% = P + P \times 0.045$
	$= P(1 + 0.045)$
end of year 2,	$P(1 + 0.045) + P \times (1 + 0.045) \times 4.5\%$
	$= P(1 + 0.045) + P \times (1 + 0.045) \times 0.045$
	$= P(1 + 0.045)(1 + 0.045)$
	$= P(1 + 0.045)^2$
	(make sure you can follow the arithmetic here)
end of year 3,	$P(1 + 0.045)^3$ (following the same argument as for year 2)

It looks as though there is a general pattern emerging here, and indeed what we are building up is the general compound interest formula which says that an amount P invested for n years at $r\%$ per annum compound interest will total $P(1 + r/100)^n$ by the end of the n years. Thus we can say that the second payment, which is only in the account for two years, will have increased to $P(1 + 0.045)^2$, while the third, which is only invested for one year, will amount to $P(1 + 0.045)^1$ or just $P(1 + 0.045)$ by the end. So the total in the account by the end of the three-year period will be

$$P(1 + 0.045)^3 + P(1 + 0.045)^2 + P(1 + 0.045) = 60{,}000$$

since this total has to cover the £60,000 replacement cost.
   Some arithmetic then enables us to simplify the equation to

$$3.278191P = 60{,}000.$$

We need to retain plenty of decimal places at this stage to ensure an accurate answer, so don't be tempted to round off the 3.278191.

Solving the equation

We have now *expressed the relationship between known and unknown quantities in algebraic terms* – in fact, in the form of a linear equation like those we solved in Chapter 5. The next step is to *solve the equation*, which is a simple matter here: dividing both sides by 3.278191 gives:

$P = 60,000/3.278191 = 18,302.777$

Interpreting and checking the answer

However, this is not 'the answer' – don't be tempted to draw a neat line under it and move on! We need to *translate the result into terms of the original problem*. What we have found is that the amount to be invested each year must be £18,302.78 – we've rounded off to a whole number of pence at this stage, to get a realistic figure.

There is a final step which you should always carry out, and that is to ask yourself *'Does this answer look about right from a practical viewpoint?'* Of course, the three payments of £18,302.78 amount to £54,908.34, and not to the full £60,000 – but the remainder will come from the interest earned, so the figure seems reasonable. If we want to be even more cautious, we can go one stage further and *carry out a check calculation*. In the present case, this will consist of following through the life of the investment as follows, working to the nearest penny:

Date	Amount in account
Start of year 1	18,302.78
Year 1 interest @ 4.5%	823.63
Total at end of year 1	19,126.41
Year 2 investment	18,302.78
Total at start of year 2	37,429.19
Year 2 interest @ 4.5%	1,684.31
Total at end of year 2	39,113.50
Year 3 investment	18,302.78
Total at start of year 3	57,416.28
Year 3 interest @ 4.5%	2,583,73
Total at end of year 3	60,000.01

Thus at the end of Year 3 the account contains the £60,000 required to purchase the new oven – plus an extra 1p due to rounding of the figures!

The kind of investment discussed in this example – designed to provide for the replacement of equipment, buildings and so on – is known in accounting terms as a *sinking fund*. In practice it would not be necessary to carry out the process in such detail – in fact Excel contains some useful financial functions which can shortcut some of the calculations we've done here.

7.3 Some general principles

You may have noticed a number of items which were printed in italics in the preceding section. If we collect these together and expand them a little, they give us a set of general principles which can be applied in many problem-solving situations:

- Identify what information we can obtain (or have been given) about the problem.

- Make some assumptions (if necessary) in order to simplify the problem and make it manageable.
- Identify the unknown quantities and give them names (preferably meaningful ones so that we can easily remember what they refer to).
- Specify units clearly and make sure they are used consistently.
- Ask 'What basic relationship do I wish to express here?'
- Express the relationship between known and unknown quantities in algebraic terms.
- Solve the equation (or perhaps plot a graph to display the relationship).
- Translate the result in terms of the original problem.
- Ask yourself 'Does this answer look about right from a practical viewpoint?'
- Carry out a check calculation if possible.

We shall use this list as a guide in dealing with the other two problems in this chapter. Not all the points will be relevant in every case, and some may need modification, but overall they provide a checklist to see us through the problem-solving process – a list which is really an expanded version of the three-point process outlined in Section 7.1.

7.4 A depreciation problem

Continuing with the example of the Stuff of Life bakery introduced in Section 7.2, let's now suppose that, having purchased the £60,000 oven, the company wishes to reduce the value of this asset as used for accounting purposes (called its 'book value') by equal amounts each year, until by the end of its useful life its value has decreased to whatever can be obtained for it when sold as scrap. The problem we wish to solve is then: what is the general relationship between the age of the oven and its book value? Knowing the answer to this question will enable us to use the correct value in each year's accounts. The process of reducing the value of an asset as time goes on is known as *depreciation*, and the idea should be familiar to anyone who has ever bought or sold a car!

We begin as before by identifying the information we can obtain about the problem. The purchase price of the oven was, as we know, £60,000. The further information we need is the expected useful lifetime of the oven, and its scrap value at the end of that lifetime. Here we will have to make some assumptions, perhaps informed by experience of the behaviour of similar equipment in the past. Let's suppose that the machine can be expected to last eight years, and that at the end of that period it can be sold as scrap for £4000.

We have already made one major assumption about the problem – namely, that the value will decrease by equal amounts each year. This means that a graph of value against the age of the oven would be a straight line, and in fact this method of dealing with depreciation is called *straight-line depreciation*. The unknown quantity we're interested in here is the value of the oven at any given point in time – let's call this value £V, and denote the time in years since the purchase of the oven by t. Notice how, as required by our general principles, we are using meaningful letters for the variables, and being careful to specify the units in which they are measured.

The basic problem here is rather different from that in Section 7.2. There, we wanted to find one single value of an unknown quantity, so we needed to find an equation which could be solved. Here, we have a more general requirement – to establish the relationship between V and t in the form of an equation. The assumption of linearity means that, as we saw in Chapter 4, the equation will have the form $V = mt + c$, where m and c are constants. So our problem reduces to that of finding the values of m and c.

The data we already have enables us to identify two points which satisfy the equation: when $t = 0$ at the time of purchase, $V = 60{,}000$, and when $t = 8$ at the end of the oven's lifetime, $V = 4000$. The first of these points tells us that $60{,}000 = m \times 0 + c$, giving $c = 60{,}000$ immediately. So the equation is of the form $V = mt + 60{,}000$. Substituting the second pair of values into this equation gives $4000 = 8m + 60{,}000$, whence $8m = -56{,}000$, so $m = -7000$. The final version of the equation is therefore

$V = -7000t + 60{,}000$, which looks better written as $V = 60{,}000 - 7000t$.

There is no question of solving this equation – to begin with, it has two unknowns and not just one, and in any case, our objective here was not to find a numerical solution to a problem, but to obtain the general form of the relationship between V and t, which we've now done. So we can proceed to the next step, interpreting the result in practical terms. The 60,000 in the equation gives us the value of the oven when new. What about the other constant? The fact that the coefficient of t – the slope of the line – is negative should come as no surprise, since it shows that the value of the item decreases each year, as we would expect. The 7000 is the amount by which the value goes down over one year, so we can say that the linear depreciation model in this case suggests an annual reduction in the book value of £7000. (You may have spotted that we could have arrived at this figure more directly by saying that the value decreases by an amount £56,000, from £60,000 to £4000, over eight years – that's £7000 a year.)

Does this result seem sensible? The negative slope is certainly correct. The equation should, of course, only be used within the lifetime of the machine; if we put $t = 10$, we get $V = -£10{,}000$, which is not very sensible, as the machine was scrapped when $t = 8$, so $t = 10$ is not a feasible value for t.

This is a very simple type of depreciation model. If you study accounting during your course you may encounter other more complex models involving fitting a curve rather than a straight line – though in such a case, further assumptions about the precise form of curve will be required.

Pause for reflection

Go over the example in this section once more, making sure that you can identify where each of the principles of Section 7.3 is being applied.

7.5 A stock-control problem

Our final example relates to the cost of obtaining and storing goods. Most organisations have to do this, whether they are supermarkets obtaining supplies of tinned goods from a warehouse, or steel-mills obtaining raw materials to go into the steel production process. Management then needs to decide how large a quantity should be ordered at one time – is it better to order large supplies at infrequent intervals, or small amounts more often? We would like to construct a mathematical model to help in answering this question.

Compared with our earlier problems, this one seems rather ill-defined. However, a little thought shows that what we really want to know is how to determine the order size which makes costs as low as possible – in other words, to minimise total costs. After your work in Chapter 6, the word 'minimise' should immediately cause you to think of calculus – and indeed, we are going to use differentiation to help find the cost-minimising size of order (though if you have not worked through Chapter 6, do not worry – we shall also be pointing out alternative ways of arriving at the solution).

Before we can start trying to minimise the costs, we need to derive an equation showing how they relate to the size of the orders. Our first step, as in both the earlier problems, is to identify known information about the problem.

Historic records will probably enable us to estimate the current demand for the item – let us say it is 12,000 items per year. We have to start making assumptions immediately by assuming that this figure will not alter too much in the near future.

Then we move to the costs. There will be a cost associated with raising an order (administrative cost, delivery charge and so on). With the aid of an accountant we should be able to get an idea of this cost – suppose it is in the region of £40. Now we need another assumption: order cost does not vary with the size of the order. (Since I am aiming to help you learn mathematics rather than operations management, I shall not spend time considering how likely the assumptions are to be true, but you might like to give this question some thought.)

The other element of cost will be connected with the storage of the items; if we order in bulk, we will have a lot more items to store than if we order small amounts at a time. Again, we need to estimate this storage or stockholding cost; we might discover that to store one item for one month costs 2p.

Following the usual procedure, we next decide what the unknown quantities are, and what we are going to call them. There are two things in the problem which may vary – we may choose to change the order size, and the total cost of placing orders will vary as a result. Making sure we include the units in our definition, we say:

let C = total cost in £ per annum
let q = number of units per individual order.

As before, we use meaningful letters rather than the ubiquitous x and y.

At this point we consider the basic relationship we are trying to express; here it is quite simply stated in words:

total cost = ordering cost plus stockholding cost.

Translating this into an algebraic equation is not quite so simple, and needs to be broken down into manageable steps. The LHS is no problem: total cost is what we have called C. On the RHS, the first term is ordering cost, which will depend on how many orders we place per year. We know that demand is 12,000 items per year, and we also know that the quantity being ordered at a time is q. But how can we link these to give us the number of orders in a year?

You may be able to see immediately that the number of orders will be $12,000/q$. If making the leap directly to this formula seems difficult, think about what would happen if q were 3000 items; then you would need 4 orders to last the year. Similarly, if q were 4000, the number of orders would be 3. So to find the number of orders per year, we are dividing the size of each order into the total demand of 12,000. Thus for a general size of order q, the number of orders would be $12,000/q$.

What we have done here is so useful that it almost deserves the status of another general principle:

Try out calculations with simple numbers before attempting to express them in general algebraic terms.

Having found the number of orders per year, we just multiply it by the cost of each order to find the annual ordering cost. So altogether,

annual ordering cost in £ = $12,000/q \times 40 = 480,000/q$.

The other contributor to total cost is the stockholding cost. This is 2p per month for each item held – but the number of items being held will vary as orders are delivered and used up. To get a definite expression for stockholding cost, we need a further assumption: stocks are used up at a steady rate from a maximum of q (just after an order is delivered) to a minimum of zero. At this point there is instant replenishment of the stock, and the whole process starts over again. Figure 7.2 is a graph showing how stocks vary with time if this assumption is made.

If you accept this assumption (which, we agree, takes some swallowing, especially the 'instant replenishment' part) then it follows that in the long term the average amount in stock will be $q/2$. (If you cannot see this immediately, note that this is the stock level half way through the period between replenishments; higher stock levels early on in the period are balanced exactly by lower stocks later in the period.) Since each of the $q/2$ items costs 2p to store for a month, the stockholding cost will be $q/2 \times 2$ pence per month.

However, we need to be careful again here about the units. We already decided to express total cost C in £ per year, so we cannot have stockholding cost in pence per month. Making the change to £ per year gives $q/2 \times 2 \times 12/100$ or $0.12q$ £ per year.

Now at last we can write down the complete equation relating C and q; it is:

C = order cost + stockholding cost = $480,000/q + 0.12q$

You may have lost sight of the original objective in the lengthy process of obtaining this equation; what we actually set out to do was to find the size of order which makes cost a

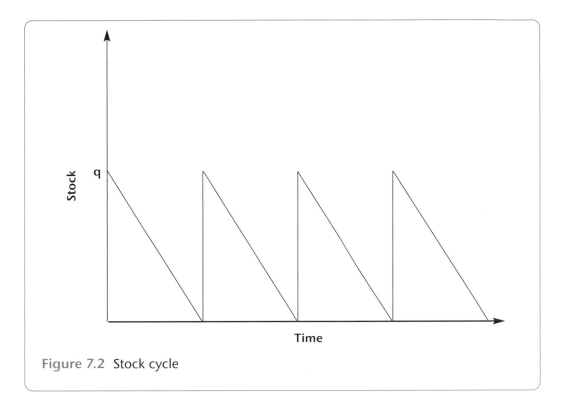

Figure 7.2 Stock cycle

minimum. Rephrasing this in terms of our mathematical expression of the problem: we want to determine the value of q (if any) which minimises C.

We have said 'if any', but a look at the equation above should show that there certainly will be a minimum value of C. As q gets bigger, the first term – the order cost – gets smaller; a sensible result, since with bigger orders we need to order less frequently. On the other hand, the second term – the stockholding cost – grows linearly with q. So there must be a point representing a 'happy medium', where the two costs balance out. This will be our minimum cost policy. We have a choice of methods for determining the value of q which produces this minimum cost. We can use calculus and say that C will have a minimum (or maximum) when $dC/dq = 0$. Applying the differentiation rules of Chapter 6 we get:

$$dC/dq = -480,000/q^2 + 0.12$$

and this is zero when

$$-480\,000/q^2 + 0.12 = 0$$

which solves to give $q = \pm2000$. Clearly a negative value of q makes no practical sense, so the value we are looking for must be $q = 2000$. If you want some practice in differentiation, you can find the second derivative of C with respect to q, and show that it is positive when $q = 2000$, so that C is indeed a minimum at this point.

The alternative method, if you do not want to use calculus, is to plot a graph of C against q and use this to read off the value of q making C a minimum. You should recognise that the graph will be a curve, since its equation contains a $1/q$ term. So you will need to plot quite a few points to get an accurate picture; the realisation that annual demand is measured in thousands should suggest that values of q of the order of several hundred, rather than $q = 1, 2, 3, \ldots$, are sensible ones to choose.

Whatever means we use to find the best value of q, we need to translate the solution back into a practically useful form. We have found that ordering 2000 items at a time minimises the total cost of ordering and storing them. Given that 12,000 items a year are needed, this means that six orders will need to be placed each year – that is, one every two months.

The problem we have examined in this section is an example of an *inventory problem*. In the Exercises at the end of the chapter, you will find a more general problem of the same type, the solution of which gives a formula for determining the cost-minimising order quantity for any demand and cost structure.

7.6 Conclusion

We observed at the start of this chapter that there are really no standard 'methods' for applying mathematical techniques to the solution of real problems. Nevertheless, we hope that the framework of general principles developed and illustrated in this chapter will stand you in good stead in applying the mathematical and statistical methods you learn in the future. Perhaps the most important principle of all is to take things steadily, step by step, and never to let go of your common sense!

What have I learned?

Look back at the examples which you identified in the 'Before you start' section at the beginning of this chapter. Can you identify the various stages of the problem-solving process in those examples?

In tackling the Exercises in the following section, try to keep the general principles in mind. Although they don't constitute a 'method', they will help to ensure that you don't omit any important points.

Exercises

1. You know that five years from now you will need to buy a replacement car costing £8000. Interest is currently available at 11.5% per annum (compounded annually). How much do you need to invest now as a single lump sum, in order to accumulate the necessary amount by the end of the five years? What assumptions do you need to make to reach your solution, and how realistic are they? (The answer you obtain – assuming it is correct! – is what is known as the *present value* of a sum of £8000 payable in six years at a *discount rate* of 11.5% per annum. If you take courses in accounting or finance, you will learn about the use of net present values as one method of investment appraisal).

2. Suppose that in the inventory problem of Section 7.5, the annual demand was for D items, the cost of placing one order was £R and the cost of holding a single item in stock for a year was £H. Follow through the argument of Section 7.5 using these general values for the quantities, and thus obtain a formula giving the cost-minimising quantity q in terms of R, H and D.

3. (a) Use the formula you have derived in Question 2 to determine the cost-minimising quantity to order if the demand for an item is 200 per month, the cost of placing an order is £4 (irrespective of size), and the cost of holding an item in stock for a year is 12p. How often will you need to place an order?

   (b) Suppose you subsequently find out that your estimate of the order cost is wrong, and in fact it should have been £3.50. What percentage error in the cost have you made? What should the correct order size be, and how much extra per year will you be paying in inventory charges as a result of your error? What general implications does your conclusion have for the usefulness of this method?

4. When a price of 40 pence per unit is charged for a commodity, annual demand for the commodity is 20,000 units. If the price is increased to 50 pence per unit, demand falls to 18,000 units per annum.

   (a) Assuming that demand varies linearly with price, determine the equation linking them.

   (b) Hence find at what price the demand would fall to zero. How likely do you think this is in practice? Where might the linear model break down?

   (c) Also determine what the demand would be if the commodity were free of charge.

5. A direct-sales firm uses the following rule of thumb for determining postage and packing charges: 5% of order value for orders up to £50, 3% for orders above £50 but below £75, and free of charge thereafter. Devise a chart from which staff can easily read off the charge for any given order value.

For further exercises and multiple choice revision questions visit the companion website: www.palgrave.com/business/morris

Statistics: organising data

8.1 | What is statistics?

Before you start

The word 'statistics' is often mentioned in the media, in many different contexts. Find three references to 'statistics' in recent news reports, and try to identify what, if anything, there is in common between the topics being covered under this heading. Could you derive a definition of 'statistics' from what you've read? Do the items you've looked at give you a positive or a negative view of the subject?

In Chapters 1 to 7 of this book, we have been looking at concepts and techniques which could be classed under the general heading of mathematics. In the last two chapters, we shall be looking at a slightly different area – that of statistics. Statistics as a subject is closely related to mathematics, and uses many mathematical ideas and methods. However, in statistics we are dealing with a different class of problems, and so it is worth spending a little time examining the nature of those problems.

The successful operation of businesses and organisations is very dependent on a supply of reliable information. The technical term *data* is often used to describe the large quantities of information involved. Here are a few examples to illustrate the importance of good data:

- A consortium of leading clothing retailers in the UK (including household names such as Marks & Spencer and John Lewis Partnership), with the support of the UK government, commissioned the National Sizing Survey, known as SizeUK, to look at the body shapes of a representative sample of 11,000 adults. 140 measurements were taken from each person – that's 1,540,000 altogether – a lot of data! The data, when suitably analysed, will enable the companies involved to ensure that they can supply clothing to fit their customers. (You can find more information about the survey at http://www.sizeuk.org/.)
- Bar-code scanning at the checkouts of large supermarkets such as Sainsbury and Tesco not only enables accurate records of stocks to be maintained – it also generates a huge volume of data which, if properly analysed, can give invaluable insights into customers' buying habits, and help to inform advertising and promotional activity. For example, if analysis of the data shows that many customers who bought fresh pasta also bought Italian wine, then a promotion could be developed which gives buyers of the pasta 50p off their wine purchase.
- Electricity supply companies like Powergen keep continuous records of the level of demand for power and the way that level varies over time. Analysis of the data enables them to plan the supply to meet peaks and troughs in demand: on an annual basis they can predict how much the demand is likely to increase or decrease with falling or rising temperatures, while in the short-term they can estimate the increase in demand which

occurs at the end of a major premiership football match, when thousands of households put the kettle on!

In all these examples, a very large volume of data is gathered, but it needs to be processed to make it more informative. The discipline of statistics provides the techniques for carrying out that processing, and for interpreting the results.

Pause for reflection

In each of the three examples given above, think about what kind of summary information you would need to obtain. For example, in the case of the SizeUK survey, it is obviously not sufficient merely to know the average height of all the people involved in the survey – what else would the retailers want to know?

Statistics is a very large subject, and in a book of this kind I can only introduce you to some of the simpler and most commonly used methods. If you are studying for a business or management degree, then it is very likely that you will have the opportunity to study more advanced statistical methods later on in your course.

8.2 Data and where to find it

As the examples given in the previous section have hinted, most organisations now have relatively easy access to large quantities of data – the problems lie in organising the data so that it can be used effectively. Nevertheless, it's worth spending a little time thinking about the different sources of data which are available to organisations, and how they can be accessed.

Data is often subdivided into *primary* and *secondary* data. Roughly speaking, primary data is that which is collected directly by the organisation, either as a matter of routine or for a specific purpose. Examples might be:

- The data on demand for power gathered by Powergen, as mentioned in Section 8.1. This is captured routinely, and can be used for a range of purposes within the company.
- Market research data collected by a food manufacturer who is thinking of introducing a new type of packaging for a well-established product (you may remember changes to the shape of Cola bottles which attracted quite a lot of attention some time ago). This data will be targeted specifically at providing information relevant to the particular development being considered, and will be collected directly either by the company itself, or by a market research agency working on its behalf.
- Data concerning the effectiveness of a new drug to treat a serious illness. Such data will be gathered from carefully designed investigations, often taking months or even years to carry out; this is why the development of new drugs is such an expensive process. There have been some high-profile cases reported in the media relating

to drug developments of this kind – one of the most recent was concerned with Herceptin for the treatment of breast cancer.

In contrast, secondary data is that which has already been collected by another person or organisation, and which is made more widely accessible either in paper or electronic format. For instance:

- An enormous range of statistical information is gathered by the government, and published both in various hard-copy formats and on-line. This includes business, sociological and economic data. To get a feel for the range and variety of statistics published in this way, try visiting http://www.statistics.gov.uk/, the website of National Statistics.
- On the international level, the United Nations Statistics Division produces a large volume of statistical information, some of which you can see at http://unstats.un.org/unsd/default.htm.
- Data about specific business sectors is often gathered and published by the relevant trade association, though access may be restricted to members of the association and/or have a high price-tag attached.
- Data about individuals and households, relating to demographics (variables such as age, gender and so on) and to lifestyle factors is collected by commercial agencies who charge other organisations, such as direct mail companies, for access to the data. One of the best-known data sets of this kind is Mosaic, which you can read about at http://www.experian.co.uk/business/products/data/113.html.

When faced with a need for information in order to deal with a business problem, there are a number of factors which need to be considered in deciding whether to look for secondary data or to set about collecting primary data. These include the following:

- If the data is very specific to your organisation, then it is likely that you will need to collect it directly. Be aware, however, that large organisations do routinely gather a lot of data, much of which is not fully exploited, and so the information you need may well already be available elsewhere in the organisation. For example, if you want to know about the location of your customer base, the accounting department is likely to have access to customer addresses which are needed for billing, and which could provide what you need.
- Secondary data, particularly when gathered by a government agency, is likely to be very reliable, not least because there is a statutory obligation on organisations to provide data on issues such as hours worked by employees, rates of pay and so on. However, such data is also likely to be out-of-date, sometimes considerably so, because of the time taken in preparing it for publication.
- Much primary data, particularly that related to customers' views, political opinions and so on, is collected by means of questionnaire-based surveys. Designing and carrying out a good questionnaire is neither quick nor simple, and can also be a costly business, while data obtained from badly designed surveys can be useless if not totally misleading. The analysis of primary data so as to be able to draw valid conclusions also requires a good understanding of statistical methods.

There are many good books on the subject of survey methods, so if you find yourself having to design a serious statistical investigation you should have no shortage of sound advice. Fortunately, methods for presenting and summarising data are much the same irrespective of the origin of the data, so we shall now proceed to examine some of those methods.

Pause for reflection

Think of some examples of surveys which you have either taken part in or read about – for example, the kind of newspaper poll which asks readers to phone in with their answers to the question 'Does the England football team need a new manager?' How reliable do you think the results of your chosen examples would be? Where might the sources of unreliability lie?

8.3 Types of data

We have already seen that data comes in various forms, some more obviously quantitative, some more qualitative or descriptive. We need to think about this in a bit more detail before we go on to look at methods for organising and presenting the data.

Qualitative and quantitative data

The term qualitative refers to something which cannot be measured, but must simply be classified – like region of residence, or hair colour. Quantitative data, on the other hand, can be assigned a measurement on some kind of numerical scale. However, we need to distinguish two sub-categories of quantitative data.

Discrete data

Measurements which consist of counts, such as the number of customers visiting the various stores of a retail chain on a given day, provide one example of what is called *discrete* data (note the spelling!). This is usually defined as data which can only take on certain definite values – thus a count must be a whole number. Other examples would be UK women's clothing sizes (8, 10, 12, 14, ...) or the weights in which some foodstuffs are packaged (for example, margarines generally come in packages weighing 250 g or 500 g). The key feature of discrete data is that there are gaps between the data values.

Continuous data

In contrast, a quantity such as the pressure in a chemical reactor, or the length of a piece of steel sheet, can take absolutely any value (though it may be limited to lie within a certain range). Such data is called *continuous*. You can begin to see why we need to make the slightly technical-seeming distinction between discrete and continuous data if you realise that, whereas discrete data can only take values from a fixed set which can be written down, there is an infinite range of possibilities for an item of continuous data. So we need to adopt rather different methods for presenting the two types.

Some terminology

Statisticians use the term *population data* to indicate that the data has been gathered from every single unit of interest (not necessarily a human population). So if we were to weigh every packet of detergent which comes off a production line, we would have data about the population of packages.

If on the other hand, as often happens, we cannot gather data from every item of interest (perhaps because it would be too expensive or take too much time), then we will have to fall back on data obtained from a *sample* – that is, a subset of the population, usually defined in some specific way. Most statistical measurements are effectively based on samples; clearly, the way a sample is selected will have a big effect on the reliability of the conclusions we can draw from it, and so the question of sampling theory looms large in many business statistics courses. We shall be returning to the question of population versus sample data in the next chapter.

The quantity we are interested in measuring, and which differs from one member of the population to the next, is often referred to as a *variable*, a term we came across in earlier chapters in its algebraic context. Statistical variables are used in a rather different way from those algebraic variables, though they are often denoted in the same way by letters such as x or y. Thus we might use h to represent the continuous variable obtained by measuring the engine capacity of a sample of cars, while n might stand for the discrete variable 'number of potatoes in a 3 kg bag'.

Test your understanding

Classify the following variables as qualitative or quantitative, and for the quantitative ones, as discrete or continuous:

Time taken to process a customer's order.
Location of branches of a supermarket chain.
Number of plant seedlings per square metre in a commercial nursery.
Monthly salary of a group of workers.
Type of job held by an employee – management, clerical or technical.
Number of nights stayed by customers of a hotel chain.
Engine capacity of different models of cars.

8.4 Presenting data using tables

When we have gathered a large amount of data, for example by carrying out a survey, it will be necessary to present it in a concise way if we, or anyone else, are to make sense of the data and be able to make sensible use of it. Large sets of data are generally presented either by means of tables, or by using diagrams, or both. In this section we look at effective ways of tabulating data.

Tabulating qualitative data

Suppose you have a set of individual responses to the question 'Please indicate whether you are male or female'. You would probably come up with a summary table for the results looking something like this:

Gender	Number of respondents
Male	36
Female	44

The same kind of table can be used for most qualitative variables. The usefulness of the table can be enhanced by including extra information, such as a total, and perhaps percentages indicating what proportion of the total fell into each category:

Gender	Number of respondents	Percentage
Male	36	45
Female	44	55
Total	80	100

Notice how the total and the percentages have been clearly distinguished from the actual figures in the table, so as not to create confusion.

A final refinement is to add a title and to indicate the source of the data (for the benefit of anyone who might want to go back and look at the results in more detail):

Gender of shoppers at XYZ Supermarket, Midtown

Gender	Number of respondents	Percentage
Male	36	45
Female	44	55
Total	80	100

(Source: Customer survey, 05/01/07)

The figures in the 'number of respondents' column are generally called *frequencies,* since they indicate how frequently values in each category occurred. The letter *f* is often used to denote the frequency.

The tabulation idea can be extended to data which has been categorised by more than one variable. For example, if in the survey mentioned above the customers had also been asked, 'How long on average do you spend on each visit to XYZ Supermarket?' then the responses to this question could be *cross-tabulated* with the gender response, giving a table like this:

Cross-tabulation of gender against length of visit

	Length of visit (minutes)			
Gender	<10	10 but <30	30 and more	Total
Male	15	11	10	36
Female	8	22	14	44
Total	23	33	24	80

We could add percentages to this table, but we now have a choice of showing the percentage of the overall total, the percentage of the row (for example what percentage of males stayed less than 10 minutes) or the percentage of the column (for example what percentage of people staying 30 minutes or more were female). Which version we choose depends on which aspect of the data we wish to emphasise. You may want to experiment with different versions of the table until you find the one which best suits your needs – this can be done quickly and easily by means of software, as we shall see in Section 8.7.

There are numerous general principles which could be given for the construction of good tables – such as making sure that your categories do not overlap, arranging the categories in a logical order, using spacing to clarify the structure of the table, and clearly specifying the units in which the data is expressed. Most of these are really just common sense. The best approach, whenever you have drawn up a table, is to stand back and ask yourself whether someone looking at the table for the first time would be able to understand the content quickly without any further explanation from you.

You can use your ingenuity to construct tables to show more than two aspects of a set of data at once. However, these can get confusing, so on the whole it is preferable to use several separate tables when you have a lot of information to get across, rather than trying to cram everything into one large table.

Tabulating quantitative data – frequency tables

In the last example, the variable 'length of visit' was grouped into categories, but would have started life as a quantitative variable. Grouping is the way we generally deal with quantitative variables; so if the supermarket survey had also included the question 'How many items did you purchase on this visit?', the results could be presented as a *grouped frequency table* thus:

Number of items purchased	Number of respondents
1–5	6
6–10	15
11–15	37
16–20	12
21–30	7
31 or more	3

Notice that the classes need not all be of the same width. Note too that, although there appear to be gaps between the classes, this does not matter because, since the variable in question is discrete, we can be sure that there will be no values between, say, 15 and 16 as you can't purchase 15.6 items. It would not be correct to use 1–5, 5–10, and so on, because then there would be ambiguity as to which class to use for someone who purchased five items.

We have made use of an *open class* at the top end of this table – this is a useful device if there is uncertainty about what the highest value in the data might be, though it does of course introduce an element of vagueness into the table.

Sometimes, when we have a discrete variable which takes only a small number of values, we may not need to resort to grouping. If the supermarket survey included the question 'How many times have you visited XYZ Supermarket, Midtown in the past month?', the results could be shown as follows:

Number of visits in the past month	Number of respondents
1	15
2	19
3	22
4	20
5 or more	4
Total	80

This is an *ungrouped* frequency table (apart from the open class at the top).

You might also come across the term *frequency distribution* to describe such tables – they show the way in which the frequencies are distributed across the various groups.

Where a continuous variable is involved, we need to adopt a rather different way of specifying the groups. If you look back at the way the variable 'length of visit in minutes' has been grouped in the cross-tabulation on page 144, you will find the following.

Length of visit (mins)	Number of respondents
<10	23
10 but <30	33
30 and more	24

Since time is a continuous variable, we cannot leave any gaps between the classes. So we adopt the clumsy-sounding but safe '*x* but <*y*' format to enable us to specify the groups without gaps and without ambiguity. There are other ways to achieve the same end, but the general principle remains the same: every value which could occur should be able to be allocated unambiguously to one group.

An alternative format called the *cumulative frequency table* is sometimes adopted for the display of quantitative data. This most often takes the form:

Length of visit (mins)	Number of respondents (*cumulative frequency*)
<10	23
<30	56
<60	80

The table in this format shows the total number of people taking less than the stated time to complete their visit – thus 23 people stayed less than 10 minutes, and 56 stayed less than 30 minutes (this includes the 23 who stayed less than 10). The table gets its name because, as we go through the groups, we accumulate more of the data values, ending up with the total group of 80 staying less than 60 minutes. We've had to make an assumption that no one stays longer than an hour in order to specify this top group. (You may also come across cumulative tables constructed on a 'more than' rather than a 'less than' basis, but this is not so common.)

Whichever format of table you choose to construct – and the decision will be partly determined by the use you intend to make of the data – it is unlikely, unless you have a very small amount of data, that you will be doing the counting of frequencies by hand. We shall therefore return to the topic of table construction in Section 8.7 and see how Excel can be used to simplify the task.

Test your understanding

1. The following frequency table represents data about the numbers of people using a company canteen over a four-week period. Which column represents the frequency in this case? Convert the table into a 'less than' cumulative format:

Number of customers	Number of days with this number of customers
<20	3
20 but <30	7
30 but <40	6
40 but <50	4

2. Construct a table to show the information contained in the following report, which refers to a hotel's customer satisfaction survey data:

   'Levels of satisfaction have improved during 2006 as compared with 2005. In 2005, of 500 customers who completed questionnaires, only 120 rated their overall satisfaction as 'very satisfied', while 200 were 'fairly satisfied', 100 were 'neither satisfied nor dissatisfied' and 80 were 'dissatisfied'. Corresponding figures for the four categories in 2006 were 150, 230, 120 and 40.'

3. Sketch two alternative frameworks for a table in which you could show simultaneously the breakdown of a group of 64 retail stores into:

   (a) North/Midlands/South sales regions.
   (b) High Street/shopping precinct sites.
   (c) Franchise/directly managed.

8.5 Presenting data using diagrams

Diagrams for qualitative data

Most people find that it is much easier to understand information if some kind of pictorial or diagrammatic representation accompanies it. We have already used this idea in drawing graphs to enhance our understanding of relationships between variables. In this section we will look at some of the diagrams which can be used to represent statistical data.

Pie charts

The concept of the pie chart is very simple, which is probably why it has become one of the most popular ways of presenting statistical information. A basic circle (the pie) represents the total group under consideration, and this is subdivided into sectors (or slices) in proportion to the breakdown of the group into subgroups. So the information concerning gender of shoppers in the XYZ survey, mentioned in Section 8.4, would give the pie chart shown in Figure 8.1.

If you need to calculate the angles of the 'slices' by hand, the easiest way is to work from the percentage figures calculated above. We saw that 45% of the shoppers were male. However, the total angle in the centre of the circle is 360°, so the angle of the slice representing males should be 45% of 360°, or 162°.

The slices of the pie should if possible be arranged in decreasing order of size starting

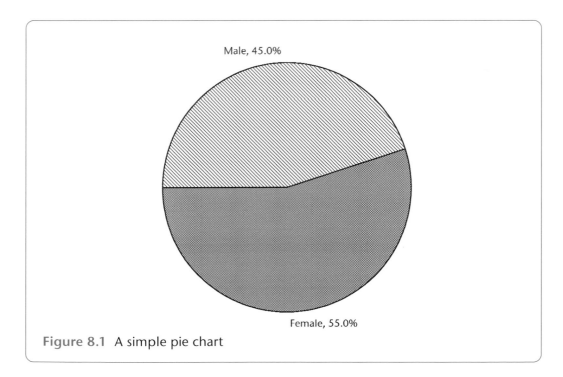

Figure 8.1 A simple pie chart

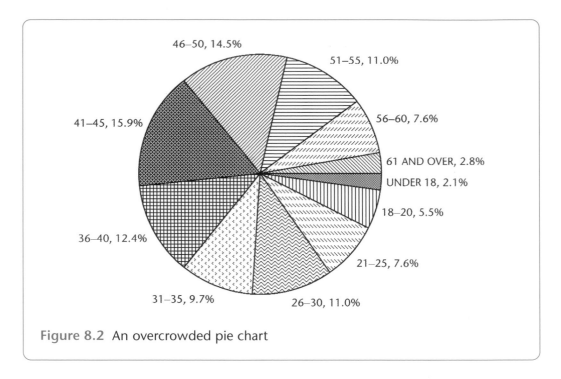

Figure 8.2 An overcrowded pie chart

from the '9 o'clock' or '12 o'clock' positions. It is not a good idea to use a pie-chart when there are a great many categories in the data, particularly if some of them are quite small; Figure 8.2 shows how cluttered such a chart can become.

There are also problems in using two or more pie charts to show the breakdown of different totals, since, strictly speaking, the sizes of the pies should be proportional to the totals involved. Thus if we want to show that last year £2.1m was distributed as dividends out of a total of £8.9m profit, whereas this year the comparable figures are £1.8m and £7.3m, the ratio of the areas of the two pies should be 8.9:7.3. If you recall that we find the area of a circle from the formula πr^2, you can see that finding the values of r to give the correct ratio will not be much fun! One way to avoid this is to show the percentage breakdown for each year, in which case both pies, representing 100%, can justifiably be the same size – but we then sacrifice the information about the *actual* profits.

To summarise: a pie chart is best used to show the breakdown of a single total into not too many categories. Software packages now available enable you to construct very attractive pie charts incorporating different colours or shadings for sectors, 'exploding' of one or more sectors, and explanatory labels. We shall look at some pie charts produced using Excel in Section 8.7.

Bar charts

A bar chart offers more flexibility than a pie-chart as a way of presenting qualitative information, while being possibly a little less eye-catching. The bar chart in Figure 8.3, which shows the data on gender/length of visit from the XYZ survey, illustrates the main advantages of the format.

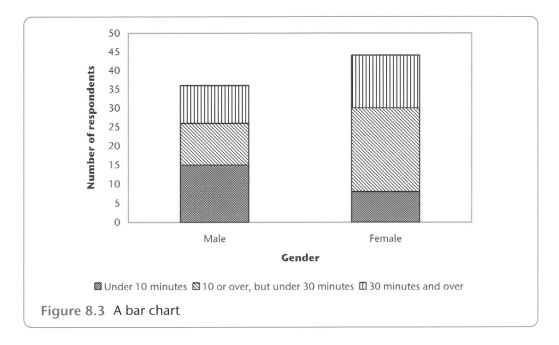

Figure 8.3 A bar chart

We have chosen to show the gender as the major bars, with a subdivision of each bar by time spent. The chart could, of course, be drawn with time as the major division – the choice, as with tabulation, depends very much on the user's needs. Notice how spaces separate the bars, and how the width of the bars is purely a matter of convenience; it has no numerical significance. Only the height of the bar – representing the frequency within the group – is important. We hope it hardly needs to be said that, however tempting it may be in terms of saving paper, it is never correct to start the vertical axis of the

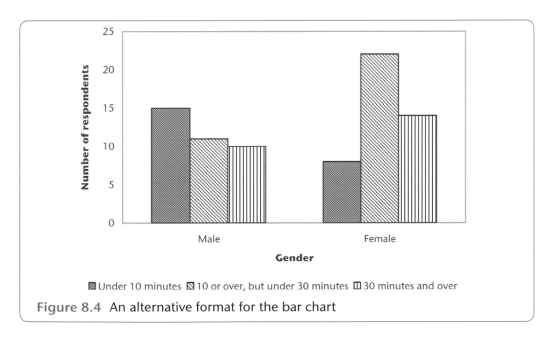

Figure 8.4 An alternative format for the bar chart

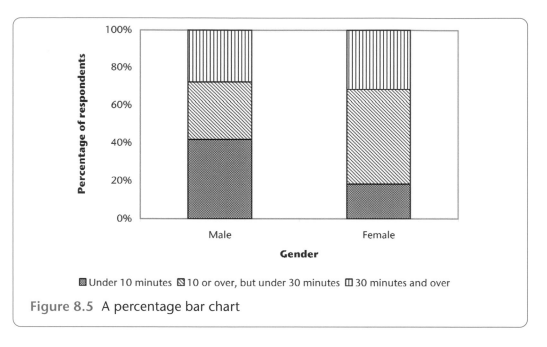

Figure 8.5 A percentage bar chart

chart from any value other than zero. (To see why this is, try putting a sheet of paper across Figure 8.3 at various levels, and notice how the proportionate heights of the bars are distorted.)

We could have chosen to place the 'time spent' components of the chart side-by-side rather than on top of each other, as in Figure 8.4.

Or we could instead adopt a percentage-based format (though, as usual, with the corresponding loss of information about the actual totals) – see Figure 8.5.

From these examples you can see that bar-charts offer a great deal of scope to the ingenious user in presenting information concisely yet accurately.

Diagrams for quantitative data

Histograms

Suppose that the XYZ Supermarket survey also included a question about the distance travelled by shoppers to reach the store. The resulting data has been summarised in the following frequency table; you can see that no one in the sample travelled more than 5 km:

Distance travelled (km)	No. of respondents
Up to 1	12
1 but under 2	16
2 but under 3	30
3 but under 4	13
4 but under 5	9

The usual way of showing this kind of data diagrammatically is by means of a *histogram*,

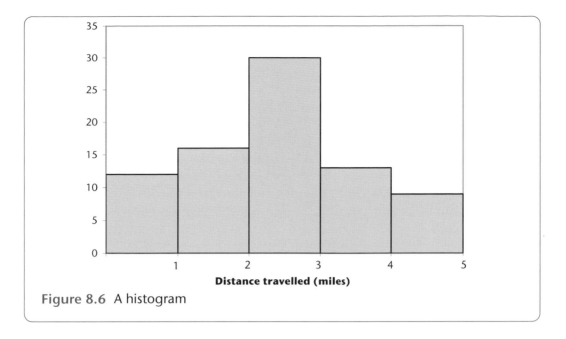

Figure 8.6 A histogram

as shown in Figure 8.6. As you can see, in many ways this histogram resembles a bar chart. However, there are no gaps between the blocks, since we now have a continuous scale of distance on the horizontal axis.

There is a more important distinction between a histogram and a bar chart which is not apparent from this example, since all the classes here happened to be of the same width. Perhaps the best way to see this distinction is to examine Figure 8.7, which shows the 'length of visit' data plotted as a histogram. In drawing this

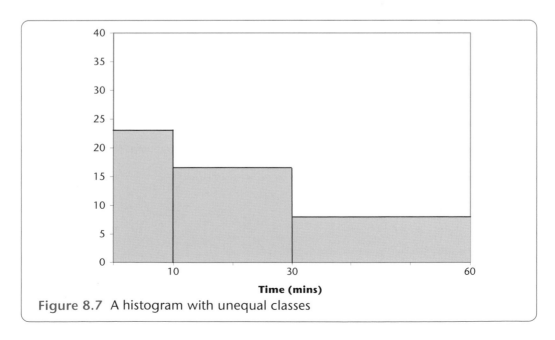

Figure 8.7 A histogram with unequal classes

histogram, we have had to assume that the longest time spent by anyone in the supermarket is 60 minutes - otherwise it would have been impossible to show the top class.

If you now compare Figure 8.7 with a bar chart such as Figure 8.3, you will notice that the bars in Figure 8.7, unlike those of the bar chart, are unequal in width, so that the unequal time-ranges are correctly represented. As a consequence, the vertical axis does *not* represent the frequency.

To see why this must be, observe that what impresses the reader when looking at the diagram is the area occupied by each of the bars. Thus in view of the unequal width of the classes, heights must be adjusted so that the area gives a correct impression. If the first class, with a width of 10 minutes, and a frequency of 23, is represented by a bar with a height of 23 units, then the second, which is twice as wide, need only have a height of 33/2 or 16.5 to show the frequency of 33 correctly. Finally the last class, with a width three times as great as the first, and with a frequency of 24, has to be given a height of 24/3 = 8.

If this seems unnecessarily complicated, compare the impression given by Figure 8.7 with that produced by Figure 8.8, where the bars have been simple-mindedly plotted with height proportional to frequency. The overall impression produced by the diagram is that there is a very large number of people spending a long time in the supermarket – a fact which we know is not true.

To avoid the difficulties created by unequal classes you can, when given the choice, always opt for equal classes as far as possible. If you do so, then heights of bars *will* be proportional to frequency, so there is no problem. You should, however, be aware that many software packages are unable to cope with histograms having unequal classes – all bars will be drawn the same width, and some widely-used packages invariably leave gaps

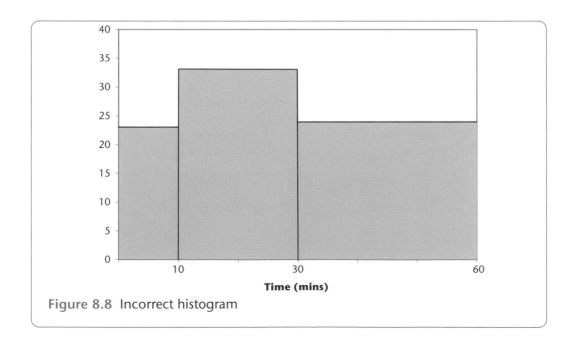

Figure 8.8 Incorrect histogram

between bars, thus effectively giving a bar chart even when a histogram is what is required.

Ogives (cumulative frequency graphs)

The histogram is obtained from the ordinary frequency table. If instead you want a diagram to show cumulative frequency information, then you need an *ogive*, which is a great deal easier to plot than a histogram. Look at the ogive in Figure 8.9 for the 'length of visit' data – what we have is simply an ordinary graph, showing the number of customers who spent less than a given length of time at the supermarket. Joining the points of the ogive with straight lines makes the assumption that values are evenly spread within the classes (for example, that of the 24 customers spending between 30 and 60 minutes, 12 spent under 45 minutes and the remainder spent between 45 and 60 minutes). This may or may not be the case, but in the absence of more detailed information it is probably the most reasonable assumption.

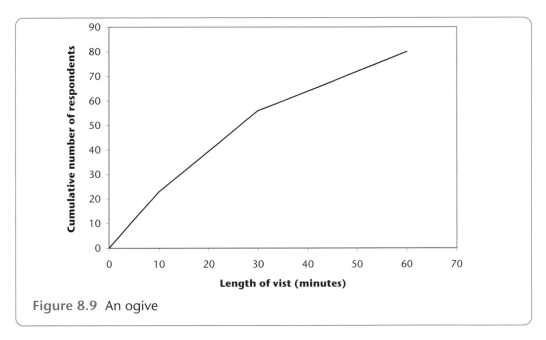

Figure 8.9 An ogive

Having plotted the ogive, we can use it to read off intermediate values; for example, about 31 customers spent 15 minutes or less on their visit to XYZ. We will see in the next chapter that this can be very useful when we come to finding summary measures for the data.

Other statistical diagrams

There are many other types of statistical diagram which you may come across: *pictograms* (using scales such as 'one drawing of a little person = 100 jobs lost'), *statistical maps*, and so on. Keep your eyes open when reading books and articles for imaginative uses of graphic presentation of data. As far as drawing your own diagrams is concerned, the same warning applies as with tabulation: ask yourself whether a reader, looking at the diagram for the first time, would obtain the impression you really want him or her to get. If not, think again!

Test your understanding

1. Sketch (do not plot accurately) a histogram and an ogive to represent the data in Question 1 of the Section 8.4 'Test your understanding' examples. Use the ogive to determine on how many days there were fewer than 25 customers.
2. Sketch a suitable diagram to display the customer satisfaction data given in Question 2 of the Section 8.4 'Test your understanding' examples.

8.6 Putting it all together

You should have no difficulty in finding examples of the use of the methods we've examined in this chapter: newspapers, magazines and web pages are full of tables of numerical data and statistical charts, and you should keep an eye open in your everyday reading for good examples. Be critical, too – diagrams in particular lend themselves to being used in a confusing, or even plain misleading, way.

We shall conclude with a couple of good examples drawn from the corporate webpages of Tesco, the UK's largest food retailer. The bar charts in Figure 8.10 show Tesco's sales and profits over a five-year period to 2005. You can access this data via Tesco's corporate website at http://www.tescocorporate.com.

Notice that no units are specified for the 'Sales' diagram, though we are told that the profits are in millions. It would also be preferable to have included a vertical axis with a scale, though looking at the heights of the bars suggests that the vertical scale does start from zero as it should. The bar chart format shows clearly the steady growth in both sales and profits.

Table 8.1 presents data about Tesco's international activities.

Notice the care with which the date at which the data was assembled, the units for sales area, and the fact that 'store openings' includes acquisitions, are spelled out. Also commendable is the fact that the 'planned store openings' figures are clearly distinguished from the rest of the data by being in italics and in a different colour. This is to show that, whereas all the other figures represent actual achievements in the past, the planned figures may or may not be achieved, so there is an element of uncertainty about them.

Try looking at the corporate websites of other large companies – they often include information, particularly financial data, presented using tables and charts.

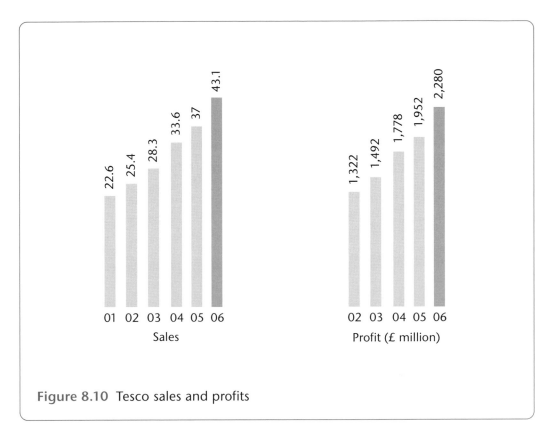

Figure 8.10 Tesco sales and profits

Table 8.1 Tesco's international activity

	Year of entry	Number of stores	Sales area (million sq ft)	Planned store openings 2006/07 (inc acquisitions)
UK		1,897	25.9	*124*
Czech Republic	1996	35	2.5	*50*
Hungary	1994	87	4.3	*22*
Poland	1995	105	4.8	*39*
Rep. of Ireland	1997	91	2.1	*8*
Slovakia	1996	37	2.3	*12*
Turkey	2003	8	0.6	*22*
China	2004	39	3.5	*12*
Japan	2003	111	0.3	*11*
Malaysia	2001	13	0.9	*4*
South Korea	1999	62	4.1	*32*
Thailand	1998	219	6.8	*180*
		2,710	58.7	*516*

(correct to end of last financial year – 25 Feb 2006)

8.7 For Excel users

Constructing tables using Excel

Excel can be used to tabulate both qualitative and quantitative data. For qualitative data, suppose that in the XYZ supermarket survey, discussed earlier in this chapter, we have entered the genders of the 80 respondents into column A of the spreadsheet, in the random order in which they were questioned, using 'm' to denote male and 'f' to denote female. We want to draw up a table to show the total number of males and females in the sample. Enter 'f' into cell C2 and 'm' into cell C3. Then enter the formula =COUNTIF (A1.A80, "f") into cell D2. You should find that the result of the formula is 44; it is counting the cells in the range A1 to A80 which contain an 'f'. In the same way, putting =COUNTIF(A1.A80, "m") into cell D3 gives the result 36, the number of males in the sample. A screenshot of this is shown in Figure 8.11. Of course, you would probably want to make the table rather more self-explanatory, perhaps by putting 'number of females' and 'number of males' instead of just 'f' and 'm'.

To tabulate quantitative data in the simplest way, you need to have the Data Analysis

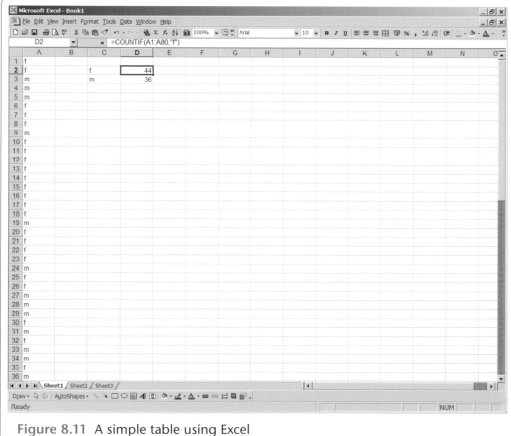

Figure 8.11 A simple table using Excel

Tool available within Excel. This is an add-in; to find out whether it's been added to your version of Excel, click on 'Tools' in the main menu. If Data Analysis does not appear, click on 'Add-Ins' and then click the tick-box next to 'Analysis ToolPak'.

The tool to be used for setting up a frequency table is called Histogram, which, rather oddly, does not actually plot a histogram unless you specifically request this. Before you can use the tool, you have to decide what your groupings are going to be, and set up what are called *bins* in Excel-speak, but are really just the limits of the groups. To reproduce the table for 'number of items purchased' in Section 8.4, we need to enter the raw data – that is, the individual figures obtained in the survey – into column A of the spreadsheet. (If you want to follow this explanation using Excel as we go along, you will find the relevant data on the companion website.) We then put the upper limits of the groupings into another column of the spreadsheet. In this case, we put the figures 5, 10, 15, 20 and 30 into cells C3 to C7; don't worry about the '31 or more' group, as Excel will sort that out.

We now click on 'Tools' in the main menu, then choose 'Data Analysis' followed by 'Histogram'. A dialogue box appears, which requires us to give the input range – that's the range where the raw data is situated, which in this case is A1 to A80. The 'bin range' is the range of cells where we have placed the limits for the groupings: in our case, these are in C3 to C7. Finally, we need to specify where the results are to go – the default is in a

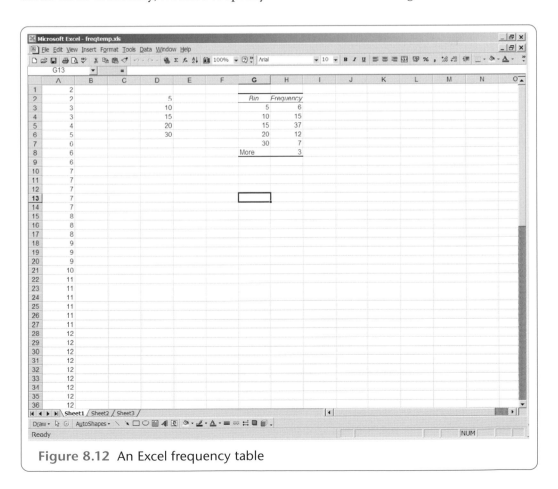

Figure 8.12 An Excel frequency table

new worksheet, but you can specify a location in the existing sheet as long as you make sure the results won't overwrite existing data. You can ignore the other parts of the dialogue box – once you have specified these three ranges, just click on 'OK'. (There is scope at the bottom of the dialogue box to tick if you want 'chart output' – that is, a histogram – but we'll come back to that a bit later in the section.)

The screenshot in Figure 8.12 shows the results of this process, with the output placed in columns G and H. As you can see, Excel has constructed a table giving the frequencies in the groups 'up to 5', '6–10' and so on, and has added a group 'more' at the end, which covers the open class at the top of the distribution. Again, you would probably want to tidy up the table by overwriting the bin labels with the more meaningful definitions of the groups, and perhaps adding a row for the total at the bottom. But the basic work of counting the number of values in each group is done quickly and easily.

It is possible to produce cross-tabulations, like the table in Section 8.4 showing length of visit by gender, with Excel using something called a Pivot Table. However, these are quite tricky to construct, so if you need to do so we suggest that you work through one of the many excellent online Excel tutorials available – you will find some useful links on the companion website.

Test your understanding

If you wish to practise using the Excel processes we've been discussing, then you need to have some raw data available. To save you from having to enter long columns of raw values, you will find some ready-made sets of data on the companion website, including the data from the XYZ Supermarket survey.

Statistical diagrams with Excel

The best way to plot a whole range of diagrams using Excel is via the Chart Wizard, the icon for which – a little coloured picture of a bar chart – you will find on the toolbar at the top of the Excel screen.

Pie charts

To plot a pie chart of the data about gender from the supermarket survey, we start with the summary table shown in Figure 8.10, indicating that there were 44 females and 36 males. Select the whole of this 2×2 table, and then click on the Chart Wizard icon. You will be presented with a long list of standard chart types, from which you need to select 'pie'. Six variants of a pie chart then appear – choose the first and simplest. (The only other one you might wish to use is the 'exploded' form – the perspective versions can be misleading, and I would not recommend their use.)

At this point, there is a button available which you can press and hold to get a preview of your chart, just to make sure that it really is the one you want. Clicking on 'Next' then takes you through a series of dialogue boxes which allow you to customise your chart by

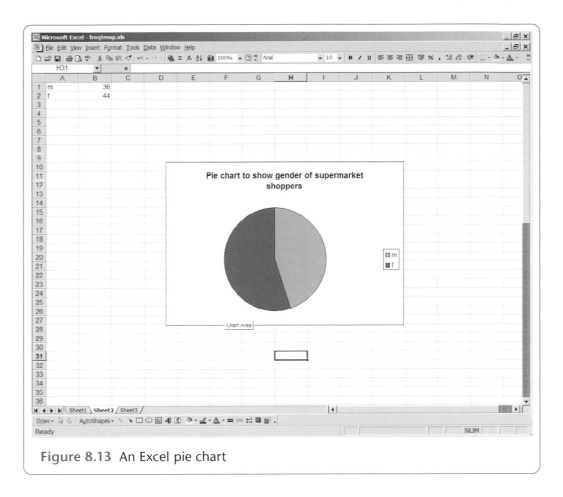

Figure 8.13 An Excel pie chart

adding a title, modifying the legend and so on. Once you click 'Finish' the final result should be something like that shown in Figure 8.13.

Bar charts

If you click on the Chart Wizard, you will see that Excel offers a whole range of different types of bar chart – conventional vertical bar charts come under the heading 'Column', whereas 'Bar' gives you the horizontal format. As with pie charts, we do not recommend the use of the perspective versions, where the third dimension adds nothing to the information and can make it harder to judge the relative heights of bars. The genuinely 3-D chart (the last in the 'Column' display) is ingenious, but for many purposes it would be preferable to use two or more separate 2-D charts for clarity.

That leaves three types of chart, described by Excel as 'clustered columns' – as in Figure 8.4 above – 'stacked columns' (like Figure 8.3) and '100% stacked columns' (like Figure 8.5). Suppose that we want to reproduce Figure 8.4 using Excel; we need to work with the summary cross-tabulation of length of visit by gender, as obtained in Section 8.4, but without the 'Totals' column and row. We then select the table, and click on the Chart Wizard.

As it originally appears, the display is in the reverse format, with length of visit as the major grouping and gender as the subgrouping. However, if in the second Chart Wizard dialogue box you choose 'Series in Columns' rather than 'Series in Rows' you will obtain the chart exactly as in Figure 8.4 (see Figure 8.14). As with the pie chart, you can then improve the appearance of the plot by adding titles, changing the colours of the bars and so on.

You should try displaying the chart in the other formats just to make sure that you have got the hang of using the Chart Wizard.

Histograms

As mentioned above, the 'Histogram' procedure in the Data Analysis Tool includes an option to check a box for 'Chart Output'. Doing this for the 'number of items purchased' data from the XYZ survey produces the result in Figure 8.15.

As you can see, this is not really a histogram: the horizontal axis is not properly labelled, no account is taken of the unequal class widths, and there are gaps between the bars. It is possible to remove the gaps by editing the chart, but the unequal class widths cannot be remedied in this way. We would therefore not recommend the use of this form of chart in Excel.

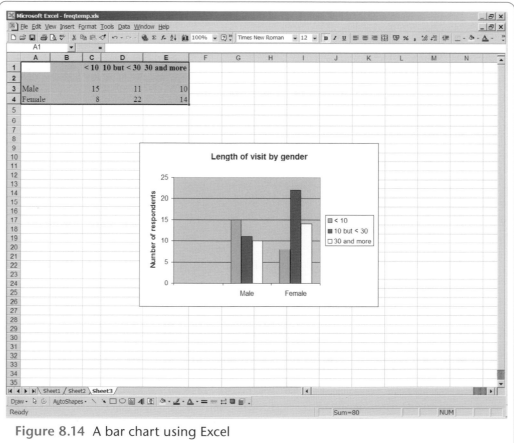

Figure 8.14 A bar chart using Excel

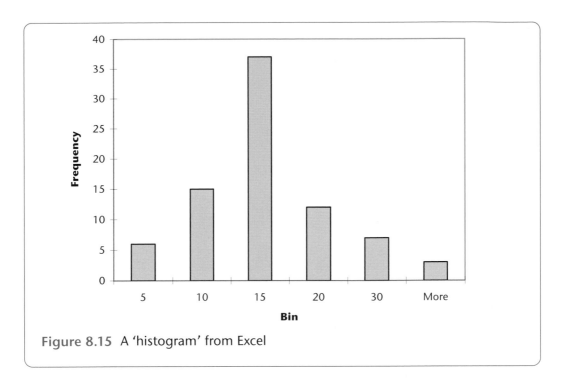

Figure 8.15 A 'histogram' from Excel

Other types of chart

Of the many other types of chart provided by the Excel Chart Wizard, the most important is that designated XY (scatter), which can be used to produce graphs of mathematical functions, and which has already been discussed in Chapter 4. Ogives like the one in
Figure 8.9 can be constructed using this format; the screenshot in Figure 8.16 shows the
cumulative frequency table for the length of visit data, and the corresponding ogive
produced using the XY (scatter) format. Notice that we have had to add a row indicating
that no respondents stayed less than zero minutes, to ensure that the ogive starts from
the origin.

If you wish to display what is often called *time series* data – data which represents the
value of a variable at equal time intervals over a period – then the 'Line' chart type may
be useful. Examples of such data would be monthly sales figures, annual profits, or quar-
terly turnovers. As an illustration, suppose that a newsagent has kept a record of the
demand for a particular monthly do-it-yourself magazine over a two-year period, with
the following results:

Year	Jan	Feb	Mar	Apr	May	Jun	Jul	Aug	Sep	Oct	Nov	Dec
2005	17	24	38	41	37	30	21	15	23	25	20	11
2006	18	27	40	44	40	32	25	19	22	28	23	16

A line chart representing this data is shown in Figure 8.17. Note that the data had to
be rearranged into a single column before Excel could produce the correct version of
the chart. You can see how the line joining the monthly figures emphasises the

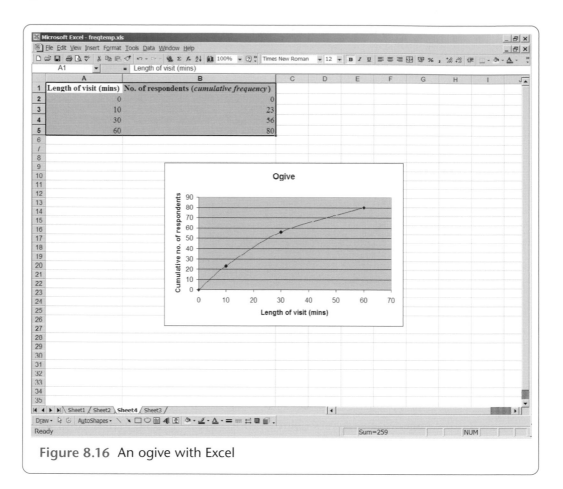

Figure 8.16 An ogive with Excel

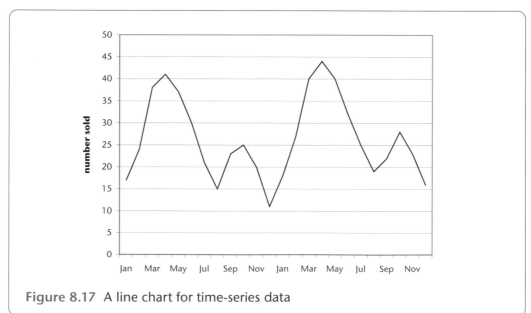

Figure 8.17 A line chart for time-series data

repeating annual pattern, and shows that overall sales in 2006 were somewhat up on those for 2005. However, it's important to realise that the line chart is only appropriate when the data values are equally spaced in time, as Excel automatically plots them in this way.

What have I learned?

To remind yourself of what you have learned to do in this chapter, imagine that you have been asked to carry out a survey which will inform a 'no frills' airline about the views of passengers on its service. What kind of data might you be collecting, and how could you get hold of it? How might you summarise the data once you've collected it? What kinds of diagrams or charts would you now be able to use to present the data more effectively?

Exercises

In all these exercises, you may either construct the tables and charts by hand, or use Excel to do so.

1. The following data shows the lengths of a random sample of 50 calls to a computer company's Helpline, in minutes to the nearest whole minute (thus values of zero represent calls which lasted less than half a minute).

   2, 1, 3, 6, 5, 6, 0, 3, 5, 1, 2, 0, 1, 1, 0, 1, 2, 2, 3, 2, 2, 2, 6, 3, 3,
   2, 7, 5, 8, 2, 6, 1, 4, 5, 7, 3, 2, 4, 2, 5, 0, 1,1, 2, 3, 3, 2, 7, 0, 2

   Organise this data into a suitable frequency table, and present the frequency data in the form of a chart which could be used to help management in planning its call handling policy.

2. Present the data contained in the following extract in the form of a table, accompanied by a suitable chart.

   'We do our best to answer all calls as quickly as possible. A recent study by independent consultants showed that, in a sample of 80 calls, 30 were answered when the telephone had rung 3 times or fewer; 20 were answered after 4 or 5 rings, and 20 after 6 or 7 rings. The remainder took longer, but only in 4 cases did the caller ring off before the phone was picked up. This contrasts with industry norms, where studies show that only 15% of calls are answered within 3 or fewer rings; 25% within 4 or 5, 25% within 6 or 7, and 10% of calls go unanswered.'

3. The Chief Executive of a small charity is writing his annual report for the trustees, and states that 'out of every £1 we receive, 80p goes directly into funding projects,

10p goes towards political campaigning, 8p towards other publicity, and only 2p to administration'. Plot a suitable diagram to show this data.

4. A city-centre hotel with 60 rooms has summarised the numbers of rooms which are occupied each night for a three-week period, with the following result:

	Mon	Tues	Wed	Thurs	Fri	Sat	Sun
Week 1	54	58	60	60	42	44	23
Week 2	52	55	55	60	39	41	17
Week 3	56	52	54	58	44	45	21

Plot a graph, or use Excel's 'Line' chart, to show this data, and comment on the pattern which is revealed.

5. A publishing company is concerned about the cost of making changes to books at the proof stage (the final stage before full production), and so has checked a sample of pages from two typical books, one a technical volume and the other a novel, to see how many corrections per page are required. The results have been summarised in the following frequency table:

Number of changes	Number of pages – technical book	Number of pages – novel
0	17	46
1	24	42
2	31	35
3	36	19
4	27	11
5	18	6
6	12	1

No pages required more than 6 corrections. Plot a bar chart to show this data, and comment on the difference between the distribution of the number of changes for the two types of book.

Case Study: Heron Marsh nature reserve

Heron Marsh is a private nature reserve close to a medium-sized town in the Midlands. It offers various outdoor activities including birdwatching and wildflower trails, and has a small cafe and a classroom for use by educational groups. The owner intends to apply for a grant from the Department of the Environment to enhance the facilities, and has carried out a survey among users of the reserve to provide evidence to back the grant application. The survey was conducted by placing questionnaire forms along with the free information leaflets in 'help yourself' boxes at various points in the reserve over a two-week period, and inviting visitors to complete and return them to a box in the car park.

You have now been asked to draft a short report summarising the results of the survey in an accessible format, to be included as part of the documentation for the grant application. You have been provided with the following details of the survey outcomes:

192 people responded to the survey. Of these, 111 were female and 81 were male. Also, 86 indicated that the primary purpose of their visit was 'birdwatching'; 54 indicated 'wildflower trail'; 37 indicated 'attending educational event' and the remainder selected 'other', giving reasons such as 'visiting cafe' and 'exercise in pleasant surroundings'.

When visitors were asked to rate the facilities, the results were:

	Excellent	Good	Fair	Poor
Cafe		12	66	47
Information	53	72	41	8
Toilets		15	94	52
Signage	27	69	50	12

Note that the totals for each facility are different, as some visitors had not used a particular facility.

Respondents were asked for their age-group: 53 of the females and 36 of the males were under 30, 38 females and 32 males were in the range 30 to 65, and the remainder were over 65.

Draft the report based on this data, including suitable tables and diagrams to display the results, in a form which the owner of Heron Marsh can include in the funding bid.

For further exercises and multiple choice revision questions visit the companion website: www.palgrave.com/business/morris

Statistics: summarising data

9.1 The need to summarise data

Before you start

Notice how many times the word 'average' is used in the media. Collect a number of examples of the use of the term from newspapers, magazines or TV news reports, and think about why the average is being quoted in each case, how representative it is of the set of data in question, and whether or not the use being made of the measurement is appropriate. (Some examples to get you started might be references to the goal average of a football team, the average wage in a particular industry, or the average waiting time for an operation under the NHS.)

The tables and charts which we constructed in Chapter 8 were very helpful in enabling data to be presented in a simple and meaningful way. However, for many purposes, further simplification is required. For example, if we want to compare two or more sets of numbers – perhaps comparing the 'number of items purchased' data from the XYZ Supermarket survey of Chapter 8 with similar data from another supermarket in a different location – doing so by looking at a chart or a table is not easy. We need to be able to reduce the large number of individual measurements to just two or three numbers which will sum up the key features of the data.

But just what are those key features of a dataset? We can get some ideas by looking at the histograms which we constructed in Chapter 8 – for example, the one shown in Figure 8.7 for the data giving the length of customers' visits to the supermarket.

It would be useful to have a way of describing what a typical length of visit might be; this will give us an idea of the kind of figures we are looking at overall. From Figure 8.7 it seems that the 'typical' value for this data is likely to be somewhere in the 10 to 30 minute range. Such a figure is often referred to as a measure of the *location* of the data, because it tells us roughly whereabouts, overall, the figures are located.

This figure on its own won't be sufficient however, because it gives us no idea how much the individual values in the data set are spread out. We could have two sets of data with the same 'typical' value, one of which has a very narrow range of variation, while the other is very spread out. For example, with the 'length of visit' data, it might be that at busier times, the overall typical value is much the same, but some people take 90 minutes or even longer to complete their shopping. So we also need to devise a way of measuring *spread*. An alternative name for such a measure is a measure of *dispersion*, because it tells us how dispersed the individual values are.

Finally, and rather less importantly, we might be interested in whether the data is distributed in a fairly symmetrical way (like the 'distance travelled' data in Figure 8.6) or is noticeably unsymmetrical, like that in Figure 8.7. The technical name for lack of symmetry is *skewness*, and we talk about a *skew* distribution of data. The use of actual numerical measurements of skewness is less common than are the measures of location and dispersion, and so we shall limit our discussion of this aspect to qualitative description.

9.2 | Measuring the typical value

We've been deliberately using rather vague language in the preceding section, talking about 'location' or the 'typical value'. This is because there is in fact no one universally used measure for location – or indeed, for dispersion and skewness either. A number of different measures have been devised, each of which has its positive and negative features. The decision as to which measure to use with a given set of data depends partly on the nature of that data, and partly on the use to which you wish to put the measure.

We shall focus on the three most widely used measures of location; they are those which you are likely to come across in your future studies, and indeed you may already have encountered some or all of them.

The (arithmetic) mean: definition

The word which has probably been hovering at the back of your mind while reading Section 9.1 is 'average'. We could have talked about 'the average length of visit' to the supermarket, rather than the 'typical' length of visit. However, the term 'average' does have a particular mathematical definition, more technically known as the arithmetic mean (or just the mean; there are other kinds of mean, but if you come across the term 'the mean' it should be understood as referring to the arithmetic mean).

The arithmetic mean, then, is nothing other than the familiar average, which you probably learned to calculate at your primary school. The definition of the mean is very simple: add together all the values you've got, and divide by the number of values in the set of data. For example, if a sample of five shoppers at XYZ respectively spent £12, £14, £22, £34 and £48, then the mean (average) amount spent is (12 + 14 + 22 + 34 + 48)/5 = 130/5 = £26.

The mean has many advantages as a way of measuring location. It has a simple interpretation: in this case, it is the amount which each person would have spent had they all pooled their expenditure and each paid the same amount. A consequence of this fact is that, given the mean of a sample of values and the number of values involved, we can always recover the total for the sample: if we are told that the mean expenditure of the five shoppers is £26, then we know that the total spent must have been 5 × £26 = £130.

A more important, though slightly technical, advantage is that if we only have data about a sample, and not about the whole population, then (assuming that the sample was selected in a 'reasonable' way) the sample mean is a reliable guide to the value of the population mean, and behaves in a predictable manner. Since most data is actually obtained from samples rather than whole populations, the question of just what can be appropriately deduced about the population mean from the sample data is an important one, which you are likely to encounter in more detail if you follow a specialised statistics course later in your studies.

However, the mean does have one drawback. It can be rather misleading if our set of data contains a few 'rogue' or extreme values. For example, if in the sample of customers' expenditures mentioned above the person who spent £14 happened to be replaced by someone throwing a party who spent £120, then the mean would become (12 + 120 + 22 + 34 + 48)/5 = 236/5 = £47.20. The change to a single figure has resulted in a large increase in the mean; moreover, the resulting value is not really 'typical', either of the four more modest spenders or of the one who spent £120.

The same situation arises whenever we have a noticeably skew (unsymmetrical) set of figures, where one or a few values are very different from the majority. In such a case we might want to use one of the other measures of location (see below).

The arithmetic mean: calculation

Now let's turn to how the mean is calculated when we have a more extensive set of data. We shall illustrate the process with the 'number of items purchased' data from the XYZ survey. The data was summarised in Section 8.4 as follows:

Number of items purchased	Number of respondents
1–5	6
6–10	15
11–15	37
16–20	12
21–30	7
31 or more	3

So what we need to do is add up all the 80 values in the sample and then divide by 80. There is just one problem with this: although we know that 6 people purchased between 1 and 5 items, we don't know the exact figures – all 6 could have purchased a single item, or they could all have purchased 5, or any combination in between. Moreover, once the data has been summarised in this way, it is quite likely that we no longer have access to the original data. So we have to make an assumption, and choose a single value to represent each class.

The most reasonable assumption is to use the midpoint of the class, which we can find by adding the class limits and dividing by 2. Thus we will assume that all 6 people in the first class bought 3 items, all 15 in the second class bought 8 items, and so on. Of course, the result we get by doing the calculation in this way is not guaranteed to be exactly the same as what we would get from using the original data, but the discrepancy should not be too great.

We also need to close the last class at a sensible value – we shall use 50 here, though other values such as 40 would be equally reasonable. We can then extend the table above as follows:

Number of items purchased	Number of respondents (f)	Class midpoint (x)
1–5	6	3
6–10	15	8
11–15	37	13
16–20	12	18
21–30	7	25.5
31 or more (50)	3	40.5

Some of the midpoints have turned out not to be integers, but that doesn't matter since they are only theoretical values, and are not intended to represent reality. We are using the letter x here to represent the mid-points, and f, as before, for the frequency in each class.

Now we want to add together the six values of three, the 15 eights, and so on. But of course there is no need to actually work out $3 + 3 + 3 + 3 + 3 + 3$ – we get the same result much more simply if we multiply 3 by 6. The same applies to the other classes, so in general we want to multiply each x by its corresponding f, and then add the whole lot together.

At this point, we introduce a new symbol to stand for 'add up'. It is printed Σ, and called 'sigma', a Greek capital letter 'S'. This particular letter was chosen to stand for 'sum', and the sign is often called the *summation sign*. Thus if we write Σfx, this is to be understood as meaning 'multiply all the x's by their corresponding f's, and then add the results together'.

Using this notation, we can write a concise formula for finding the mean. The mean is, as already stated, sum of values/total number of values, and since the total number of values is equal to the sum of all the frequencies, Σf, the final formula becomes:

Mean $= \Sigma fx/\Sigma f$

The detailed calculation using this process is set out in the table below.

Number of items purchased	Number of respondents (f)	Class midpoint (x)	fx
1–5	6	3	18
6–10	15	8	120
11–15	37	13	481
16–20	12	18	216
21–30	7	25.5	178.5
31 or more (50)	3	40.5	121.5
Σ	80		1135

Notice that there is no need to add up the column of class midpoints. Using the formula $\Sigma fx/\Sigma f$ now gives $1135/80 = 14.1875$ items as the mean.

Is this a sensible value? We can't say that it is exactly correct simply by inspection, but it is certainly reasonable – the number of items purchased ranges from 1 to 50, with a lot more values at the lower end of the distribution, so an average around 14 is about right.

Various letters are used to stand for the mean, the most common being $\bar{x}$ (read as x-bar) for the mean of the sample, and the Greek letter μ (called 'mew', and actually a Greek m standing for mean) for the mean of a population. The convention that Roman letters stand for sample values and Greek ones for population values is widely used.

If you have a calculator with a memory, then the addition of the fx values can easily be done by adding each product into the memory as you go along. Many calculators now have the ability to find the mean automatically, but you will need to read the instruction leaflet for your particular machine to find if you can do this and how it works. The process is also very simple using Excel, as we shall see in Section 9.6.

Of course, finding the numerical value of the mean is generally not the end of the story – we probably wish to use this value to tell us something about the data, or to inform a decision. Here the average number of items purchased could tell XYZ Supermarket something about the likely time taken to scan shoppers' purchases, and so help in planning the staffing of checkouts. We will discuss the use of the mean, and indeed the other summary measures, in more detail in Sections 9.4 and 9.5.

The median

We have seen that for very skew distributions, the mean can be somewhat misleading as a measure of the 'typical' value of the data. An alternative 'typical' value which is often used in such cases is provided by the *median*, which is the middle value in the distribution when all the data is arranged in ascending or descending order. Take the case cited earlier, of the five shoppers who respectively spent £12, £120, £22, £34 and £48. In this case, the £120 had a distorting effect on the mean; however, if we arrange these values in ascending order we get 12, 22, 34, 48 and 120, so the middle value or median is £34. You can see that this is not affected by the one 'rogue' value of £120.

In this case we had five values, so the middle one was clearly the third. In general, if we have n values in the set of data, the median will be the $(n+1)/2$th value. If n is an odd number, this formula gives an integer answer – for example, for a sample with 11 values, the median will be the 6th. However, if n is even, then the formula gives a fraction; with $n = 10$, for instance, we get the median as the 5.5th value, which doesn't exist. In this case, we take the value halfway between the 5th and 6th as the median, and the same applies whenever n is even. In practice, if n is reasonably large then the +1 term makes little difference; if $n = 100$, for example, the difference between using the 50th and the 50.5th value as the median would be small. So you really only need to worry about the +1 for smallish samples – say, of 30 or fewer items.

For a grouped frequency table, we have the same problem in finding the median as we did with the mean – namely, that we don't know what the actual values in each class are. The simplest way to find the median in such a case is graphically from the ogive. Go up the vertical axis to the $(n+1)/2$th point, then across to the graph, and hence read off the median value on the horizontal axis. If you do this with Figure 8.9 (the ogive for the 'length of visit' data) you should find that the median is about 20 minutes.

A good way to interpret this value is to say 'half the customers spent less than 20 minutes in the supermarket, and the other half spent 20 minutes or over'. The fact that the median has this simple interpretation, and that it is resistant to extreme values in the data, are its main advantages.

If you do not want to go to the trouble of plotting an ogive, then the exact position of the median within its group can be calculated by a simple proportion argument. Recall the cumulative frequency table for our 'length of visit' data:

Length of visit (mins)	Number of respondents (*cumulative frequency*)
<10	23
<30	56
<60	80

With $n = 80$ values, we can forget about the +1 in the formula and say that the median will be at the $80/2 = 40$th value. This clearly does not come in the first group, since that only contains 23 values; however, it is included in the second group, since by the top of that group we have accumulated 56 values. To find the exact position of the median within the group, it may be helpful to look at Figure 9.1.

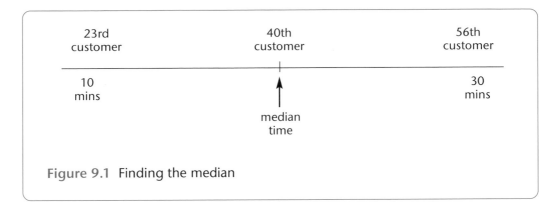

Figure 9.1 Finding the median

This shows that up to 10 minutes, we have 23 customers; up to 30 minutes, we have 56, and the median value, the 40th, is 17 people up from the bottom of the group. So, assuming that the customers' times are spread out evenly through the range 10 to 30 minutes, we can say that the 40th customer will be at a point $(40 - 23)/33$ of the way through the class. The corresponding time is therefore 10 minutes + $(40 - 23)/33 \times 20$ minutes = 20.3 minutes, agreeing with the rough value we got from the ogive.

Medians are often used in preference to means with data such as house prices, where the distribution tends to be highly skew, with a lot of reasonably priced houses on the market but also a small number of extremely expensive ones.

The mode

If you look at a frequency table, such as the one below for the 'number of visits' data, one of the things you probably notice immediately is that the 'peak' frequency occurs at three visits:

Number of visits in the past month	Number of respondents
1	15
2	19
3	22
4	20
5 or more	4

So if you were asked to say how many visits a 'typical' shopper makes over a month, you might well answer '3', because more people made 3 visits than any other number.

This most common value is formally called the *mode* of the data, and is easily found in this case where we have an ungrouped frequency table. With a grouped table, probably the best course to adopt is simply to state the modal class. Moreover, there may be more than one mode, or indeed none at all (as with the sample of five customer expenditures, all different). So on the whole the mode, being rather ill-defined, is not a very useful measure of location.

Test your understanding

1. A transport campaigning group carries out a check on the number of passengers using a train service, and finds that on a day when there are nine trains in total, the numbers travelling on each are: 32, 77, 111, 64, 28, 25, 116, 83, 47.

   (a) Find the mean number of people per train over the day. What use could be made of this figure by the campaigning group?
   (b) What is the median of the sample? Comment on how it compares to the mean.

2. XYZ Supermarket, in addition to carrying out the survey described in this chapter, has examined the time taken for customers to be processed through the checkout, and has summarised the resulting data as follows:

Time to pass through checkout including queuing (mins)	Number of customers
Under 2 minutes	7
2 but under 5 minutes	23
5 but under 10 minutes	12
10 minutes and more	8

   (a) Assuming that no one takes more than 20 minutes to get through the check-out process, find the mean time taken by this sample of customers.
   (b) Either by sketching the ogive, or by carrying out a proportion calculation as in Figure 9.1, find the approximate value of the median in this case, and comment on what its value as compared to the mean tells you.
   (c) What is the modal class here?

3. The data about the number of visits to XYZ Supermarket in the past month, given in Section 8.4, is repeated below:

Number of visits in the past month	Number of respondents
1	15
2	19
3	22
4	20
5 or more	4

(a) Choose a reasonable value for the maximum number of visits.

(b) Calculate the mean number of visits per customer per month. (Note that although, with the exception of the last class, the data is not grouped, the same formula for the mean can be used – but only for the last class will you need to compute a mid-point.)

(c) What is the value of the median for this set of data?

9.3 ## Measuring the spread

Each of the measures of location which we have looked at has its corresponding measure of spread; we will look at them in the same order.

The standard deviation: definition

If you have studied some elementary statistics before, you will almost certainly have come across the standard deviation.

Pause for reflection

If you have encountered the standard deviation before, could you define what it is, and what it can be used for (not just how it's calculated)? Try explaining your ideas to someone in your group who is not familiar with this measure.

The standard deviation is one of the most important and widely-used concepts in the whole of statistics, but because it can't be displayed on a simple chart, or interpreted in a very direct way in relation to the data, newcomers to the topic often find that it's not easy to grasp. In particular, the formula for the measure looks quite complicated. So, rather than jumping straight in, we will build up the method of calculation from scratch, using the data about the expenditure of the five XYZ customers as an illustration.

This data (in its original version before we introduced the high-spending customer) consisted of the values £12, £14, £22, £34 and £48. The mean, as we calculated it in Section 9.2, was £26. We now want to construct a way of measuring how dispersed the individual values are; one reasonable way to do that is to ask how far they are from the mean. Clearly, if the data is very widely spread, then some of the values will be very different from the mean; if the data is all quite closely 'bunched', then all the values will be near to the mean.

So we look at the differences between individual values and the mean, denoting the values as usual by x and the mean by $\bar{x}$. The differences are then found by taking $x - \bar{x}$. It's best to set this calculation out as a table:

x	x – $\bar{x}$
12	–14
14	–12
22	–4
34	8
48	22

Some of the $x - \bar{x}$ values (called the *deviations* of the x's from the mean) are negative – because the values are smaller than the mean – and some are positive. The result of this is that if we try to find the total of all the deviations, to get an idea of the overall spread, we actually find that the total is zero, because the positive and negative values have cancelled each other out. And this is not just a quirk of this particular set of numbers; the total will always be zero, because of the way the mean is calculated. Roughly speaking, the deviations above and below the mean always 'balance out'.

So, if we want to devise a measure of dispersion based on these deviations, we will have to eliminate the negative values in some way. One possibility is simply to ignore them; there is a measure of dispersion based on this idea, called the mean absolute deviation, which you might encounter. However, just ignoring information is not a very satisfactory procedure; a better way is to recall from Chapter 2 that if we square a negative quantity we get a positive one, and so to take the squares of the deviations. This eliminates the minus signs, while preserving the information about large and small deviations.

We then get an extra column in our table:

x	x – $\bar{x}$	$(x - \bar{x})^2$
12	–14	196
14	–12	144
22	–4	16
34	8	64
48	22	484
Total		904

So the average squared deviation is 904/5 = 180.8. We still haven't quite finished; there is a bit of a problem with the units of this answer. We started out with measurements in £, but by squaring the deviations we have ended up with a measure in 'square £'! To get back to the original units, therefore, we take the square root of 180.8, to arrive at a final result of £13.45, which is the standard deviation of the amounts spent.

If we recap the process by which we arrived at this figure, we obtain a formula for standard deviation. We took the square root of the average of the squared deviations from the mean, which in symbolic terms gives

$$\text{standard deviation} = \sqrt{\frac{\sum(x - \bar{x})^2}{n}}$$

where n denotes the number of items in the set of data.

The letters generally used to represent the standard deviation are 's' if it's calculated from a sample, and σ (a little Greek sigma, not to be confused with the capital Σ used for summation) if we have population data.

There is one slightly technical point which is worth mentioning here. We have mentioned before the need to be able to get reliable information about a population when we only have data relating to a sample. It turns out that the standard deviation calculated from the formula above gives a biased estimate of the population standard deviation – it is a bit too small. It can be demonstrated mathematically that you get a better, unbiased estimate if you divide by $n-1$ rather than n when you only have sample data. This explains why many statistical calculators have two keys for finding standard deviation, one labelled something like σ_n and the other σ_{n-1}. In fact, for samples where n is bigger than about 30, the two formulae give pretty much the same answer, but a safe rule of thumb is always to use the σ_{n-1} version, since we are nearly always working with sample data.

The standard deviation: calculation and interpretation

The formula we derived above is fine as a definition of the standard deviation, but as a way of calculating its value it is rather clumsy. It becomes simpler if you expand the expression (you can work it out if you would like some practice at algebra) to get:

$$\text{standard deviation} = \sqrt{\frac{\Sigma x^2}{n} - \bar{x}^2}$$

And if we have frequency table data, so that each x occurs not just once but f times, then the formula can be further modified to get:

$$\text{standard deviation} = \sqrt{\frac{\Sigma f x^2}{\Sigma f} - \bar{x}^2}$$

This is the version of the formula which is most widely used – though it has to be said that in this era of statistical software packages you will hardly ever find yourself calculating standard deviations by hand.

To illustrate the use of this formula, let's return to the data on number of items purchased from the XYZ survey, for which we've already found the mean to be 14.1875 items. Table 9.1 shows the data, with an extra column added for the fx^2 terms. Incidentally, the easiest way to calculate fx^2 is to multiply the fx by another x – your recollection of Chapter 3 should tell you that $fx \times x = fx^2$.

Table 9.1 Calculating the mean and standard deviation

Number of items purchased	Number of respondents (f)	Class midpoint (x)	fx	fx^2
1–5	6	3	18	54
6–10	15	8	120	960
11–15	37	13	481	6253
16–20	12	18	216	3888
21–30	7	25.5	178.5	4551.75
31 or more (50)	3	40.5	121.5	4920.75
Σ	80		1135	20627.5

Thus the standard deviation = $\sqrt{[20{,}627.5/80 - 14.1875^2]}$ = 7.52 items (remember that the standard deviation always has the same units as the original data).

Having found this figure, we need to think about what it might mean in practical terms. One way to get a handle on this is to consider a comparative situation: if shoppers at another supermarket had a mean of 12.2 items with a standard deviation of 4.1 items, that would indicate that not only are they buying fewer items on average, but also that there is less variation between customers in the number of items bought.

Another fact which may be helpful in getting a 'feel' for what the standard deviation is telling you is based on the theory of the *normal distribution*, which you may study later on in your course. This indicates that, as long as the distribution is not too skewed, virtually all the data will lie within a range of about 3 standard deviations either side of the mean. So in the present example, we could expect the number of items bought by all shoppers to range between $14.1875 - 3 \times 6.68$ and $14.1875 + 3 \times 7.52$, or from about 0 to 37 items. (The calculation actually gives a negative lower limit – that's because this particular distribution is somewhat skewed.)

The quartiles

Just as we divided a set of data into halves using the median, so we can divide it into quarters by values known as the *quartiles*. The lower quartile, sometimes called Q1, cuts off the bottom 25% of the data, while the upper quartile Q3 cuts off the top 25% (the 50% point or Q2 is of course the median). The quartiles can be found in the same way as the median – either by reading from the ogive, or directly from the cumulative frequency table. To illustrate, we will find the median and quartiles for the 'number of visits' data from the XYZ survey.

Here is the data again:

Number of visits in the past month	Number of respondents (*f*)	Cumulative frequency
1	15	15
2	19	34
3	22	56
4	20	76
5 or more	4	80

The median will be the 40th value, which is 3 visits (there is no need to do a proportion calculation here, since the table is not grouped). The lower quartile is the 20th value, which is 2, and the upper quartile is the 60th value, namely 4. So we could say that 25% of customers make 4 or more visits per month to XYZ, and 25% make 2 or fewer visits. The quartiles, like the median, are not affected by the extremes – they give us an idea of the spread of the central 50% of the data. Using quartiles rather than the standard deviation to indicate spread also avoids the need to make any assumptions about where the open top class finishes.

The median and quartiles, taken together, can provide useful information about the shape of a distribution, as well as its location and spread. For example, if you calculate the median and quartiles for the 'length of visit' data from the XYZ survey (closing the top class at 60 minutes), you should find that the quartiles are at about 9 and 35 minutes (we already calculated the median as roughly 20 minutes). So the lower quartile is a bit nearer to the median than the upper quartile, indicating that there is a longer 'tail' at the upper end of the distribution.

The range

The most obvious way to indicate the spread of a set of data is simply to state its range, which is just the distance from the smallest to the largest value in the data. Thus we might make a statement such as 'the wages of these workers range from £220 to £400 per week' or (less usefully) 'the range of these wages is £180'.

However the range, like its companion measure of location the mode, is not actually a terribly useful measure. Just one extreme value can give the range a very misleading value, and of course, where there are open classes at the top or bottom of a frequency distribution, it's very difficult to say what the range is at all with any degree of accuracy. So the range is not very widely used.

Test your understanding

These questions relate to the 'Test your understanding' questions in Section 9.2.

1. For the train usage data in Question 1 of Section 9.2, find the range and the standard deviation of the numbers of passengers. Which of these do you think would be most useful to the transport lobby group in making its case to support the train service?
2. For the 'time to pass through checkout' data in Question 2, use the ogive to find the upper and lower quartiles, and give a practical interpretation for your answers.
3. (a) For the 'number of visits' data in Question 3, calculate the standard deviation. If this data was collected in July, and data collected in December has a mean of 3.4 visits and a standard deviation of 1.62 visits, what can you conclude about the numbers of visits in the two months?
   (b) Find the quartiles for this data, and use them together with the median found in Section 9.2 to confirm whether or not the data is noticeably skewed.

9.4 Choosing a measure

We've now looked at three different ways of measuring location and dispersion, each of which has its own plus and minus points. So, given a particular set of data, you need to think carefully about which measures to use. There are no 'rules' for making this decision, but as a rough guide:

- If your data is reasonably symmetrically distributed, and/or you want to draw conclusions about population values based on your sample – use the mean and standard deviation. This is the default choice.
- If your data is markedly unsymmetrical (skew) – use the median and quartiles.
- If you just want a quick idea of the location and dispersion without doing any calculations – use the mode and range.

You may have noticed that in places, when giving the value of one of these measures, we have used words like 'roughly' and 'approximately'. This may surprise or even worry you – after all, isn't statistics an exact science? The answer is yes and no; quite often there are slightly different ways of doing calculations – for example, some textbooks get very excited about the exact positions of class boundaries, particularly with discrete data; some software treats all variables as continuous, and so on. So small discrepancies are quite likely to arise, particularly where small samples of data are involved. Use your common sense to decide whether, if there is a difference between your answer and someone else's, it's small enough not to really matter, or so large that it suggests someone has made a serious mistake.

9.5 Putting it all together

The Bootle Building Society is a small mortgage provider, which at present has business concentrated in Merseyside. It is interested in opening up a new office in Bristol, and so has used the free Internet tool Nethouseprices (http://www.nethouseprices.com/) to look at two random samples of house prices over the past year, one within a suburban area near to its offices in Liverpool and the other in a comparable part of Bristol. The two samples of prices, in £000, are shown in full below; all relate to houses, not flats, and they exclude newly built houses:

Liverpool: 215, 170, 204, 195, 345, 260, 170, 220, 275, 294, 167, 190, 170, 375, 145, 195, 242, 250, 195, 255, 230, 135, 205, 190, 173, 220, 210, 168, 180, 266, 190, 200, 219, 110, 138, 146

Bristol: 395, 684, 325, 320, 278, 270, 605, 335, 402, 495, 645, 535, 325, 626, 615, 570, 595, 628, 695, 262, 382, 380, 277, 300, 240, 530, 460, 250, 492, 250, 295, 470, 199, 470, 430, 455, 329, 165

It is immediately obvious that the houses in Bristol are much more expensive than those in Liverpool. However, to get a clearer picture of what's going on, the building society should turn the two sets of data into frequency tables.

To decide exactly how to arrange the table for the Liverpool data, look at the smallest and largest values; they are 110 and 375 respectively. We want to choose a class width which will cover this range in about six to ten classes. In this case, starting from 100 and going up in steps of 50 will do the trick:

Price	Frequency
100 but less than 150	5
150 but less than 200	13
200 but less than 250	10
250 but less than 300	6
300 but less than 350	1
350 but less than 400	1
Total	36

Doing the same for the Bristol data, one possibility is as follows:

Price	Frequency
150 but less than 200	2
200 but less than 250	1
250 but less than 300	7
300 but less than 350	6
350 but less than 400	3
400 but less than 450	2
450 but less than 500	6
500 but less than 550	2
550 but less than 600	2
600 but less than 650	5
650 but less than 700	2
Total	38

Histograms for the two distributions are shown in Figure 9.2 (a) and (b). These show that, in addition to being more widely spread, the Bristol data exhibits a much less regular pattern than the Liverpool data, looking almost as though there is evidence of two or three distinct subsets in the prices.

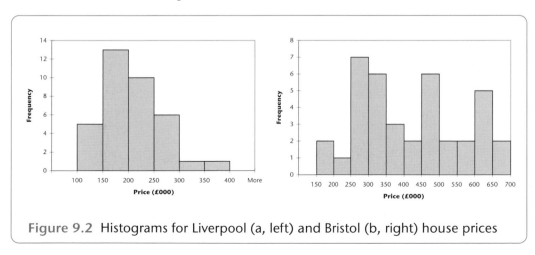

Figure 9.2 Histograms for Liverpool (a, left) and Bristol (b, right) house prices

Now we will calculate the mean, standard deviation, median and quartiles for the two sets of data, to see how these reflect the observations we've already made just by looking

181

at the tables and charts. The table for calculation of the mean and standard deviation for the Liverpool data is shown below:

x	f	fx	fx²
125	5	625	78,125
175	13	2275	398,125
225	10	2250	506,250
275	6	1650	453,750
325	1	325	105,625
375	1	375	140,625
Total	36	7500	1,682,500

This gives the mean as 7500/36 = 208.333, or £208,333, and the standard deviation as $\sqrt{[1,682,500/36 - 208.333^2]}$, which works out to 57.735 or £57,735.

The ogive for this data is shown in Figure 9.3, and from it we can read off the value of the median as the price corresponding to the 18th value (or the 18.5th if you want to be fussy) – that's about £200,000. Similarly the quartiles are the 9th and 27th values, giving around £165,000 and £245,000 respectively.

Figure 9.3 Ogive for Liverpool house prices

We will leave the calculations for the Bristol data as an exercise; you should find that the results are: mean £419,737, standard deviation £144,545, median £400,000, and quartiles £296,000 and £537,500.

What useful information can the mortgage lender glean from all these measurements? A short report prepared for the Bootle Building Society might read something like this:

> **The mean price of the Bristol sample of houses is more than twice that found in the Liverpool sample, and the spread, as measured by the standard deviation, is also much larger. This shows that prices in Liverpool are much more**

consistent, perhaps reflecting a more homogeneous housing stock in the area surveyed. The Liverpool distribution is slightly skewed, as seen from the fact that the upper quartile is a little further from the mean than the lower quartile; however, the effect is not marked. The skewness is more pronounced with the Bristol data, the lower and upper quartiles being respectively about £104,000 and £137,000 from the median. The Bootle Building Society therefore, should it enter the Bristol market, will have to be prepared for borrowers who are seeking much larger loans than in Liverpool, and for some very high house prices to be encountered.

One final cautionary note can be drawn from this example. We put the Bristol data into £50,000 bands for consistency with the way we'd treated the Liverpool data. However, it might be argued that this gives rather too many classes, thus accounting for the 'bumpy' appearance of the histogram. If we re-group the data into bands 150 but less than 250 and so on, we get the histogram shown in Figure 9.4, which definitely suggests that there are two distinct groups within the data. This demonstrates that sometimes the impression given by a chart may be as much a product of the way the analyst has chosen to arrange the data, as of any real features within the data itself.

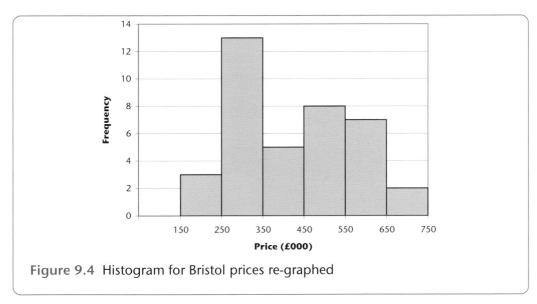

Figure 9.4 Histogram for Bristol prices re-graphed

9.6 For Excel users

Excel has built-in functions which will calculate most of the measures we've discussed in this chapter. You can see a list of them by clicking on the Function Wizard icon, f_x, in the top menu bar, and then on Statistical. The relevant functions are as follows:

AVERAGE gives the mean
MEDIAN gives the median

MODE   gives the mode

STDEVP   gives the population standard deviation (corresponding to the formula with the n divisor, as mentioned above), while STDEV gives the standard deviation based on a sample (using the $n-1$ divisor).

All of these functions simply require you to specify the range where the raw data values are to be found.

QUARTILE   This is slightly different; it has the format QUARTILE(array, quart). The *array* is simply the list of data values, as with the other functions, whereas *quart* is a parameter which can have the values 0, 1, 2, 3, 4. If you give it the value 0, you get the minimum value in the data; 1 gives the lower quartile, 2 the median, 3 the upper quartile, and 4 the maximum value in the data.

No function is provided for the range, though you can find it by using MAX and MIN.

The screenshot in Figure 9.5 shows the process for finding the lower quartile of the set of Liverpool house prices given in the previous section. Of course, the value obtained is

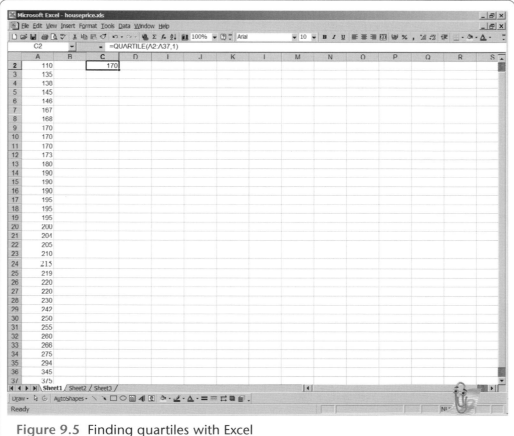

Figure 9.5 Finding quartiles with Excel

not exactly the same as the one we got from the grouped frequency table, since Excel is using the individual prices. However, the discrepancy should not be large.

You might like to test your facility in using these functions by finding the other measures for the Liverpool and Bristol house prices, and comparing them with the values obtained 'by hand'; the data is available on the companion website to save your having to enter all the individual values. It is worth noting that, while Excel will not calculate these measures directly from data which has already been arranged into a frequency table, the layout of the hand calculation – with columns for x, f, fx and fx^2 – lends itself to very efficient calculation using a spreadsheet. The necessary formulae can simply be entered into the top row of the table and then copied down the columns.

What have I learned?

Describe in your own words the measures to which you have been introduced in this chapter, and indicate why each of them might be useful. Don't quote formulae or formal definitions – imagine that you are trying to get the gist of the ideas across to someone who is totally non-numerate!

Exercises

1. Find the mean and standard deviation of the two samples of data 4, 7, 9, 10, 15 and 40, 70, 90, 100, 150. What do you notice? How might this be useful?
2. A company is seeking a building contractor to carry out major alterations to its premises. It examines information provided by the two contractors who have put in similar tenders for the project, and finds that for similar projects contractor A took a mean time of 8.4 weeks, with a standard deviation of 3 weeks, while contractor B took a mean of 9.1 weeks with a standard deviation of 2.4 weeks. How might this information be useful to the company in reaching a decision whether to use contractor A or contractor B?
3. Refer to the data in Question 1 of the exercises for Chapter 8, and to your solution to that question. Find the mean, median and mode of the call times, and explain the difference between them. Which do you think would be the most useful measure in this case?
4. Refer to the data in Question 5 of the exercises for Chapter 8. Calculate the mean, standard deviation, median and quartiles for the two distributions of the numbers of corrections per page, and explain how these relate to the shapes of the distributions. Which of the measures could be useful to the publisher, and in what way?
5. (a) Suggest three variables which might have a fairly symmetric distribution, best summarised by the mean and standard deviation.
   (b) Suggest three variables that might have a skewed distribution, best summarised by the median and quartiles.

Case Study: The Bill Oates Foundation

The billionaire businessman Bill Oates has set up a Foundation dedicated to the relief of worldwide poverty. As a researcher for the Foundation, you have been asked to analyse some data relating to Gross National Income per head of population in the various countries of the world.

You have located this information on the Wikipedia website at:
http://en.wikipedia.org/wiki/
List_of_countries_by_GDP_%28nominal%29_per_capita

(a) Use the list provided at this web address to determine the median and quartiles of the set of values, and identify the corresponding countries.

(b) What do these values tell you about the shape of the distribution of per capita income across all countries? Sketch or plot accurately a histogram of the data to confirm your findings.

(c) How might you make use of these figures in promotional literature for the Foundation?

For further exercises and multiple choice revision questions visit the companion website: www.palgrave.com/business/morris

Solutions and hints

Chapter 2

Section 2.2

Some other examples of the use of negative numbers in a practical context:

- In geography, the height of land above sea level is represented by positive measurements – so the height of Mount Everest is, according to Wikipedia, 8840 m. In some low-lying parts of the world, such as Holland, land is actually below sea level; this could be represented by saying that the level is, say, –10 m. Industries such as mining also make use of this concept.
- In discussing the motion of vehicles, the concept of velocity is often used. Suppose a shuttle bus regularly travels backwards and forwards between an airport and a hotel. If the velocity is measured in a direction away from the airport, then it will be positive when the bus is travelling in that direction. However, when it is returning, and thus travelling towards the airport, the velocity will be negative.
- Some of you may have come across the concept of negative marks in multiple-choice tests: to discourage students from guessing answers, a wrong answer results in your total being reduced by 1 mark (whereas no attempt would give a zero mark). A very poor and unlucky student who guessed every answer in a 10-question test, and got them all wrong, could finish with a mark of –10!

Section 2.3

Page 15

1. 29	2. 9	3. –4	4. –3	5. 6
6. 36	7. 9	8. –28	9. 28	10. –5

Page 16

1. 5	2. 19	3. 2	4. 4	5. 72

Page 17

1. 21	2. 13	3. 54	4. –22	5. 4	6. –4.

Section 2.4

Page 20

1. 16/15 or 1 1/15   2. 5/18   3. 4/10 or 2/5   4. –3/12 or –1/4
5. 43/12 or 3 7/12   6. 14/9 or 1 5/9   7. 5/24 8. 13/20

Page 21

1. 33/84 or 11/28   2. 6/75 or 2/25   3. 3/4   4. 64
5. 8   6. 24/36 or 2/3   7. 117/8 or 14 5/8
8. 2/5   9. You need to work out 22 1/2 ÷ 3/4 = 30 batches.
10. 28/1000 = 7/250, whereas 8/1000 = 2/250. The rate has thus decreased by a factor of 7/2 = 3 1/2.

Section 2.5

Page 23

1. $4 \times 100 + 6 \times 10 + 2 \times 1$
$5 \times 1000 + 0 \times 100 + 0 \times 10 + 3 \times 1$
$1 \times 10 + 1 \times 1 + 4 \times 1/10$
$7 \times 1 + 1 \times 1/10 + 2 \times 1/100$
$5 \times 10,000 + 3 \times 1000 + 2 \times 100 + 8 \times 10 + 9 \times 1$.
2. 0.17, 0.141, 0.14, 0.03, 1.14.
3. 5.37E+07, 4.42E+08, 7.75E–04

Page 25

1. 4.031   2. –4.32   3. 12.34   4. 3.73   5. 20
6. 208   7. 0.8355   8. 1445.17
9. 0.8888... (the division process never stops, so we get a recurring decimal)
10. 1240.59 kroner (there is no point in quoting more than 2 decimal places, since this is an amount of currency and smaller subdivisions than 1/100 of a kroner don't exist)
11. 13/40 (325/1000 can be cancelled by 25)
12. £7101.05.

Section 2.6

1. 8.927, 24.369, 0.005, –32.660
2. 10,200, 0.0306, 2.67, –17.9
3. There are several ways of looking at this question. You might argue that, as the least accurate figure is only quoted to the nearest £50, the other figures should be rounded in the same way. This would give £24,300 + £18,750 + £19,350 = £62,400. This figure will then be accurate to the nearest £50.

   Or you could say that £24,279 to the nearest pound could result from an actual figure anywhere between £24,278.50 and £24,279.49; £18,730 to the nearest £10 could be between £18,725.00 and £18,734.99; and £19,350 to the nearest £50 could be between

£19,325.00 and £19,374.99. So the true total could be anywhere between £62,328.50 and £62,389.47 – that's £62,359 with a margin of about £30.50.

What you certainly should not do is just add the three original figures and quote the result as £62,359 without any kind of qualification as to its accuracy.

Section 2.7

1. 9, 24, 6, 22.4, 6.4.
2. 37.5%, 40%, 180%, 20%, 37.5%.
3. £2.90. Note that there is no need to work out 16% of £2.50 and then add it to £2.50; it is more efficient to find 116% of £2.50 – that is, to realise that the answer will be 116% of the original figure.
4. £19,756 (simplest to find 88% of £22,450; that is, 100% – 12%).
5. £76.60 to the nearest penny (£90 is 117.5% of the original price; if you got £74.25 as your answer, you have applied the 17.5% to the final price instead of the original price).
6. 59.5% (there are 398 employees in total).
7. 19.4% (to 1 decimal place; the actual decrease is 67, which as a percentage of last year's total is 19.4%). This figure is not very useful unless we also know the total numbers of mortgage holders involved. If (admittedly a rather extreme case) the society had 3460 customers last year, and only 558 this year, then last year's 346 defaulters constituted only 10% of the total, whereas this year's 558 form 50% of the total – a serious position totally obscured by saying 'the number of defaulters fell by nearly 20%'. So generally a fairer comparison could be made by stating what percentage of customers defaulted in each year.
8. Remember that you cannot simply say 'increase over 10 years = 10 x 3% = 30%'. Instead, using the hypothetical population of 10,000 as a base, you need to work as follows:

> Population after 1 year = 10,000 x 103% = 10300
> Population after two years = 10300 x 103% = 10,609,
> ...
> Population after ten years = 13,439 to the nearest whole number

So the increase is 34.39%. (There are actually quicker ways of working out this kind of calculation, as we'll see later in the book.)
9. 0.42, 0.03, 0.625, 1.2, 1.1.
10. 22.5%, 4%, 240%, 75%, 65%.

Exercises

1. –1/4 (remember that the multiplication is done before the subtraction)
2. 14.16   3. 2   4. 128
5. 12 (if you got 60 as the answer, you have done the operations in the wrong order)
6. 45%   7. 63   8. 49.9   9. 108   10. 9

Case study

(a) It appears that the figures are being quoted to the nearest £1000, since they are all integer multiples of 1000.

(b) The growth year on year is just over 3%; 3.3% correct to 1 decimal place between 2004 and 2005, 3.2% between 2005 and 2006.

(c) PrinTidy's turnover appears to be growing by a flat amount of £3000 per year – though it would be rash to be too firm about this conclusion on the basis of data covering only three years.

(d) Assuming that the rate of growth continues at 3.2% per year, the turnover should exceed £250,000 in the year 2010. (Just extend the table given, adding 3.2% to each year's figure to get the estimate for the next year.)

(e) If 3.2% per year is added to the N-Press figures, while the PrinTidy figures continue to rise by a flat £3000 per year, then we get the following continuation of the table (figures to the nearest whole number of £):

Year	N-Press	PrinTidy
2006	227000	237000
2007	234264	240000
2008	241760	243000
2009	249497	246000
2010	257481	249000
2011	265720	252000

It therefore appears that N-Press will overtake PrinTidy in 2009. However, as we've only got three years of data to go on, the assumption that N-Press is growing at a steady percentage rate, while PrinTidy is only growing by a constant amount per year, is not very securely based. In practice you would probably want to have data for several more years before drawing such a conclusion – and even then, making predictions several years into the future like this is obviously a risky procedure: all kinds of market conditions, changes of ownership of the companies, new technology, and so on could intervene to invalidate your calculations. Nevertheless, this is the kind of projection which businesses do have to make in order to plan for the future.

(f) The management of N-Press could use this data to help in setting budget targets for future years. Actual achievements could then be monitored against those targets.

Chapter 3

Section 3.1

Page 37

1. (a) £500   (b) £625   (c) £125 – you need to write 50p as £0.5 here.
2. If we say that the number of shares is represented by n, then

Total (in £) received for shares $= n \times P$

(You could have used other letters, such as Q for quantity.)

Page 38

1. Replace Q by 12 and P by 450 to give a cost of £5400.
2. This is a bit trickier! Putting the numbers we are given into the formula gives $8000 = 400 \times Q$, so Q is the number which when multiplied by 400 gives 8000: that's 20. This means that 20 tonnes should be purchased. We are really approaching the idea of *solving an equation* here – something to which we'll be returning in Chapter 5.

Section 3.2

Page 40

1. $2xy - 4x + y$ 2. $7s + 3t - st$.
3. $-2x + 3y - 11$ 4. $a - 2b - ab$
   Note that you could have the terms in a different order (for example, number 1 could be $2xy + y - 4x$) as long as the signs are still correct.

Page 41

1. 243   2. 49   3. 0.001
4. Because the 2 is inside the brackets, this means 2a multiplied by itself 4 times – that's $2a \times 2a \times 2a \times 2a$. Since the order in multiplication doesn't matter, this can be rewritten as $2 \times 2 \times 2 \times 2 \times a \times a \times a \times a = 16a^4$.

Page 43

2   (a) p^5q^5 or $(pq)^5$ (b) x^3y (c) $4t^8$

Page 44

1. 196   2. 25   3. 1296   4. 5   5. –7
6. This root does not exist within the real number system
7. $a - 2$ 8. $4x^2$ 9. 1/5 or 0.2 10. 1

Section 3.3

Page 46

Answers (b) and (d) are both correct – (b) is the same as (d) but with the brackets removed.

Page 47

1. $2 \times 6 = 12$ 2. $-(-2) = 2$

3. $a - 8 + 2b$ or $a + 2b - 8$ (the order doesn't matter, but the signs must be correct)
4. $4b - 4a$ 5. $-2a^2 + ab$ or $ab - 2a^2$ 6. $a^2 - b^2$
7. $bc - b^2cd - b^3$ (remember to remove the inside brackets first).
8. $-x + 5y$ or $5y - x$.
9. $0.1(R + M) + 0.2S$, or $(R + M)/10 + S/5$.
10 $80 \times 0.25 + (x - 80) \times 0.12$. Cost for 100 miles is £22.40.

Section 3.5

1. The formula =0.1*A1 should be put into cell B1. This can then be copied down the column. Be careful not to forget the = sign in front of the formula.
2. The formula =1200*A1+800*B1 should be put into cell C1, and then copied down the column to find the amount for the remaining months.

Exercises

1. 1/4 or 0.25; also –1/4 or –0.25, since the square root of a number can be positive or negative.
2. $x^2 - xy + y^2$. If you have $x^2 + 2xy - 3xy + y^2$, then you have forgotten that the two terms in xy can be combined.
3. $12x^3y^4$ 4. $6x^2 - xy - y^2$ 5. $0.5q/p$ or $q/2p$.
6. This can't really be simplified, since the terms can't be combined. You could write it as $a(1 + b - bc)$, but that isn't really any simpler.
7. 3600. If you got 1,440,000, you have squared the whole expression, but the square actually only applies to the value of y.
8. The expression would be negative if b is bigger than 2, or less than –2.
9. Your friend has forgotten that the 3 and the –1 in front of the brackets multiply everything inside the bracket, not just the first term. The correct version should be:

$$3(x + 2y) - (x - y) = 3x + 6y - x + y = 2x + 7y.$$

10. The negative sign in front of the power 'turns the result upside down' – in other words, you need to work out 1/corresponding positive power. So $4-2 = 1/42 = 1/16 = 0.0625$.

Case study

1. 6.4 million, 3.76 million, 1.58 million.
2. The population seems to be declining. This is in line with the formula, because when t is bigger than 1, t^2 is bigger than t. So $t/(t^2 + 1)$ will be less than 1, and will get smaller as t gets bigger. Thus the population will decline as time goes on. (Can you see why this argument does not depend on the value of A?)
3. After 16 hours the population is just below 1 million. The figures do indeed decline as time goes on, as argued in Part 2.

Chapter 4

Section 4.2

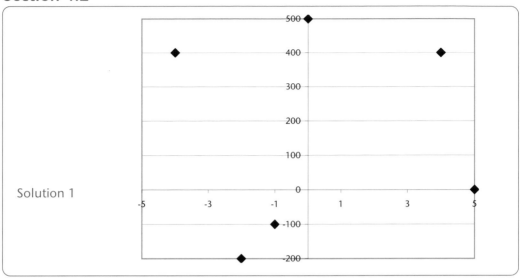

Solution 1

Section 4.3

Page 60

1. (a) Slope = 4, intercept = 11
   (b) This equation can be rearranged as $y = 2x - 2$, so slope = 2, intercept = –2.
   (c) This equation can be rearranged as $y = 1.5 - x$, so slope = –1, intercept = 1.5.
   (d) This equation can be rearranged as $y = 10x + 15$, so slope = 10, intercept = 15.
   (e) Slope = 4, intercept = 0 (the graph passes through the origin).
   (f) Slope = 0 (because there is no x term, so coefficient of x = 0), intercept = 7.

The lines represented by (a) and (e) are parallel, since both have slope 4.

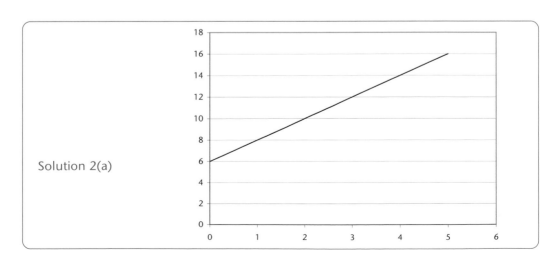

Solution 2(a)

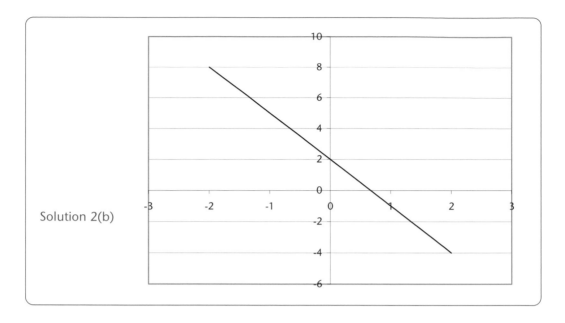

Solution 2(b)

Page 64

1. $P = 1.5 + 0.75d$

   This graph shows that for £7.50 you can travel 8 miles (try checking this using the equation if you know something about solving equations).

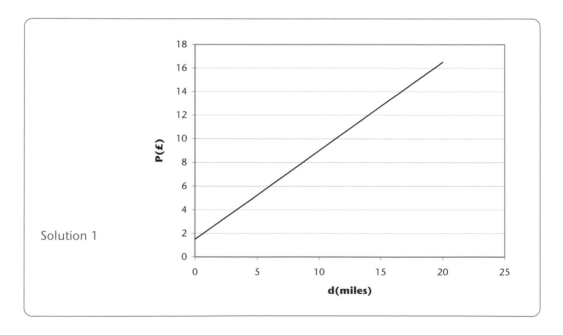

Solution 1

2. $C = 1500 + 25n$

   When 50 orders are placed, the total cost will be £2750 (check this from the eqaution.

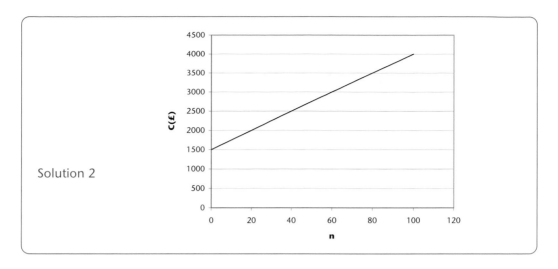

Solution 2

Section 4.4

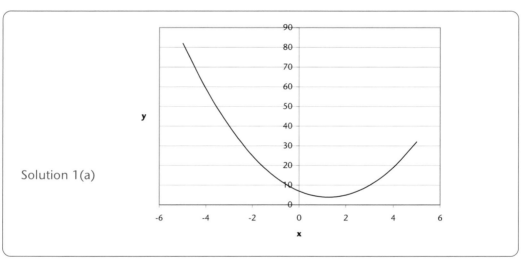

Solution 1(a)

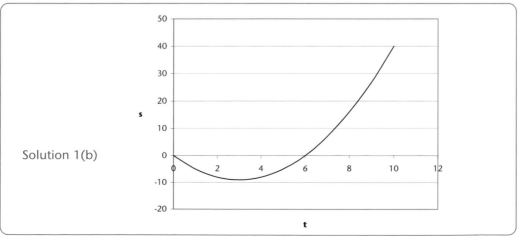

Solution 1(b)

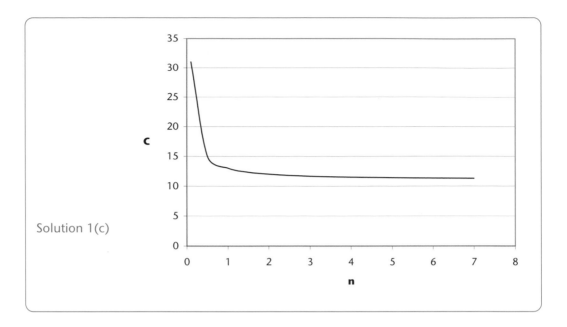

Solution 1(c)

(a) and (b) are parabolas, (c) is a hyperbola.

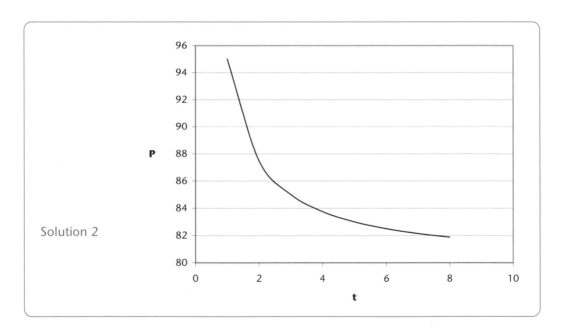

Solution 2

Awareness falls to less than 83% on day 6.

3. (a) Revenue R = price per copy × copies sold = $(0.65 + P) \times (500 - 600P)$. (The units here are thousands of £ because the number of copies $500 - 600P$ is in thousands of copies).

So $R = 325 + 110P - 600P^2$.

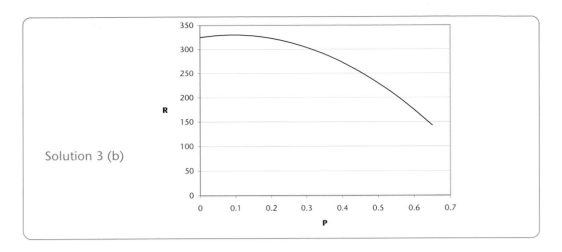

Solution 3 (b)

(b)   The curve is a parabola.
(c)   As the value of P rises from zero (that is, the price charged for the paper rises from £0.65) the amount of revenue increases very slightly – the maximum revenue is about £330, attained when P is about 0.1 so that the price is £0.65 + £0.10 = £0.75 or 75 pence per copy. After this, the revenue falls, because the extra revenue generated by the increased price is more than offset by the falling numbers of customers who buy the paper – the more expensive it gets, the fewer people will buy.

Exercises

1. (a)   Passes through $x = 0$, $y = -3$ and through $x = 1.5$, $y = 0$; slope is 2.
   (b)   Passes through the origin, with slope 2.5
   (c)   Passes through $x = 0$, $y = 4$ and through $x = 10$, $y = 0$; slope is $-2/5$ or -0.4.
   (d)   A parabola with its vertex downwards, passing through $x = 0$, $y = 0$ and $x = 0$, $y = 8$. Minimum value of y is -16 when $x = 4$.
   (e)   A hyperbola, shaped very much like $y = 1/x$ (see Section 4.4 above).
2. For graph, see below. It appears that, as d continues to increase, p falls, but very slowly

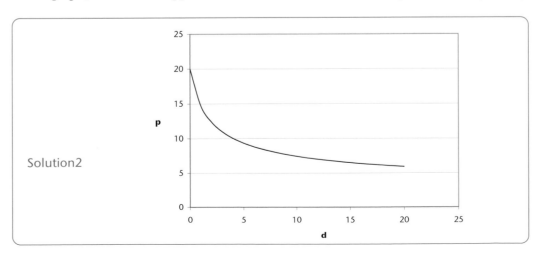

Solution2

(it will actually approach the value 2%; can you see why this is by looking at the equation?). However, in practice, this one retail park is not operating in isolation – as d gets bigger, towns will start to fall into the catchment of other, closer retail parks, and so the relationship will break down – or rather, a much more complex model is needed, which includes the effects of competition between neighbouring parks.

Case study: C21 Graphic Design

Your report should be properly structured, with a management summary addressed to the intended recipient.

The graph should look something like this:

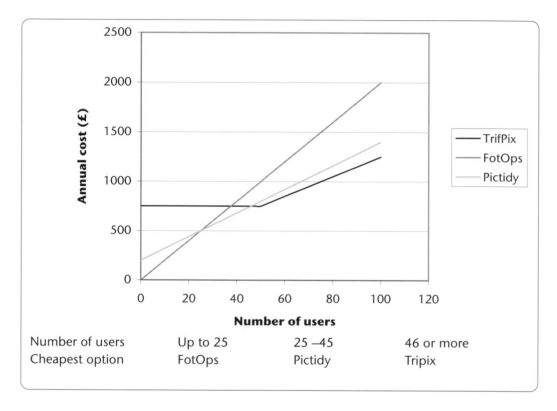

Number of users	Up to 25	25 –45	46 or more
Cheapest option	FotOps	Pictidy	Tripix

Note that for exactly 25 users, the cost of FotOps and Pictidy is the same. The actual point at which the Pictidy and TrifPix graphs cross is at 45.83 users, but of course this makes no practical sense – users can only have a whole number value, and the information should be reported in those terms.

Given the likely number of users over the year – which, assuming that all non-administrative staff need access to the software, is likely to be at least 50, it seems that TrifPix is clearly the best choice. However, noting that the gap between TrifPix and Pictidy is pretty narrow for up to 100 users, it might be worth looking more closely at any 'extras' which are included in the two deals, and which might make Pictidy a better choice in practice.

Chapter 5

Section 5.1

1, 3, 6 and 9 are equations which could be solved, since they contain only a single unknown quantity.

2, 5, 7 and 10 are algebraic expressions, they do not contain an = sign.

4 and 8 are formulae linking more than one unknown quantity.

Section 5.2

Page 81

1. $5x - 4 = 16$

   $5x = 16 + 4 = 20$ adding 4 to each side

   $x = 4$ dividing both sides by 5

2. $10 - 2x = 7$

   $10 - x = 7/2 = 3.5$ (dividing by 2) This is where the error has arisen – the student has forgotten that you need to divide the whole of the left-hand side by 2. That includes the 10 as well as the x term.

   $10 = 3.5 + x$ The rest of the process is correct.

   $10 - 3.5 = x$

   $6.5 = x$.

   You can tell that this answer isn't right because if you substitute it into the original equation you get $10 - 2x = 10 - 2 \times 6.5 = 13$, not 7 as should be the case.

   Correct solution:

   $10 - 2x = 7$

   $-2x = 7 - 10$ (subtracting 10 from each side)

   $-2x = -3$

   $2x = 3$ (multiplying both sides by -1)

   $x = 3/2 = 1.5$.

   Check: $10 - 2x = 10 - 2 \times 1.5 = 10 - 3 = 7$, so the equation is satisfied.

3. $3x + 2 = 20$

   $3x = 20 - 2 = 18$ This is correct

   $x = 18 - 3 = 15$ To eliminate the 3 in front of the x, we need to divide by 3, not subtract 3. The correct version is:

   $x = 18/3 = 6$.

   Check: $3x + 2 = 3 \times 6 + 2 = 18 + 2 = 20$, so the equation is satisfied.

Page 83

1. $x = 12$	2. $x = -3$	3. $x = 2$	4. $x = 18$	5. $z = 6$
6. $p = 3$	7. $m = 3$	8. $x = -7/3$	9. $x = 1.5$	10. $a = 4$

Section 5.3

Page 86

For each of these questions, you need to determine whether b^2 is bigger than, smaller than or equal to $4ac$.

1. $b^2 = 16$, $4ac = 44$, so $b^2 < 4ac$ and there is no real solution.
2. $b^2 = 36$, $4ac = -264$, so $b^2 > 4ac$ and there are two real solutions.
3. $b^2 = 36$, $4ac = 0$ (because $c = 0$), so $b^2 < 4ac$ and there are two real solutions.
4. $b^2 = 100$, $4ac = 100$, so $b^2 = 4i$ and there is one real solution.

Page 88

1 (a) $x^2 - 6x + 8 = 0$

$a = 1, b = -6, c = 8$

$$x = \frac{-(-6) \pm \sqrt{[(-6)^2 - 4 \times 1 \times 8]}}{2 \times 1} = \frac{6 \pm \sqrt{(36 - 32)}}{2} = \frac{6 \pm 2}{2} = 4 \text{ or } 2$$

You can check this solution by substituting these values, one at a time, back into the original equation.

(b) $5x - x^2 = 0$ can be re-arranged as $x^2 - 5x = 0$.

It's pretty clear that one solution here will be $x = 0$. We have $a = 1$, $b = -5$ and $c = 0$ (no constant term), so the formula gives:

$$x = \frac{-(-5) \pm \sqrt{[(-5)^2 - 4 \times 1 \times 0]}}{2} = \frac{5 \pm \sqrt{25}}{2} = 0 \text{ or } 10/2 = 5$$

(c) $3x^2 + 4x + 8 = 0$.

$a = 3, b = 4, c = 8$.

$$x = \frac{-4 \pm \sqrt{[16 - 4 \times 3 \times 8]}}{2 \times 3}$$

However, the expression under the square root sign works out to $16 - 96 = -80$, a negative quantity, so the square root does not exist, and there are no real solutions to the equation.

Your graphs should show that the parabola $x^2 - 6x + 8 = y$ cuts the x-axis at the points $x = 2$ and $x = 4$, confirming the solution to (a).

The parabola $x^2 - 5x = y$ touches the x-axis at $x = 5$, the single solution to (b).

The parabola $3x^2 + 4x + 8 = y$ doesn't intersect the x-axis at all, so there are no solution to (c).

2. Putting $y = 0$ into the equation $y = 80t - 2t^2$ gives $80t - 2t^2 = 0$., or $2t^2 - 80t = 0$ (multiplying through by -1).

Thus $a = 2, b = -80, c = 0$.

Using the formula gives $t = 0$ or $t = 40$.

So the yield of the process is zero after 0 hours – that is at the very start, which seems sensible – and again after 40 hours.

The graph opposite shows $y = 80t - 2t^2$

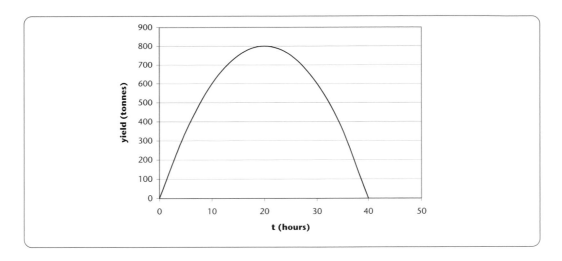

It appears that the yield is maximised by letting the process operate for 20 hours. This kind of behaviour is quite common in operations where, if allowed to run for too long, the chemical process actually begins to use up the product. But you can see that it could also apply, suitably varied, to modelling things like the yield of strawberries from a field, with harvesting too early giving a lower yield, because not all the fruits will have developed, while harvesting too late also reduces the yield due to some fruit being overripe. More sophisticated versions of these models can be used to help companies maximise the yield obtained.

3. (a) total cost per hour = fixed + variable cost = 5000 + 50n (remember we want the result in pence).

   (b) Profit, P = revenue – costs = $(400n – 2n^2) – (5000 + 50n) = 400n – 2n^2 – 5000 – 50n = 350n – 2n^2 – 5000$.

   (c) To find where a profit begins, and ceases, to be made, we need to put $P = 0$ into the equation $P = 350n – 2n^2 – 5000$; that is, to solve $350n – 2n^2 – 5000 = 0$. This can be rearranged as $2n^2 + 5000 – 350n = 0$, or, dividing throughout by 2 to make the numbers a bit more manageable:

   $$n^2 – 175n + 2500 = 0$$

   With $a = 1$, $b = –175$ and $c = 2500$, you should be able to substitute into the formula to get $n = 15.69$ or $n = 159.31$. Since n is a number of chickens, which cannot be fractional, a sensible answer is therefore that a profit will be made when between 16 and 159 chickens per hour are processed.

Section 5.4

Page 93

1. $2x – y = 7$
   $x + 4y = 17$

$2x - y = 7$

$2x + 8y = 34$ Second equation multiplied by 2 so as to get the same coefficient of x as in equation 1

$(2x - y) - (2x + 8y) = 7 - 34$ Second equation subtracted from first

$2x - y - 2x - 8y = -27$ Remove brackets and simplify

$-9y = -27$ Collect terms; x terms cancel as intended

$9y = 27$ Multiply through by -1

$y = 3$ Divide by 9

$2x - 3 = 7$ Substitute $y = 3$ into first original equation

$2x = 7 + 3 = 10$ Add 3 to each side

$x = 5$. Divide through by 5

2. (a) $x = 16, y = 2$.   (b) $x = 0, y = 3$.   (c) $s = 4, t = 2$.
   (d) In the equations

$$2x + 5y = 13$$
$$4x + 10y = 15$$

if we multiply the top equation by 2 to get the same number of x's in both equations, we obtain:

$$4x + 5y = 26$$
$$4x + 5y = 15$$

But both of these equations can't be true at once – the sum of two quantities can't simultaneously be 26 and 15. We say that the equations are inconsistent, and they have no solution. If you try to go further with the solution method by subtracting the second equation from the first to eliminate the x-term, you find that the y-term disappears as well, and you end up with $0 = 26 - 15$, which is clearly not true.)

(e) $a = b = 1/7$.
(f) In the equations

$$x + y = 4$$
$$2x + 2y - 8$$

the second equation is simply the first multiplied by 2, so the equations are essentially identical. There is thus really only one equation, and so there are any number of combinations of x and y which satisfy it: $x = 1, y = 3$ and $x = y = 2$ are just two possibilities.

3. Call the two numbers a and b. Then $a + b = 7$, and $a - b = 15$. These equations can be solved to get $a = 11$ and $b = -4$.

4. If L is the price of a large pad, and S is that of a small pad, then
   $2S + L = 6.6$

$3S + 2L = 11.4$

Solving these gives $S = £1.80$, $L = £3.00$.

Page 97

1. $q = \sqrt{(2CD/H)}$
   Square both sides to get rid of the square root sign: $q^2 = 2CD/H$
   Multiply through by H: $Hq^2 = 2CD$
   Divide by q^2: $H = 2CD/q^2$
2. $A = P(1+r/100)^n$
   This is quite tricky. We need to get rid of the term $(1+r/100)^n$ on the right-hand side. So we divide throughout by this term, in exactly the same way as we would if it were just a single number or variable:

$$\frac{A}{(1 + r/100)^n} = P$$

If you think back to Chapter 3, you may recall that another way of writing $1/x^n$ is x^{-n}. So we can rewrite the left-hand side here to get:

$A(1+r/100)^{-n} = P.$

This formula would enable us to work out how much (P) we need to invest now in order to accumulate an amount A after n years at r% per annum compound interest.

Section 5.6

Page 98

1. $0 \le x \le 10$
2. $-4 \le y \le 4$.
3. $s + t > 5$.

Page 99

1. Two children count as one adult, so when A adults and C children are on the ride, this is equivalent to $A + C/2$ adults. If you find it hard to see this, or if perhaps you wanted to say $A + 2C$ adults, think about what would happen if there were 4 children – that's clearly equivalent to 2 adults, so we're dividing the number of children by 2 to find the equivalent number of adults.
   The H&S requirement then says that $A + C/2 \le 40$.
   If $A = 25$, then $25 + C/2 \le 40$, so that $C/2 \le 15$ (subtracting 25 from each side).
   Thus $C \le 30$ (multiplying by 2).
2. The total time taken up by R routine cases and C complex cases, together with the 20-minute break, is $10R + 15C + 20$.

This must fit within the three-hour period, which needs to be expressed as 180 minutes since the appointment times are given in minutes.

Thus $10R + 15C + 20 \leq 180$, or $10R + 15C \leq 140$ (subtracting 20 from both sides), or $2R + 3C \leq 28$ (dividing by 5).

When $R = 7$, we have $14 + 3C \leq 28$, so $3C \leq 14$.

So $C \leq 14/3$. This means that in practical terms, since C must be a whole number of patients, the maximum number of complex cases which can be added is 4. This will however leave some spare time (how much?).

Page 101

1. The health and safety inequality was $A + C/2 \leq 40$. This is shown on the graph below.

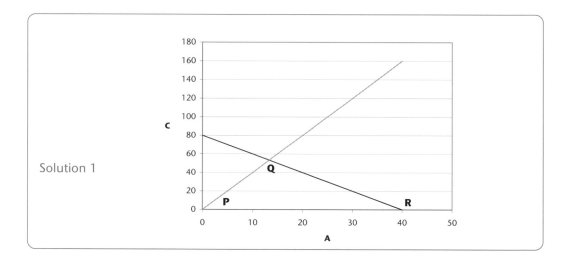

So 60 children and 10 adults, 40 children and 20 adults, or 20 children and 30 adults would all be possible solutions which use the full capacity of the ride.

If there must be at least one ad ult per four children on the ride, then $A \geq C/4$, or $4A \geq C$. This line passes through the origin, and is as shown on the graph (Solution 1). The constraint is satisfied *below* the line (for example, 20 adults and no children would satisfy the constraint). So the feasible region meeting both constraints is the triangle PQR.

2. The consultant's inequality was $2R + 3C \leq 28$. This is shown on the graph (Solution 2).

The feasible (that is, whole number) solutions which lie on the line are as follows:

R	C
2	8
5	6
8	4
11	2
14	0

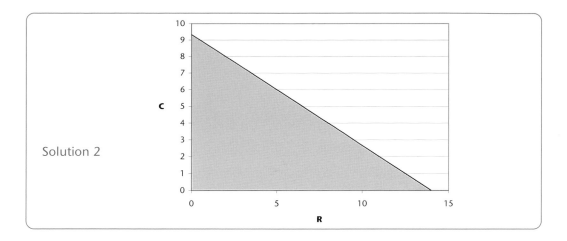

Solution 2

Exercises

1. $3x + 4 = 12$
   $3x = 8$
   $x = 8/3$ or 2.67 to two decimal places.
2. $0.4a - 1 = 1.6$
   $0.4a = 2.6$
   $a = 6.5$
3. $3x - 4y = 25$
   $2x + y = 24$

   $3x - 4y = 25$
   $8x + 4y = 96$, multiplying by 4
   $11x = 121$, adding the two equations to eliminate the y term.
   $x = 11$

   $33 - 4y = 25$, substituting for x in the first equation.
   $33 - 25 = 4y$
   $8 = 4y$
   $y = 2$

   Solution is $x = 11$, $y = 2$.
4. $3p^2 - 6p + 2 = 0$
   $a = 3, b = -6, c = 2$.
   The formula then gives $p = 1.58$ or $p = 0.42$ to two decimal places.
5. $2s^2 - 1 = 0$
   Although this could be solved using the formula with $a = 2$, $b = 0$, $c = -1$, it is simpler just to say:
   $2s^2 = 1$
   $s^2 = 1/2 = 0.5$
   $s = \pm 0.707$.
6. 40 km/hour means that each km covered takes 1.5 minutes.
   So total time $t = 20 + 1.5d$.

When $t = 1$ hour 40 minutes = 100 minutes, $100 = 20 + 1.5d$.

So $1.5d = 80$

$d = 80/1.5 = 53.33$ km.

So in 1 hour 40 minutes a delivery lorry could load and reach a store just under 54 km from the depot.

7. $T = 8 + 1.8n$ for Infitech.

    $44,000 is 44 when expressed in thousands of dollars. So $T = 44$, whence

    $44 = 8 + 1.8n$

    $36 = 1.8n$, so $n = 20$.

    Turnover reaches $44,000 in month 20 after startup.

    When the two companies have equal turnover, $8 + 1.8n = 17 + 1.5n$.

    So $1.8n - 1.5n = 17 - 8$, or $0.3n = 9$.

    This gives $n = 30$: from 30 months onwards, Infitech's turnover will exceed that of XX Technologies.

    These calculations are based on the assumption that both companies will continue their linear rate of growth into the foreseeable future, which in practice is unlikely – a company might, for example, saturate the market early on so that its growth will slow down; or it might 'take off' in such a way that growth becomes faster than linear.

8. $3x - 4 \geq 2$, $-4x - 6 \geq -14$, and $4x - 2 \geq 1$

    $3x - 4 \geq 2$ gives $3x \geq 6$, so $x \geq 2$.

    $-4x - 6 \geq -14$ gives $4x + 6 \leq 14$ (the direction of the inequality changes because we are multiplying through by a negative number, namely -1).

    Thus $2x + 3 \leq 7$, and so $2x \leq 4$, $x \leq 2$.

    The final inequality $4x - 2 \geq 1$ gives $4x \geq 3$, so $x \geq 0.75$.

    The only value of x which meets all three of these inequalities at once is $x = 2$.

Case study: The Voice Friend Trust

Let's denote the number of calls made by n, and the amount generated in donations by £D.

To find the equation of the line which passes through the points $n = 250$, $D = 1200$, and $n = 120$, $D = 800$, recall that the general equation of a straight line is $y = mx + c$, or $D = mn + c$ in this case (donations depend on number of calls, so we want the equation in the form $D = ...$).

Since $D = 1320$ when $n = 250$, $1320 = 250m + c$

Since $D = 800$ when $n = 120$, $\quad 800 = 120m + c$

We can solve these two equations simultaneously; if we subtract the second from the first, the term in c vanishes and we have $1320 - 800 = 250m - 120m$, so $520 = 130m$. Thus $m = 520/130 = 4$.

Substituting this in the first equation we get $1320 = 1000 + c$, so $c = 320$.

The linear equation is thus $D = 4n + 320$.

(a) The level of giving without any telephoning would therefore appear to be £320 per week. In order to generate £2000 per week, we will need n calls where 2000 = 4n + 320.

4n = 1680 so n = 420 calls.

The slope of the linear equation here is 4; this means that on average each extra phone call generates £4 in donations.

(b) If you substitute the values of n into the equation in turn, the arithmetic looks rather unpleasant but you should find that, within the limits of accuracy due to rounding, the corresponding values of D are indeed given by the equation. (This can be done very easily using Excel simply by entering the quadratic into a cell of the spreadsheet.)

The equation is a quadratic, and a sketch shows that it is of the form with the vertex pointing upwards. This means that, as n increases, eventually the values of D will start to decrease. This is probably not very realistic in this situation, where giving might level off but is unlikely to start falling just because large numbers of phone calls are made. So the model should be used with caution.

Chapter 6

Section 6.3

Page 110

Slopes are as follows:

1. $5x^4$ 2. $11x^{10}$ 3. $-3x^{-4}$ 4. $-x^{-2}$ or $-1/x^2$ 5. $1/2\, x^{-1/2}$ or $1/2\sqrt{x}$

6. Slope is $6x^5$, so when $x = 2$ the slope is 192, and when $x = -1$ the slope is -6. The graph would thus have a steep upwards slope at $x = 2$, and a less steep downwards (negative) slope at $x = -1$.

7. $1/x^2$ can be written as x^{-2}, so slope in general is $-2x^{-3}$. When $x = 1$, this gives a slope of -2. When $x = 0$, $-2x^{-3} = -2/x^3$ is not defined, since we cannot divide by zero.

The graph is as follows:

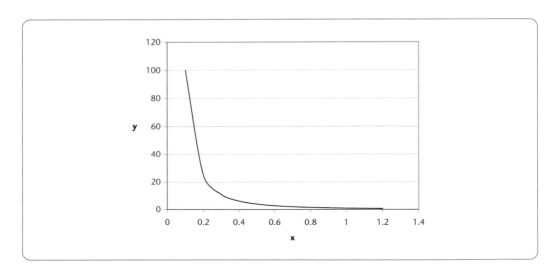

So as x gets smaller, y gets very large, but the value of y at $x = 0$ is not defined – this is why the slope is not defined either.

Section 6.4

1. $2x + 2$ 2. $6x + 6$ (remove the brackets before differentiating)
3. $1 - 1/x^2$ 4. $2x - 4$ 5. $1/\sqrt{x} - 2$ or $x^{-1/2} - 2$
6. $dy/dx = 6x - 7$, so at $x = 0$ this gives -7.
7. $dy/dx = 2x + 1$, so at $x = -1$ this gives -1.
8. $dv/dt = 8$, which does not change with the value of t. (The corresponding graph is a straight line.)
9. $dy/dx = 75 - 3x2$, so at $x = 2$ this gives 63.
10. $dy/dx = 2x + 6$. When $dy/dx = 2x + 6 = 0$, we can solve to get $x = -3$. Where the slope of a curve is zero, the tangent to the curve is horizontal; such points have special properties which will be examined in Section 6.6.

Section 6.5

1. $d^2y/dx^2 = 6$ 2. $d^2y/dx^2 = 0$ 3. $d^2y/dx^2 = 30x^4$
4. $d^2y/dx^2 = -1/4\, x^{-3/2}$ or $-1/(4\sqrt{x^3})$ 5. $d^2y/dx^2 = -1/x^2 + 2/x^3$ 6. $d^2y/dx^2 = -4$
7. $d^2y/dx^2 = 24x - 6$

Section 6.6

1. $dy/dx = x + 2$, which is zero when $x = -2$. $d^2y/dx^2 = 1$, which is positive, so there is a local minimum at $x = -2$.
2. $dy/dx = 3x^2 - 12x + 12$, and using the formula for solving a quadratic tells us that this expression is zero when $x = 2$. $d^2y/dx^2 = 6x - 12$, which is also zero when $x = 2$. So we probably have a point of inflection. To be sure, look at what happens to dy/dx on either side of $x = 2$. At $x = 1$, $dy/dx = 3$, and at $x = 3$, $dy/dx = 3$ also, so there is no change of sign, which confirms that this is a point of inflection.
3. $dy/dx = 3x^2 - 12x$, so $dy/dx = 0$ when $x = 0$ or $x = 4$ (you can get this either by using the quadratic formula, or by noting that $3x^2 - 12x = 3x(x - 4)$). There are thus turning points at $x = 0$ and $x = 4$. $d^2y/dx^2 = 6x - 12$. At $x = 0$, this is -12, so that point is a maximum; at $x = 4$, it is 12, so that's a minimum. The function thus has a maximum at $x = 0$ and a minimum at $x = 4$.
4. $dy/dx = 2x - 8$, which is zero when $x = 4$. $d^2y/dx^2 = 2$, which is positive, so there is a minimum at $x = 4$.
5. $dy/dx = 1 - 1/x^2$. When this is zero, $1 - 1/x^2 = 0$, so $x^2 - 1 = 0$, whence $x = 1$ or -1. $d^2y/dx^2 = 2/x^3$, which has the value 2 when $x = 1$, and -2 when $x = -1$. There is thus a minimum at $x = 1$ and a maximum at $x = -1$. Of course, this function is not a quadratic or a cubic, since it contains a $1/x$ term. Its graph is in fact as shown below; the value of the function at $x = 0$ is not defined, since this would involve a division by zero.

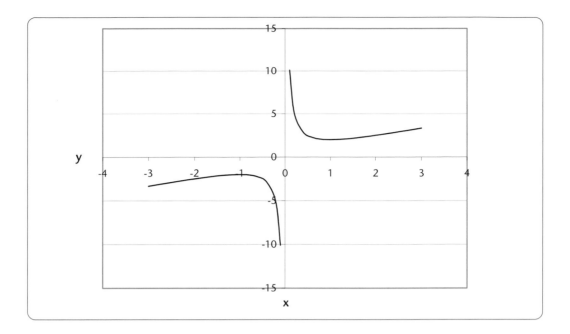

Exercises

1. (a) $dy/dx = 2x - 2$ (b) $ds/dt = -1/t^2 + 6t$ (c) $dy/dx = 2x + 1$

2. (a) $dy/dx = x^2 - x - 6 = 0$ when $x = -2$ or $x = 3$ (use the formula for solving a quadratic). $d^2y/dx^2 = 2x - 1$. So at $x = -2$, $d^2y/dx^2 = -5$, indicating a maximum, and at $x = 3$, $d^2y/dx^2 = 5$, indicating a minimum.

   (b) $dy/dx = 4x^3 + 3x^2 + 2x$. When $dy/dx = 0$, $4x^3 + 3x^2 + 2x = 0$, so $x(4x^2 + 3x + 2) = 0$. This means that either $x = 0$, or $4x^2 + 3x + 2 = 0$. However, if you try to solve this quadratic using the formula, you will find that it has no real solutions, so the only turning point of the function y is at $x = 0$. $d^2y/dx^2 = 12x^2 + 6x + 2$, which is equal to $+2$ when $x = 0$, so this point is a minimum. (Try plotting the curve using Excel – you will see that it looks rather like a parabola, but with a very 'flat bottom'.)

3. (a) and (b) To find the maximum and minimum of C, we need to find the points where $dC/dt = 0$. $dC/dt = t^2 - 12t + 32 = 0$ when $t = 4$ or $t = 8$. $d^2C/dt^2 = 2t - 12$, which has the values -4 at $t = 4$ and $+4$ at $t = 8$. So the cost has a local maximum at $t = 4$ and a local minimum at $t = 8$.

   However, if you sketch (or plot with Excel) the graph of the function (shown overleaf), you can see that of course the overall (as distinct from the local) minimum cost occurs when no paint is made – that is, at $t = 0$, where the cost is $C = 25$ or £25,000. And furthermore, the value of C when $t = 10$ is the same as that at $t = 4$, so both of these are maximum values.

   (c) If the value of t must lie between 5 and 10, then the minimum cost is clearly at $t = 8$ tonnes, and the maximum is at $t = 10$ tonnes.

   This question shows the difference between local and what are generally called global maximum and minimum values of a function.

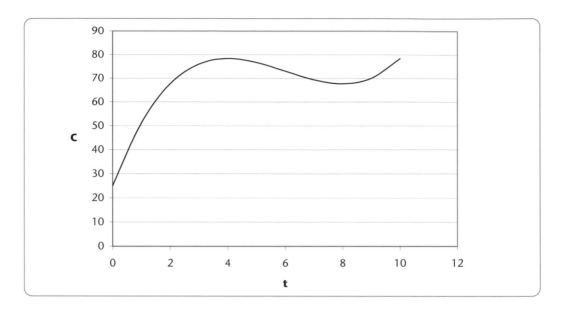

4. (a) If $C = 200 - 20P$, then revenue $R = P \times \overline{C} = P(200 - 20P) = 200P - 20P^2$.

(b) To find the maximum (or minimum) of R in terms of P, we need to find where $dR/dP = 0$. $dR/dP = 200 - 40P = 0$ when $P = 5$. At this point, $d^2R/dP^2 = -40$, so the point is a local maximum. As the function is a quadratic, it will only have one turning point, so we can be confident that this point is also the global maximum. When $P = 5$, we have $C = 200 - 20P = 200 - 20 \times 5 = 100$, so there will be 100 customers.

(c) Marginal revenue = $dR/dP = 200 - 40P$ as before. When $P = £4.50$, $dR/dP = 20$, and when $P = £5.50$, $dR/dP = -20$. So the slope of the function is positive just below $P = 5$, and negative just above, confirming that this is indeed a local maximum. The values also have the practical interpretation that if the price is increased a little above £4.50, revenue will rise, but if the price is increased a little above £5.50, then revenue will fall.

5. (a) When the belt is at rest, $s = 0$, so $0.001t(80 - t) = 0$. The speed is thus zero at $t = 0$ (when the belt is switched on) and at $t = 80$. So the belt returns to rest after 80 seconds.

(b) $ds/dt = 0.08 - 0.002t = 0$ at $t = 40$. There is thus either a local maximum or minimum at $t = 40$. Since $d^2s/dt^2 = -0.002$, the point is a maximum, so maximum speed is attained after 40 seconds. At that time, the speed is $0.04(80 - 40) = 1.6$ m/s.

Case Study: ToysisUs

(a) The graph of the predicted sales is as shown.

(b) The sales will reach their maximum in the middle part of the graph, where the equation $n = 12t - t^2 - 18$ applies. We can find $dn/dt = 12 - 2t$, so when $dn/dt = 0$, $12 - 2t = 0$ and $t = 6$. The maximum is thus reached after the product has been on the market for 6 months. (Strictly speaking we should check by looking at d^2n/dt^2 that this is a maximum rather than a minimum, but in practice we can see from the graph that this is the case.)

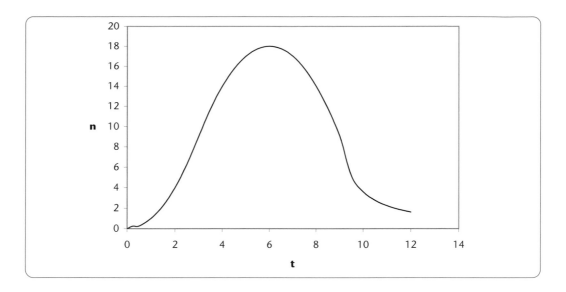

The maximum sales are given by substituting $t = 6$ into the equation, to obtain $n = 12 \times 6 - 6^2 - 18 = 18$. So maximum sales are $18 \times 10,000$ or 180,000 (remembering that the units were tens of thousands).

(c) The slope of $n = t^2$ at $t = 3$ is $dn/dt = 2t = 6$ when $t = 3$ and the slope of of $n = 12t - t^2 -18$ is $dn/dt = 12 - 2t = 6$ when $t = 3$. So the graphs of the two equations have the same slope at $t = 3$; thus they joint together smoothly at that point. If the slopes were different there would be a sharp 'bend' in the graph.

(d) The sales in the long-term will eventually fall closer and closer to zero, though they will never quite get there – the graph approaches the t-axis asymptotically.

(e) The model shows a continuous graph, but of course the data is really discrete – n gives the sales at the end of each month, so only the integer values of n actually have a meaning.

Another point is that if the product remains on the market then sales are not likely to fall ever closer to zero; it is more likely that they will reach a small but steady level.

Chapter 7

Exercises

1. We want to find the sum to be invested now at 11.5% per annum, to give a total of £8000 after 5 years. That means that in the notation of the compound interest formula developed in this chapter, we want to find C. We have $t = 5$, and $r = 11.5$. So we can say:

$$C(1 + 11.5/100)^5 = 8000$$

Thus C x $1.115^5 = 8000$, so that $C = 8000$ x 1.115^{-5}.

Working this out using the x^y key of a calculator gives $C = £4642.11$ to the nearest penny. You can check that the compound interest formula with $C = 4642.11$ does indeed give an amount of 8000 when $t = 5$ and $r = 11.5$.

In arriving at this result we have had to assume that the interest rate of 11.5% will remain constant – not a very likely assumption over a five-year timescale – and that the purchase will take place exactly at the end of the fifth year. We say that the present value of £8000 payable in five years time is £4642.11 at a discount rate of 11.5%.

2. As before, let q denote the quantity in each order. Then to meet a demand for D items per year, we will need to place D/q orders, at a total cost of $D/q \times £R$, or $£DR/q$.

The average stock held (with the assumptions of steady consumption and instant replenishment which we made in Section 7.5) will be $q/2$, at an annual cost of $q/2 \times £/H$, or $£qH/2$.

So the total inventory cost for the year, $£C$, is given by:

$$C = DR/q + qH/2.$$

To find where this has a maximum or minimum, we compute:

$$dC/dq = -DR/q^2 + H/2$$

(remember that the D, R and H are treated as constants in this differentiation). We then set this equal to zero:

$$-DR/q^2 + H/2 = 0$$

which can be solved to give:

$$q = +/- \sqrt{(2DR/H)}$$

You can verify that $d^2C/dq^2 = 2DR/q^3$, which is positive, indicating a minimum, when q is positive (the negative root makes no sense from a practical point of view, since we cannot have a negative order quantity). Thus an order size of:

$$q = + \sqrt{(2DR/H)}$$

gives the minimum-cost inventory policy. This is the well-known *economic batch quantity* (EBQ) or *economic order quantity* (EOQ) formula of operations management theory. You can check that if you substitute $D = 12,000$, $R = 40$ and $H = £0.24$ into this formula, you get the value $q = 2000$ which we obtained in Section 7.5.

3. (a) You need to be careful with units in this question – the stock-holding cost is given in pence per year, but the demand is monthly, and the order cost is in £s. If we standardise on £s and years as our units, then in the notation of the previous question we have $D = 200 \times 12 = 2400$ units per year, $R = £4$, and $H = £0.12$ per year. Substitution in the formula then gives $q = 400$ units. This means that orders will have to be placed every two months.

   (b) Our estimate of order costs was out by 50p, so we have overestimated the true cost of £3.50 by 0.5/3.5 = 14.3% – quite a serious error. We therefore wrongly decided to order 400 items at a time. The annual inventory cost for this policy would be:

number of orders × order cost + average stock held × SH cost
= 6 × 3.5 + 200 × 0.12 = 21 + 24 = £45.

If we had got the cost right, the true value of q would be given by
$\sqrt{(2 \times 2400 \times 3.5/0.12)}$ = approximately 375 units. With this size of order, there will be 2400/375, or 6.4, orders in a year, so that the annual inventory cost falls to:

6.4 × 3.5 + 187.5 × 0.12 = £44.90.

So although we made an error of nearly 15% in our estimate of the order cost, we are only paying 10p extra as a result – an error of less than 0.3%. This is good news, suggesting as it does that the outcome of our calculation is very stable to even quite large errors in the estimated figures.

Here we have been investigating the sensitivity of the solution to changes in the quantities involved. This kind of sensitivity analysis forms an important part of more advanced mathematical problem-solving methods.

4.(a) Let price charged in pence be p, and annual quantity demanded at this price be q units. Then if the relationship between price and demand is linear, we will have:

$$q = ap + b$$

where a and b are constants. There are two ways of finding the values of a and b; we give both.

(i) Since $q = 20,000$ when $p = 40$, we can say that:

20,000 = 400 + b.

Similarly, since $q = 18,000$ when $p = 50$, $18,000 = 500 + b$.

These equations can be solved simultaneously (see Section 5.5) to give $a = -200$ and $b = 28,000$. So the equation linking demand and price is:

$$q = 28,000 - 200p.$$

The fact that a, the slope, is negative should come as no surprise – demand will decrease as price increases.

(ii) Alternatively, we can say that when price increases by 10 pence, demand falls by 2000 units. So if the relationship is linear, the fall in demand for unit increase in price will be 200 units. But this is simply the slope, or rate of change of demand with respect to price – the a of the linear equation. Thus $a = -200$.

To find b, we note that when $p = 40$, $q = 20,000$. So, $20,000 = 40a + b = -200$

× 40 + *b*, using the value of *a* we just found. Solving this linear equation for *b* gives *b* = 28,000 as before.

(b) Using the equation $q = -200p + 28{,}000$ we have just derived, we want to find the value of *p* when *q* = 0. Thus we need to solve $0 = -200p + 28{,}000$, which gives $p = 140$ pence, or £1.40. However, it is unlikely that a firm would ever increase its prices to the level where demand fell to zero. It is also likely that for any commodity there will be a small market who will purchase the commodity whatever its price, so that the true relationship is unlikely to be linear over the full range of values of *p* – the picture will probably be more like that shown in the graph below. The precise point at which the linear relationship breaks down will, of course, depend on the nature of the commodity in question. Using the terminology of Section 4.1, we could say that the domain of the linear function is unlikely to include *p* = £1.40.

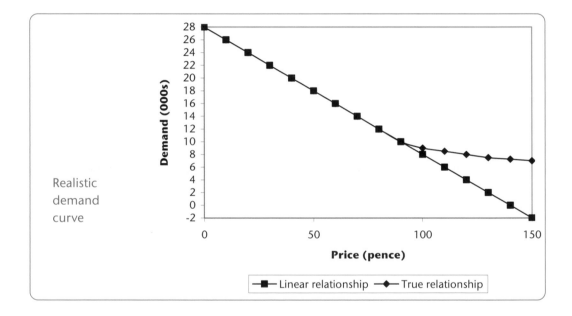

Realistic
demand
curve

(c) As already noted in (a) above, the value of *q* when *p* = 0 is given by *b* and is 28,000. This represents a ceiling above which demand for the product will apparently not rise even if it is free – however the validity of the linear equation in this region must again be questioned, as the domain may not include *p* = 0.

5. The graph overleaf shows order value on the horizontal axis against p&p charge on the vertical.

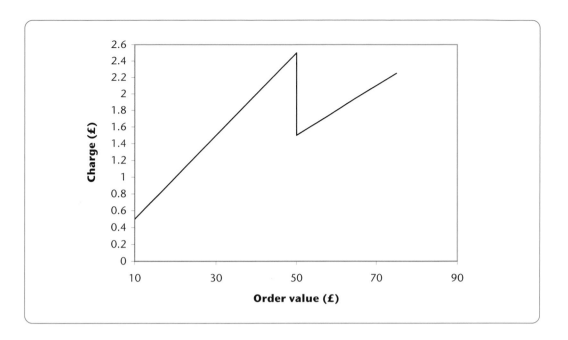

Chapter 8

Section 8.3

Time taken to process a customer's order – quantitative, continuous.

Location of branches of a supermarket chain – qualitative.

Number of plant seedlings per square metre in a commercial nursery – quantitative, discrete (though possibly taking a large number of different values).

Monthly salary of a group of workers – quantitative, and strictly this is discrete, since it must be a whole number of pence. However, since the 'steps' of 1p are very small compared with the overall size of the salaries, the variable could effectively be treated as continuous.

Type of job held by an employee – management, clerical or technical – qualitative.

Number of nights stayed by customers of a hotel chain – quantitative, discrete.

Engine capacity of different models of cars – in principle the engine capacity is a continuous quantitative variable, but in fact most popular models of car have engine capacities which fall into standard categories – 1.2 litres, 1.4 litres, and so on. So the variable is a actually discrete.

These examples should demonstrate that the discrete/continuous classification is by no means a cut-and-dried one, and can depend on your understanding the context for the data in question.

Section 8.4

1. The 'number of days' represents the frequency in this case – telling us how frequently each level of customer demand occurred.

Number of customers	Cumulative number of days
<20	3
<30	10
<40	16
<50	20

2. The layout given below is just one example of a number of ways in which this data could be displayed. It is, however, certainly a good idea to show the percentages, since the totals for the two years are different, and so comparison is difficult unless percentages are provided.

Overall satisfaction levels, 2005 and 2006

	2005 (number)	2005 (%)	2006 (number)	2006 (%)
Very satisfied	120	24	150	28
Satisfied	200	40	230	43
Neither satisfied nor dissatisfied	100	20	120	22
Dissatisfied	80	16	40	7
Total	500	100	540	100

Note that the percentages have been given to the nearest whole number, to avoid cluttering up the table. Rounding off like this may sometimes result in percentage figures which total 99% or 101%; don't be surprised if you come across this in published tables.

3. No solution given for this question, and there is a wide range of equally correct possibilities – compare your answers with those of others in your group, and think about what features each of the different layouts tends to emphasise.

Section 8.5

1. The diagram overleaf was produced by Excel, and so the x-axis isn't properly labelled – rather than labelling the intervals on the axis, we should have the edges of the bars labelled 10, 20, 30, 40, 50. We have chosen to start the bottom class (which was left open in the original data) from 10 so as to make all the classes the same width; thus no adjustment of the heights of the bars is needed, and it is correct to label the vertical axis 'frequency'.

The ogive opposite shows that there were fewer than 25 customers on about six days (the actual value as read off from the ogive is 6.5, but clearly the answer has to be a whole number of days).

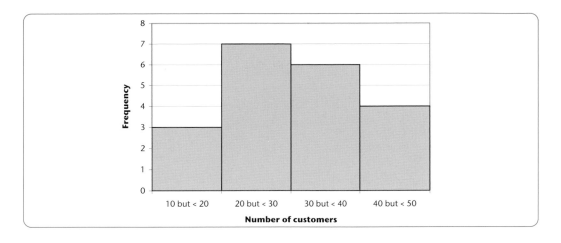

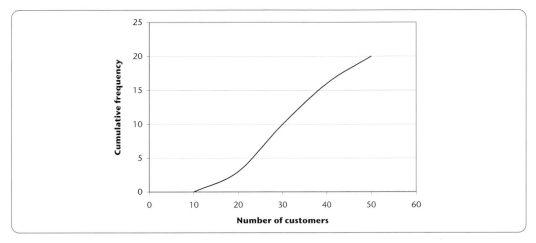

2. We have chosen to display the percentage for each year in this way so that the change in customer views over the two years can easily be seen. However, many other formats are possible.

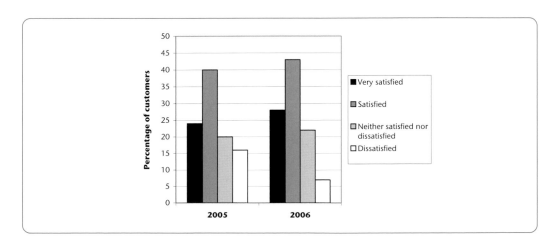

Exercises

1.

Length of call (mins)	Number of calls
0	5
1	8
2	14
3	8
4	2
5	5
6	4
7	3
8	1
Total	50

It is OK to show this data as a bar chart, since we are dealing with discrete categories.

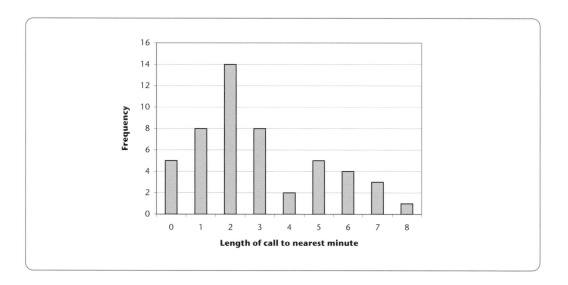

2.

No. of rings before answering	Frequency	% (industry % in brackets)
3 or fewer	30	37.5% (15%)
4 or 5	20	25% (25%)
6 or 7	20	25% (25%)
more than 7	6	7.5% (25%)
not answered	4	5% (10%)
Total	80	

The chart emphasises the fact that, while the company is comparable with the rest of the industry in the 4 to 5 and 6 to 7 groups, it does very much better in that it has a much higher percentage of calls answered within 3 rings, and a much smaller percentage which are either answered after more than 7 rings, or not answered at all.

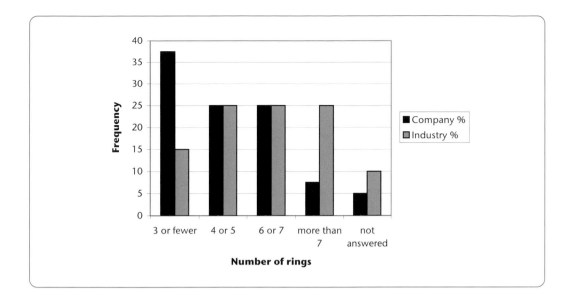

3.

This graph makes clear the fact that the great majority of expenditure goes directly into funding projects.

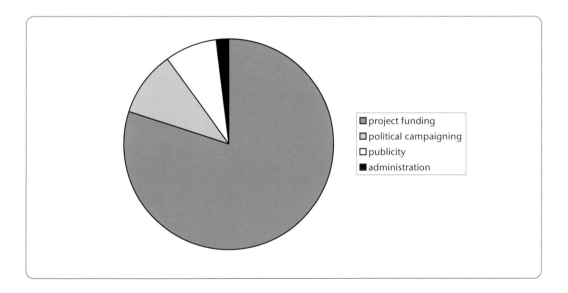

4.

The plot overleaf makes clear the pattern which persists from week to week, with week-nights (Monday to Thursday) busier than Friday and Saturday, and the lowest occupancy on Sundays. This is what you would expect with a city hotel, where there is probably a high volume of business-related occupancy during the week, a smaller number of week-end (probably leisure) visitors, and very few people using the hotel on Sunday nights.

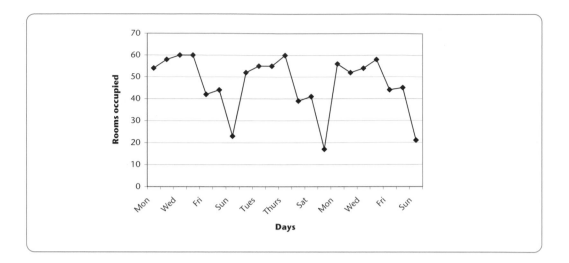

5.

This chart makes it clear that the technical book requires more corrections than the novel. The distribution for the technical book has its maximum frequency at 3 corrections per page, whereas for the novel the most common figure is zero.

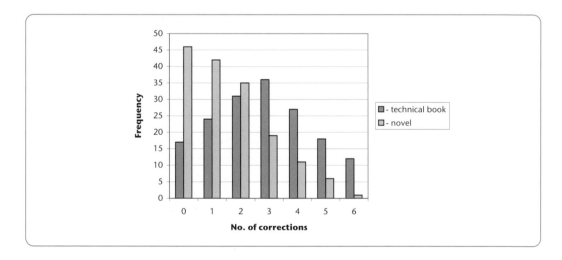

Case Study: Heron Marsh nature reserve

No detailed solution is provided for this case, since a wide range of tables and diagrams might be equally appropriate. Generally speaking, bar charts and pie charts will be suitable; in particular, for the data on ratings of facilities, it might be best to use percentages instead of, or as well as, the original figures, to overcome the fact that the size of the respondent group differs for each facility.

Chapter 9

Section 9.2

1. (a) The mean number of passengers per train is 583/9 = 64.78. The campaigning group could use this, in conjunction with the average price of ticket purchased, to examine whether or not the train service is likely to be profitable with current numbers of passengers.

   (b) The median is 64 passengers, which is very close to the value of the mean, suggesting that the distribution of the data is fairly symmetric, with no very extreme values.

2. (a) The table for calculating the mean is as follows:

f	x	fx
7	1	7
23	3.5	80.5
12	7.5	90
8	15	120
Sum 50		297.5

   So mean = 297.5/50 = 5.95 minutes.

   (b) The median is about 4½ minutes. It is considerably smaller than the mean here because the distribution is quite skewed, with a small proportion of customers taking a long time to get through the checkout.

   (c) The modal class (maximum frequency) is 2 but under 5 minutes.

3. (a) One possible choice for the maximum number of visits is 8, which would correspond to someone who visits the supermarket twice per week. However, you could make a case for other choices.

   (b) Using 8 as the upper limit, the mean becomes 225/80 = 2.8 visits correct to 1 decimal place. If you have chosen a larger value at which to close the top class, then your mean will be slightly larger also.

   (c) The median is the 40th value, which is 3 visits. This of course is not affected by your choice for the maximum number of visits.

Section 9.3

1. The number of passengers ranges from 25 to 116. The standard deviation is 32.6 passengers. The range is probably a more useful measure from the campaign group's point of view, as it makes clear that there are never fewer than 25 passengers, and sometimes as many as 116; it also shows that the numbers are very variable. The standard deviation might not mean much to the train company management.

2. The lower quartile is about 2½ minutes, and the upper quartile about 8 minutes. Thus the middle 50% of customers take between 2½ and 8 minutes to check out. 25% of customers take more than 8 minutes, something about which the supermarket might want to take action.

3. (a) The standard deviation is 1.35 visits per month. As compared with the December figures, this shows that in July the average number of visits paid by customers is lower, and also that the numbers of visits overall show less variability in July. This is consistent with the fact that, in the run-up to Christmas, some customers will be visiting the supermarket more frequently, while others will stick to their usual pattern.

   (b) The quartiles are 2 visits and 4 visits. The median was 3 visits. This suggests that the data is not noticeably skewed.

Exercises

1. The mean and standard deviation of the first set of data are 9 and 3.63 respectively. For the second set, they are 90 and 36.3. Since the second set of figures is 10 times the first set, the mean and standard deviation are also increased by a factor of 10. This could be useful when changing units (such as from cm to mm), or when working with very large figures.

2. Contractor B takes a slightly longer time on average, but performance is more consistent, as indicated by the smaller standard deviation. Thus the company might be prepared to opt for the longer average completion time in return for greater predictability of the completion time.

3. The mean is 2.93 minutes, the median is 2 minutes and the mode is also 2 minutes. While the mode and the median are identical, the mean is somewhat higher, reflecting the fact that we have a rather skewed distribution here, with a longer 'tail' at the upper end – there are some calls which take quite a long time, though the majority are short. In this situation the median would give the company a better idea of the duration of a 'typical' call.

4.

	Technical book	Novel
Mean	2.81	1.71
Standard deviation	1.56	1.43
Median	3	1
Lower quartile	1	0
Upper quartile	4	2

The two sets of measures reflect the fact that there tend to be more errors in the technical book – hence the higher mean and median – and although the range of the data is the same in both cases, the distribution for the novel is more concentrated around the mean – hence the smaller standard deviation. The larger difference between the mean and the median for the sample from the novel indicates the greater skewness of that distribution, whereas for the technical book the two measures are much closer together.

   The publisher could use this data to help in estimating the cost of making changes to the final proofs of different types of book.

5. (a) Many variables which occur 'naturally', such as distributions of adult male heights, tend to follow a more symmetric pattern. This is also the case for variables

which are the result of industrial processes – such as the weights of packets of low-fat spread filled by an automatic packaging machine, or the diameters of mass-produced components like screws.

(b) Variables which are the result of human decisions, such as salaries, tend to follow a less symmetric pattern (most people earn modest salaries, but a few have very high earnings, skewing the distribution).

Counted data (like the 'number of corrections' data in Question 4, often gives a skewed picture, since the smallest value which can arise is zero, but there is no limit at the upper end.

Most of the examples of skew distributions which we have looked at had the longer tail at the top end. A familiar example of the opposite situation is the distribution of people's ages at death, which has a high mean but a long tail on the lower end, due to small numbers of people dying relatively young.

Case Study: The Bill Oates Foundation

The values of the requested measures for the September 2006 data as given by Excel are:

lower quartile = $673.5
median = $2764
upper quartile = $10,477

The striking feature of these measures is that the lower quartile and the median are very much closer together than the median and the upper quartile. They suggest a highly skewed shape for the distribution, and this is confirmed by plotting a histogram (the Excel bar chart version is shown below).

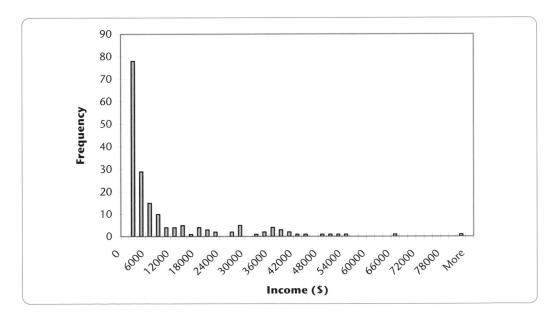

The data shows that a in a large proportion of countries, per capita income is very low when compared with that for the relatively small proportion of rich 'western' nations. This disparity helps to demonstrate the need to address such imbalances in the distribution of wealth across all countries.

Glossary of technical terms

Asymptote A line which a graph approaches, while never actually meeting it. An example would be the graph of $y = 1/x$, which has both the x and y-axes as asymptotes.

Bar chart A means of displaying frequency data using bars of varying heights to represent the frequency of occurrence in different categories of data.

Coordinates The values relative to horizontal and vertical axes which enable us to fix the position of a point on a graph.

Denominator The number or expression on the bottom of a fraction; for example, the denominator of 3/5 is 5; the denominator of $x/(x + 6)$ is $x + 6$.

Dependent variable In an expression such as $y = 3x^2 - 2x + 1$, y is known as the dependent variable because its value depends on the value we give to x. The dependent variable is generally plotted on the vertical axis of a graph.

Derivative The result of performing a differentiation. The derivative of x^4 with respect to x is $4x^3$.

Difference The result of subtracting one number from another. For example, the difference of 7 and 5 is 2; the difference of 5 and 7 is –2.

Discrete data Data which can take only certain specified values. An example would be the number of broken eggs in a box, which must be 0, 1, 2, ...

Dividend The number being divided in a division calculation. For example, the dividend in the calculation $5 \div 2$ is 5.

Divisor The number by which we are dividing in a division calculation. For example, the divisor in the calculation $5 \div 2$ is 2.

Exponent The power in an expression such as x^3; here the exponent of x is 3.

Frequency In statistics, the number of times a particular value or range of values occurs in a set of data. For example, in the set of data 1, 1, 2, 2, 2, 3, 3, 4, the frequency of 2 would be 3.

Frequency distribution A table showing the frequency of each value or range of values within a dataset. Also called a frequency table. If ranges are used, we refer to a grouped frequency distribution.

Function A relationship between a dependent variable and one or more independent variables; often represented by an equation. For example, the general linear function of a single independent variable can be written as $y = ax + b$.

Gradient   The slope of a graph. If the graph is plotted on (x, y)-axes then the slope is the increase in y per unit increase in x. A positive slope means that the graph runs uphill from left to right; a negative slope (i.e. y decreasing as x increases) means the graph runs downhill from left to right.

Histogram   A way of displaying a grouped frequency distribution by means of blocks, whose width is proportional to the width of the classes in the distribution, and whose area corresponds to the frequency of the class.

Hyperbola   The shape of graph which results from plotting a function containing a term of the form $1/x$, $1/x^2$, etc. For an example see page 69.

Inequality   An algebraic or arithmetical expression representing the relationship between the sizes of two quantities. The signs $<$, $>$, $\leq$, $\geq$ are used to represent 'less than', 'greater than', 'less than or equal to', and 'greater than or equal to'. So $2 < 6$, etc.

Integer   Whole number, such as 11, 362 or –50.

Intercept   The value of y in a linear equation when $x = 0$. Also the point where the graph of the equation crosses the y-axis, assuming the x-scale starts at 0.

Linear equation   An equation in which no variable is raised to any power other than 1 or multiplied by any other variable. A linear equation in a single variable can always be put into the form $ax + b = 0$.

Linear function   A function in which the dependent variables only occur raised to the power 1. Can be expressed in the form $y = a_0 + a_1 x_1 + a_2 x_2 + ...$

Local maximum   The function $y = f(x)$ has a local maximum when $x = x_0$ if $dy/dx = 0$ when $x = x_0$ and dy/dx is positive to the left of x_0 and negative to the right of it; or equivalently, if d^2y/dx^2 is negative at $x = x_0$. This means that $f(x_0)$ is greater than the value of $f(x)$ anywhere else in the immediate neighbourhood of x_0.

Local minimum   The function $y = f(x)$ has a local minimum when $x = x_0$ if $dy/dx = 0$ when $x = x_0$, and dy/dx is negative to the left of x_0 and positive to the right of it; or equivalently, if d^2y/dx^2 is positive at $x = x_0$. This means that $f(x_0)$ is smaller than the value of $f(x)$ anywhere else in the immediate neighbourhood of x_0.

Lowest common denominator   The smallest number into which the denominators of a group of fractions will all divide. For example, the lowest common denominator for the fractions 1/4, 1/3 and 1/6 is 12, because this is the smallest number into which 4, 3 and 6 will all divide. Used in addition and subtraction of fractions.

Mean   The arithmetical mean, which is usually contracted to 'mean', is what is colloquially called the 'average'; so the mean of 3, 4 and 5 is $(3 + 4 + 5)/3 = 4$, and so on.

Median   The central value in an ordered set of numbers (or the mean of the two central values if there is an even number of values). For example, the median in the set 21, 33, 47, 68, 74, 91 is $(47 + 68)/2 = 57.5$.

Mode   The most common value in a group of numbers. The mode in the group 1, 1, 2, 2, 2, 3, 3, 4 is 2.

Numerator   The number or expression on the top of a fraction. For example, the numerator of 11/12 is 11; the numerator of $(x + 2)/(x - 3)$ is $x + 2$.

Ogive   A graph plotted from a cumulative frequency table.

Origin   The point (0, 0) on a graph, which is often, but not invariably, the point where the coordinate axes meet.

Parabola   The shape of graph which results from plotting a quadratic function. For examples, see pages 66–8.

Percentage   A fraction expressed on a denominator of 100; the denominator is not explicitly written. Thus 25% means 25/100, etc.

Pie chart   A means of displaying frequency data using sectors of a circle to represent subgroups of the data.

Point of inflexion   A point on a graph where $dy/dx = 0$, but dy/dx does not change sign.

Power   An expression such as x^n is called the nth power of x. More loosely, we sometimes refer to n as the power of x in this expression.

Product   The result of multiplying two or more numbers or expressions. So the product of $2x$ and x^2 is $2x^3$.

Quadrant   One of the four parts into which the coordinate axes divide the Cartesian plane.

Quadratic   A quadratic expression in x is one where the highest power of x occurring is a square. A quadratic equation is one involving only quadratic expressions; a quadratic equation in one variable can always be put into the form $ax^2 + bx + c = 0$.

Quartile   A number which divides an ordered set of figures into quarters. The smallest quartile is the lower quartile, the middle one is the median (see above) and the biggest is the upper quartile.

Quotient   The result of dividing two numbers or expressions. The quotient of 12 and 3 is 4; the quotient of 3 and 12 is 0.25.

Range   The difference between the largest and smallest values in a set of data.

Rate of change   If y is a function of x, the rate of change of y with x is the increase in y per unit increase in x. A negative rate of change means y decreases as x increases.

Root of an equation $x = a$ is a root of an equation in x if substituting $x = a$ into the equation makes the two sides equal. For example, $x = 2$ is a root of $2x + 8 = 10 + x$ because when $x = 2$, both sides of the equation are equal to 12. A root is said to *satisfy* the equation in question.

Significant figures   The number of digits which actually carry information, as distinct from those which simply indicate place-value. Thus in 30,270, there are four significant figures: the 3, 2, 7 and the zero between the 3 and the 2. The last zero is, however, not significant, since it only indicates the overall place-value.

Slope   The rate of change of the dependent variable in a graph per unit increase in the independent variable.

Solution   The solution of an equation is the value or set of values of the unknown(s) which make the two sides of the equation equal.

Standard deviation   A measure of the spread of a set of data, found by taking the square root of the mean of the squared deviations of the data values from their mean.

Sum   The result of adding two or more numbers or expressions. The sum of 11, 2 and $3x$ is $13 + 3x$.

Summation sign (Σ) Σx means 'add up all the values of x'.

Tangent   A line which meets a curve only at a single point.

Turning point   A general term for a local maximum or minimum (see above).

Index

Index of symbols and Greek letters